Kodály in the First Grade Classroom

Kodály Today Handbook Series

Mícheál Houlahan and Philip Tacka

Kodály Today: A Cognitive Approach to Elementary Music Education, second edition
Kodály in the Kindergarten Classroom: Developing the Creative Brain in the 21st Century
Kodály in the First Grade Classroom: Developing the Creative Brain in the 21st Century
Kodály in the Second Grade Classroom: Developing the Creative Brain in the 21st Century
Kodály in the Third Grade Classroom: Developing the Creative Brain in the 21st Century
Kodály in the Fourth Grade Classroom: Developing the Creative Brain in the 21st Century
Kodály in the Fifth Grade Classroom: Developing the Creative Brain in the 21st Century

Kodály in the First Grade Classroom

Developing the Creative Brain in the 21st Century

Micheál Houlahan
Philip Tacka

Oxford University Press is a department of the University of
Oxford. It furthers the University's objective of excellence in research,
scholarship, and education by publishing worldwide.

Oxford   New York
Auckland   Cape Town   Dar es Salaam   Hong Kong   Karachi
Kuala Lumpur   Madrid   Melbourne   Mexico City   Nairobi
New Delhi   Shanghai   Taipei   Toronto

With offices in
Argentina   Austria   Brazil   Chile   Czech Republic   France   Greece
Guatemala   Hungary   Italy   Japan   Poland   Portugal   Singapore
South Korea   Switzerland   Thailand   Turkey   Ukraine   Vietnam

Oxford is a registered trademark of Oxford University Press
in the UK and certain other countries.

Published in the United States of America by
Oxford University Press
198 Madison Avenue, New York, NY 10016

© Oxford University Press 2015

All rights reserved. No part of this publication may be reproduced, stored in
a retrieval system, or transmitted, in any form or by any means, without the prior
permission in writing of Oxford University Press, or as expressly permitted by law,
by license, or under terms agreed with the appropriate reproduction rights organization.
Inquiries concerning reproduction outside the scope of the above should be sent to the
Rights Department, Oxford University Press, at the address above.

You must not circulate this work in any other form
and you must impose this same condition on any acquirer.

Library of Congress Cataloging-in-Publication Data
Houlahan, Micheál, author.
Kodály in the first grade classroom / by Micheál Houlahan and Philip Tacka.
pages cm. — (Kodály today handbook series)
Includes bibliographical references and index.
ISBN 978–0–19–023578–9 (paperback); 978–0–19–024848–2 (hardback)
1. School music—Instruction and study.   2. Kodály, Zoltán, 1882–1967.
3. First grade (Education)—Curricula—United States.   I. Tacka, Philip, author.   II. Title.
MT1.H835 2015
372.87′049—dc23
2014032954

We are the music-makers,
And we are the dreamers of dreams,
Wandering by lone sea-breakers,
And sitting by desolate streams;
World-losers and world-forsakers,
On whom the pale moon gleams:
Yet we are the movers and shakers
Of the world for ever, it seems.

Ode, by Arthur O'Shaughnessy

[. . .] eratque tam turpe Musicam nescire quam litteras

from *De Musica*, by Isidoris Hispalensis

"Legyen A Zene Mindenkié" [Music should belong to everyone]

Zoltán Kodály

Contents

Acknowledgments • ix

Introduction • xi

1 Framing a Curriculum Based on the Kodály Concept • 1
The Kodály Concept • 1
Multiple Dimensions of Music • 2
Grade 1 Music Curriculum • 4
Prompt Questions for Constructing a Music Curriculum • 9
Lesson Planning • 10
Key Components of Lesson Plan Design • 11

2 Developing a Music Repertoire: Students as Stewards of Their Cultural and Musical Heritage • 17
Selecting Repertoire • 17
Grade 1 Song Lists • 18
Lesson Planning • 43

3 Teaching Strategies • 54
Teaching Strategies • 54
Beat • 54
Quarter and Eighth Notes • 60
Two-Note Child's Chant • 64
Rest • 68
Three-Note Child's Chant • 72
Duple Meter • 77
Developing a Lesson Plan Design Based on the Teaching Strategies • 81

4 Students as Performers: Developing Music Skills and Creative Expression • 99
Tuneful Singing Skills • 99
Reading Skills • 102
Inner-Hearing Skills • 106
Writing Skills • 108
Improvisation Skills • 110
Musical Memory • 112
Understanding Form • 114
Part-Work Skills • 115
Instrumental Performance Skills • 118
Creative Movement Skills • 121

Listening Examples for Grade 1 Concepts and Elements • 125
Lesson Planning • 127

5 Unit Plans and Lesson Plans • 133
Transitions in Lesson Plans • 134
General Points for Planning Lessons • 139
Evaluating a Lesson • 139
Unit 1: Kindergarten Review • 141
Unit 2: Teaching Quarter and Eighth Notes • 151
Unit 3: Teaching a Two-Note Child's Chant *so-mi* • 163
Unit 4: Teaching Quarter Note Rest • 176
Unit 5: Teaching a Three-Note Child's Chant *la* • 188
Unit 6: Teaching Duple Meter • 200

6 Assessment and Evaluation • 215
Grade 1 Assessments • 215

Notes • 233

Index • 235

Acknowledgments

We owe a debt of gratitude to the many individuals who inspired, encouraged, and helped us along the way. Both of us were fortunate enough to study at the Franz Liszt Academy/Kodály Pedagogical Institute in Hungary and at the Kodály Center of America with world-renowned Kodály experts, many of whom were Kodály's pupils and colleagues, who shared their knowledge with us over many years. Among them were Erzsébet Hegyi, Ildikó Herboly-Kocsár, Lilla Gábor, Katalin Komlós, Katalin Forrai, Mihály Ittzés, Klára Kokas, Klára Nemes, Eva Vendrai, Helga Szabó, László Eősze, Peter Erdei, and Katalin Kiss. We are especially indebted to Katalin Forrai for her support and encouragement for the research contained in this publication. Our research is grounded in their many valuable insights and research.

Special thanks are due to these individuals for critically reading portions of the manuscript, field-testing lesson plans, and insightful suggestions regarding this approach to instruction and learning: Nick Holland, lower school music teacher at St. Paul's School in Baltimore, Maryland; Lauren Bain, elementary music specialist in the Northeast School District of San Antonio, Texas; Georgia Katsourides, music specialist in the Lancaster City School District, Pennsylvania; and Vivian Ferchill, retired music specialist from Round Rock, Texas.

Special acknowledgment must be made to Patty Moreno, director of the Kodály Certification Program at Texas State University, San Marcos, for her support and continued encouragement of this project. We would also like to thank Holly Kofod and Lisa Roebuck for their comments, which helped us bring this book to completion.

Many of our students in Kodály Certification Programs at Texas State University; the Austin Independent School District, Austin Texas; Belmont University in Nashville, Tennessee; and the Eastman School of Music in Rochester, New York, have all helped us shape our approach to instruction and learning presented herein. Kristopher Brown, José Pelaez, Rebecca Morgan, Loren Tarnow, and Meredith Riggs deserve special mention. Gratitude is due Rebecca Seekatz for her work on the game directions and the accompanying glossary of terms. Our many years working together have not only contributed to the information we present but also served as a continuing source of inspiration in working with the pedagogical processes we have shaped.

Regarding practical matters, we would like to thank our students at Millersville University of Pennsylvania for helping us with initial drafts of the manuscript. Special thanks are due Jamie Duca, for her technical and hands-on assistance.

This book would not be so complete in terms of pedagogy and educational content were it not for readings and comments from Blaithín Burns, Kodály instructor at the Blue Coat School. She provided invaluable assistance in the initial design of *Kodály in the First Grade Classroom* and field-tested many teaching strategies. Richard Schellhas deserves thanks for

Acknowledgments

his personal patience and understanding as well as words of encouragement and advice throughout the writing of this manuscript.

Research for this publication was supported by a grant from Millersville University, the State System for Higher Education in Pennsylvania. The university's library assistance, technical, administrative, and financial support, and overall encouragement for this project allowed us to bring this volume to completion. We would like to express our gratitude to Gabriella Montoya-Stier and Faith Knowles for their permission to include songs from their collections *El Patio de Mi Casa: Traditional Rhymes, Games and Folk Songs from Mexico* and *Vamos a Cantar*. We are very grateful to Katalin Forrai's children, András Vikár, Tamás Vikár, and Katalin van Vooren Vikár, for permission to use materials from their mother's book, *Music in Preschool*, edited and translated by Jean Sinor, Budapest, Hungary: Kultura, 1995 (original publication 1988).

We wish to thank Suzanne Ryan, Editor-in-Chief of Humanities and Executive Editor of Music at Oxford University Press, for her encouragement and critical guidance. We thank Lisbeth Redfield, assistant editor at Oxford University Press, and Molly Morrison, who oversaw editing and production. Very special thanks are due our editor, Thomas Finnegan, for his impeccable scrutiny and thoughtful editorial assistance with our manuscript.

Introduction

The primary purpose of this handbook is to give music teachers a practical guide to teaching first grade that is aligned with information contained in *Kodály Today* and national standards in music that promote twenty-first-century music learning. The foundational aspects of this book are a detailed guide for teaching children to sing, move, play instruments, develop music literacy and reading literacy skills, promote creativity skills, and enhance music listening. The hallmark of this teaching pedagogy is that it integrates the development of problem-solving, critical-thinking, and collaborative skills into music instruction and learning. The importance of this approach is identified in the National Research Council's July 2012 report, wherein the authors cite these as "21st century skills" or "deeper learning."[1] Our hope is that every teacher will absorb the process of teaching as detailed in this publication and blend it with personal creativity, which will ultimately result in a lively and valuable musical experience for children.

We have tried to give elementary music instructors a reference with information and materials about adopting a teaching approach inspired by the Kodály philosophy of music education. The handbook should not be considered a substitute for reading *Kodály Today: A Cognitive Approach to Elementary Music Education*; that volume is a practical and detailed guide for teaching a music curriculum to children in the first grade music classroom that is aligned with national and state content standards for music education. *Kodály Today* and this handbook for first grade offers teachers a step-by-step roadmap for developing students' love of music, musical understandings, and metacognition skills.

Focus discussions and surveys with music teachers reveal their concern regarding the lack of specificity relating to teaching music. Although many teachers have acquired a number of techniques for use in music activities, many are concerned about developing a more holistic approach to teaching music, one that moves beyond activities and toward developmental skill building. Teachers are looking for more direction on how to create an organic curriculum. They are looking for more guidance on how to:

- Select music materials for teaching
- Enhance skills in singing, playing music instruments, and movement that are cognitively and developmentally appropriate
- Build the foundations of music literacy skills
- Promote creativity skills
- Develop improvisation skills
- Teach active music listening lessons
- Implement evaluation and assessment tools

This text addresses these concerns. The ideas reflected here have been field-tested and shaped over a decade of collaborative work with music specialists. The innovative approach of this book, like the collaboration of music teachers with a group of researchers to design the contents of this publication, is truly pioneering.

We spell out teaching procedures that are outlined in *Kodály Today* and demonstrate how they can be used within lesson plans, in considerable detail. In this handbook, we refer to chapters in *Kodály Today* that explain in greater detail the relevant techniques adopted in lesson plans. The suggestions given should be used as a point of departure for a teacher's own creativity and personality and need not be taken entirely literally. It is expected that teachers will apply these suggestions in a way that is responsive to the needs, backgrounds, and interests of their own students. The sample lesson plans and sample curriculums are not meant to be comprehensive. We expect that music instructors will infuse these ideas with their own national, state, regional, and local benchmarks for teaching. We appreciate that teachers must develop their own philosophy for teaching music and their own repertoire of songs, procedures, and processes for teaching musical skills, as well as consider such factors as the frequency of music instruction, the size of the class, the length of the class, and current music abilities of students.

Chapter Summaries

Here are summaries of the chapters in this Grade 1 Handbook.

Introduction

Summarizes the first grade handbook with a brief outline of all chapters.

Chapter 1: Framing a Curriculum Based on the Kodály Concept

This chapter presents a sample curriculum summary statement as well as curriculum goals for first grade. The information in this chapter is aligned with Chapter 1 of *Kodály Today* and the accompanying website.

Chapter 2: Developing a Musical Repertoire: Students as Stewards of Their Cultural and Musical Heritage

This chapter has a selection of music repertoire for teaching music performance, music literacy skills, improvisation, and composition as well as listening skills. There is also a detailed review summary of how to teach games and dances to children. The content in this chapter is aligned with Chapter 2 of *Kodály Today* and the accompanying website.

Chapter 3: Teaching Strategies

This chapter presents teaching strategies for all music concepts and elements, based on the model of learning presented in Chapter 6 of *Kodály Today* for grade one. More information related to Chapter 3 can be found on a new accompanying website for the second edition of *Kodály Today*. Information in this chapter is aligned with Chapter 6 in *Kodály Today*.

Chapter 4: Students as Performers: Developing Music Skills and Creative Expression

This chapter offers music teachers guidance on how to develop skill areas in the first grade. There are lists of music techniques for teaching the music skills of tuneful singing, reading, writing, improvisation, musical memory, understanding of form, part-work activities, instrument performance, inner hearing, creative movement activities linked to games, and music listening. The content in this chapter is aligned with Chapters 3 and 4 of *Kodály Today* and the accompanying website.

Chapter 5: Unit Plans

The music curriculum for this grade is divided into units. Each unit focuses on preparation and presentation for teaching a new concept and element, and practice of a known concept or element. Each unit plan has three sections: the first furnishes a list of repertoire for teaching five music lessons, the second includes a summary of music skill activities to practice, and the third presents five sample lesson plans for teaching a new concept and element, and practice of a known concept or element for the unit. Worksheets to accompany unit plans are posted on the accompanying website.

More information related to this chapter can be found on a new accompanying website for the second edition of *Kodály Today*. The website will include more than twenty worksheets to be used for practicing reading, writing, and improvisation for music elements related to the handbook for the first grade. Information in this chapter is aligned with Chapter 10 in *Kodály Today*.

Chapter 6: Assessment and Evaluation

The chapter includes twenty-five detailed assessment rubrics to assess singing, reading, writing, and improvisation for this grade. These rubrics can form the foundation of any kind of assessment that takes place in the music classroom.

Outstanding Features

Timely Publication

In July 2012 the National Research Council challenged teachers to cultivate approaches to teaching that develop "deeper learning." This first grade handbook supplies to music teachers a model that promotes twenty-first-century skills.

Transcending All Methods of Teaching Music

The researchers have used the Kodály philosophy as a pedagogical compass for this handbook. The foundation for the approach in this first grade handbook is focused on developing children's knowledge of repertoire, performance skills (singing, moving, playing instruments), reading and writing of music, listening, and improvisation and composition skills—key components of any music curriculum. Teachers certified in Kodály, Orff, and Dalcroze training piloted this handbook. Any teacher, regardless of personal philosophy and favored pedagogy, can use these handbooks.

Writing Style

The writing style of this handbook is accessible; it instantly engages the reader. The text is filled with examples of activities as well as detailed lesson plans that translate a theoretical model for learning and instruction into a practical handbook for teaching music in the first grade music classroom.

Organic Pedagogy

The authors use an organic approach to teaching music that begins with careful selection of repertoire. This repertoire is then used to build students' skills in singing, movement, playing instruments, reading and writing, listening, and improvisation skills. This is accomplished through active music making in the classroom.

Sequential Pedagogy

Through our many years of research and classroom teaching as well as having the opportunity to work with professionals in the field, we have created a process for presenting musical concepts and developing music skills. Although several works describing Kodály-based techniques and curriculums exist, few spell out in detail teaching procedures for presenting musical concepts and integrating them with musical skill development. Some educators familiar with Kodály-inspired teaching may already know some of the teaching ideas presented in this text. However, we have combined these ideas with current research findings in the field of music perception and cognition to develop a model of music instruction and learning that offers teachers a map to follow that will develop their students' musical understandings and metacognition skills. We have worked to present a clear picture of how one develops a first grade music curriculum based on the philosophy of Kodály, the teaching and learning processes needed to execute this curriculum, and assessment tools.

Vertical Alignment of Music Classes

Because of the pedagogy used in this publication, it offers a compelling example of how to achieve vertical alignment in the elementary music curriculum. Like all other subject areas in the elementary curriculum, this handbook develops routines and procedures that are common to music lessons regardless of grade level and teaching philosophy. In this teaching handbook, we delineate the teaching process by including more than thirty-five lesson plans for first grade for teaching music according to the Kodály philosophy and based on the *Kodály Today* text. This handbook presents a clear picture of how the teaching and learning processes go hand in hand during the music lesson.

New Cognitive Model for Teaching Music

The series presents detailed instructions on how to present music concepts based on a model of learning developed in *Kodály Today*. This model builds on the accepted process of teaching music: prepare, make conscious, reinforce, and assess. The researcher has adopted these phases of learning, but each phase is further broken down into stages that allow sequential teaching of music concepts and elements as well as the means for their assessment. This model of learning inspires the music curriculum, lesson plans, and assessment rubrics for all the handbooks.

Who Should Read This Book?

This book will appeal to methods instructors, pre-service music teachers, beginning music teachers, and practicing or veteran music teachers, for a number of reasons. It is a book with a solid methodological foundation that focuses on creatively enhancing the learning environment of students. Therefore, it appeals to methods instructors who will use the handbooks over the course of a semester to show the necessary elements of a comprehensive music education. Effective methods instruction includes what to teach, how to teach, and why to teach, and this book addresses all of these areas. Second, pre-service music teachers will gravitate toward the sequencing and lesson planning included in the book, as well as specific resources (songs, books), when practice-teaching during methods courses, field experiences, and student teaching. Third, beginning teachers are often most concerned with long-term planning for each grade level; unit and lesson plans contained in the handbooks will appeal to these teachers. Finally, this book will appeal to practicing and veteran music teachers because it can be used to refresh knowledge of teaching music. The book updates traditional ideas and teaching practices associated with the Kodály concept of music education and makes them accessible, practical, and relevant for today's classrooms. Veteran teachers will use this handbook to link best practices to research.

Kodály in the First Grade Classroom

Chapter 1

Framing a Curriculum Based on the Kodály Concept

This chapter gives teachers an overview of the Kodály concept as it relates to curriculum development, and it includes a sample of a grade one curriculum. Also included is a lesson plan design that is used throughout this book to create sample lessons reflecting the content of each chapter. Chapter 1 of *Kodály Today* offers teachers a biographical overview of Kodály's life as well as an introduction to the Kodály concept of music education.

The Kodály Concept

Zoltán Kodály's philosophy of music education inspired development of the Kodály method or the Kodály concept of music education. The Kodály method was actually developed by his students and colleagues. Simply stated, the method is a comprehensive approach to teaching music skills. The composer stressed the need for all music teachers to be excellent musicians and conductors, and to have a knowledge of music repertoire to successfully develop a music program. This section identifies the essential hallmarks of the Kodály method as shaped by Kodály's philosophy of music education.

Singing

Singing is the essence of the Kodály concept, and tuneful singing is the foundation for developing music skills. Generally speaking, singing should be taught before formal instrumental lessons. Singing permits quickly internalizing music and allows students to develop the skill of audiation. Chapter 3 of this handbook offers a comprehensive overview for developing the singing voice in the first grade curriculum.

Repertoire

Everyone needs to know and celebrate his or her cultural heritage. A key component of this cultural heritage is folk music, which includes children's songs and games. These songs and games include the basic rhythmic and melodic building blocks of music that can be used to make connections to all styles of music. A music curriculum should include these materials:

> Traditional children's songs and games
> Folk songs and games of the American culture
> Folk songs of other cultures
> Art music (music of the masters)
> Pedagogical exercises written by composers
> Recently composed music written by excellent composers

In Chapter 2 of the handbook we lay out a more comprehensive overview of the repertoire that is used in the elementary music curriculum.

Reading and Writing

Musical reading and writing is another essential component of the Kodály method. Practitioners of this method use a variety of musical tools to develop a student's fluency in reading and writing music. These tools are discussed in more detail in Chapter 4 of this book. The teaching tools used include relative solmization, moveable *do* (where the tonic note is *do* in major and *la* in minor), hand signs, and rhythm syllables.

Sequencing

Another vital component of the Kodály concept is the ability for teachers to sequence materials along with presenting concepts and elements to students that are derived primarily from singing repertoire musically. This is an experience-based approach to learning. We present a thorough approach to curricular sequencing for grade one in Chapter 5 of this book.

Multiple Dimensions of Music

Music education, to quote the author Daniel H. Pink, is "fundamental, not ornamental."[1] Learning music gives students many opportunities to perform music, become stewards of their cultural heritage, develop critical-thinking skills (reading and writing music), be creative human beings, and be informed listeners and audience members. Through these multiple dimensions of their music education, students develop skills that not only will make them more accomplished musicians but will also prepare them for life as citizens of the twenty-first century.

When designing a curriculum based on the Kodály philosophy of music education, we need to develop our students':

- Performance skills through, singing, playing an instrument, and movement
- Knowledge of music repertoire
- Knowledge of critical-thinking skills about music through reading and writing
- Ability to improvise music
- Ability to listen to music with understanding

Students as Stewards of Their Cultural Heritage

Students will perform a repertoire of music that includes folk music, art music, patriotic music, and recently composed music. They will explore music from cultures such as the southern Appalachians, African American, Mexican, American frontier, British Isles, and Eastern Europe. This exposure deepens students' understanding of the various styles of music, giving them tools to compare musical styles as well as the cultures they come from. First grade students will be able to connect music to the subject areas of reading, writing, language, and math.

Students as Performers

For a music education to be complete, it must begin with singing and experiencing the production of sound daily. In fourth grade, students add to their singing a number of songs with greater vocal range and complexity of rhythms, and they will improve part-singing skills and extend their vocal range by using canons and two- and three-part song arrangements of various cultural origins. They will add double circle games, basic square dancing, and conducting of complicated meters to their movement skills. They will demonstrate melodic and rhythmic concepts on recorders as well as other classroom instruments.

Students as Critical Thinkers

In first grade, the students will analyze music that includes quarter notes and two eighth notes, quarter note rests, and melodies composed of a three-note child's chant. As critical thinkers, students reason effectively, and learn to communicate and collaborate to solve music problems.

Students as Creative Human Beings

Students express themselves through improvisation, form, and melodic and rhythmic composition using their knowledge of music as the basis for their improvisation activities and compositions in the classroom. Teachers engage students in myriad activities. For example, the teacher furnishes students with an A phrase (question) that is four beats long and asks them to improvise a four-beat B phrase (answer). This activity leads to performing melodic or rhythmic conversation. They compose and improvise simple four-beat rhythmic phrases and three-note melodic phrases. These activities permit assessment of student understanding of musical elements and musical styles as well as their skill performance.

Students as Informed Listeners

Students in the twenty-first century are surrounded every day by music from a variety of mixed media sources. The first grade musical concepts will be reinforced through an expanded listening repertoire that includes local artists, classical compositions, popular styles, and peer performances. Along with the melodic and rhythmic concepts, they will develop awareness of dynamics, tempo, and timbre through masterworks of various historical periods.

Grade 1 Music Curriculum

Here we present a sample grade one curriculum that is shaped by our understanding of the Zoltán Kodály philosophy of music education. All the sections of the curriculum will be discussed in greater detail in subsequent chapters. Of course we offer only a shell of a music curriculum; the demands placed on music teachers differ from one school district to the next. We present a sample grade one curriculum as a starting point for creating engaging music lessons. It is important to remember that, as we read in the *Oxford Handbook of Music Education*, "although disciplined practice is part of the task, a young aspiring musician's spirit can be deadened in the face of a curriculum of tasks to be done and discriminations to be learned in a standardized way, however 'age appropriate' its methods strive to be."[2] It is likely that the specific music skills in the sample will need to be modified according to the frequency of instruction. The goal of this curriculum is to make available a model for constructing your own curriculum based on the Kodály philosophy of music education. Once you have an understanding of this philosophy, you will be able to make modifications to suit your own particular teaching situations. Our goal is to show how the major tenets of the Kodály philosophy, and current practices in teaching music using techniques associated with the Kodály method, can shape a music curriculum.

Students as Stewards of Their Cultural and Musical Heritage: Repertoire

Students experience a repertoire of music that includes folk music from a variety of cultures, art music, patriotic music, recently composed music, and seasonal music. This exposure deepens students' understanding of the various styles of music, giving them tools to understand diverse music cultures and styles. Guided by a skillful teacher, they can relate their music performance to history, to society, and to culture (playing games, singing songs from an array of cultures, from the United States and neighboring countries), as well as connect the music to other subjects—reading, writing, language, and math.

Students will grow to understand how many types of music share the same "musical building blocks" as well as what makes every music composition unique. Understanding a particular music style will help them with developing their own creative style. This is an invaluable and unique aspect of music education. Students in grade one will study a core of folk song repertoire music and subsequently expand their repertoire to add to their knowledge of songs and games, folk music of neighboring and other cultures, art music, and recently composed music.

Students as Performers: Performance

A student's music education should begin with singing. Students sing while performing singing games and part music, as they develop their knowledge of music literacy along with using the voice to create their own music. Singing is the glue that connects all of the music skills and knowledge taught in the music classroom. It develops a primary skill in music: the ability to think in sound. This leads to their ability to perform musically on an instrument. Once students gain the ability to think in sound, they will be able to play a musical instrument with musical understanding. Playing an instrument is not simply about the technical aspects of learning it; playing involves learning how to translate an aural image of a piece into an acoustic sound. Therefore learning the technique of playing an instrument is only one part of the process necessary for translating notation into sound. The aural image of the piece of music should always dictate how to perform the piece of music.

Students also learn how to develop their movement and conducting skills in this grade. We believe that it's essential to create an organic connection between singing, playing instruments, movement, and conducting skills.

The curriculum will broaden performance skills:

1. Singing tunefully
   A. Students sing songs independently and tunefully in a six-note range.
   B. They become familiar with a varied repertoire of at least thirty folk songs and singing games, classical music, and recently composed music (just a few songs are sufficient here).
   C. They know by memory ten to fifteen songs and are able to sing them with solfège and rhythm names.
   D. They perform all songs with accurate intonation, clear diction, clear head tone, musical phrasing and breathing, appropriate dynamics, and tempi.
   E. They perform songs using tempo, including allegro and largo, and dynamics, including forte and piano.
2. Movement
   A. They explore music making with body percussion.
   B. They perform acting-out, chasing, winding, simple line, and circle games.
   C. They improvise words and movement to known songs.
   D. They explore games, activities, and movement in personal space or general space.
3. Instruments
   A. They play instruments independently or in a group.
   B. They play ethnic music with unpitched instruments and body percussion.
   C. They demonstrate first grade melodic and rhythmic concepts on classroom instruments.
   D. They accompany classroom singing on classroom instruments.
4. Part Work
   A. They sing songs antiphonally.
   B. They practice singing intervals simultaneously with solfège syllables and hand signs.
   C. They accompany a song with a rhythmic ostinato using quarter and eighth notes and quarter note rests.
   D. They accompany a song with a melodic ostinato using *la*, *so*, and *mi*.
   E. They chant simple rhythmic canons derived from the rhythms of familiar songs.
   F. They sing simple melodic canons derived from the melodic motifs of familiar songs.
   G. They perform two-part rhythmic exercises based on rhythmic motifs of known songs.
   H. They perform two-part melodic exercises based on the rhythmic and melodic motifs of known songs.
   I. They perform simple folksongs in canon.
5. Conducting
   A. They conduct in duple meter.

Students as Critical Thinkers and Problem Solvers: Music Literacy

Learning how to read and write music is closely connected to understanding stylistic elements of music. To develop students' music literacy skills, it is important that they study a core repertoire of songs sharing similar rhythmic and melodic characteristics. Each piece of music studied is an opportunity for the teacher to share with students the commonalities between pieces of music and also introduce them to new music elements. This can be accomplished through developing students' reading and writing of music.

As critical thinkers, students will use an inquiry-based approach to learn how to read and write music. We approach the teaching of every new music concept and element as a problem to be solved. The teacher is always asking questions about a new concept or element being studied: "What are the characteristics of the new concept or element?" How can you create a representation of the new music concept or element? Analyze your representation with the help of a friend, and draw conclusions about your representation. Share your findings with the class about what you discovered. How do we notate a new rhythmic or melodic element into notation?" Students will learn to gather kinesthetic, aural, and visual information about a new music concept or element before they learn the process of how to notate this new element. Part of their problem-solving activities is to engage in a process where they create their own notations for a new element and try to capture the characteristics of the new element in their own notations. The act of taking music apart, studying the parts, and then putting them all back together again to perform repertoire musically teaches students how to understand music thoughtfully, but the process can be applied to other subjects as well.

Critical thinking is applied in music through reading and writing music to develop music literacy skills. First grade students will gain fluency using rhythm syllables for quarter and two eighth notes, quarter rests, and solfège syllables for *so, mi,* and *la*. Students will learn how to read and write known rhythms and melodies, sight-read new melodies, and write unknown songs using stick notation, traditional notation, and staff notation. They also develop their inner hearing, knowledge of form, and memory skills while developing music literacy skills.

1. Reading and writing of rhythmic elements
   A. Students know names and written symbols for quarter and eighth notes, quarter note rests, accented beat, and bar lines. They conduct in duple meter. (This should be the final step in learning rhythms; students need to sing repertoire fluently with rhythm syllables before learning the technical names of notes.)
   B. They read well-known rhythmic patterns with stick notation and traditional rhythmic notation.
   C. They read a two-part rhythmic exercise.
   D. They write well-known rhythmic patterns with stick notation and traditional rhythmic notation.
   E. They write rhythmic patterns from memory or when dictated by the teacher in stick notation and traditional rhythmic notation.

2. Reading and writing of melodic elements
   A. They know the names and written syllables for grade one solfège syllables *so, mi,* and *la.*
   B. They read well-known melodic patterns with traditional rhythmic notation and solfège syllables, as well as on staff notation.
   C. They read a two-part melodic exercise from notation.
   D. They write well-known melodic patterns with traditional rhythmic notation and solfège syllables as well as on staff notation.
   E. They write melodic patterns found in focus songs from memory or when dictated by the teacher, using stick and solfège syllables, traditional notation, and solfège syllables or staff notation.
3. Inner hearing
   A. They silently sing melodic motifs or melody from the teacher's hand signs.
   B. They silently sing known songs with rhythmic syllables.
   C. They silently sing known songs with melodic syllables.
   D. They silently read either full or partial rhythms or melodies written in traditional notation with solfège syllables or staff notation.
   E. They sing back short known melodic or rhythmic motives from memory using text (if the student recognizes the song it is abstracted from), rhythm syllables, or solfège syllables.
4. Form
   A. They recognize same, similar, or different phrases in a song either aurally or through music reading.
   B. They recognize repeated musical motifs that are the same and the ones that differ.
   C. They use letters to label the forms in simple songs: AB, AABA, or ABAC patterns.
   D. They use repeat signs correctly in reading and writing.
5. Musical memory
   A. They echo four- and eight-beat rhythm patterns clapped by the teacher with rhythm syllables.
   B. They echo four- and eight-beat solfège patterns sung by the teacher with solfège and hand signs.
   C. They memorize short melodies through hand signs.
   D. They memorize rhythm patterns of four or eight beats from known songs from traditional rhythmic notation.
   E. They memorize melodic patterns of four or eight beats from known songs from traditional rhythmic notation with solfège syllables or from staff notation.

Students as Creative Human Beings: Improvisation and Composition

When students learn to express themselves through improvisation and composition, they learn more about who they are and what they are capable of accomplishing. The initial act of improvising and subsequently composing music gives a student a chance to engage creativity. We believe it is most valuable for students to develop creative skills by manipulating known rhythmic or melodic elements before they begin to create their own compositions. They should be given several types of rhythmic and melodic improvisation exercises, to include individual and class improvisation/composition of movement, singing, and playing on classroom instruments. The goal is to lead them to improvise with short rhythmic and melodic patterns derived from known repertoire in creating new versions of their songs.

1. Rhythmic improvisation (based on the rhythmic building blocks of sung repertoire)
   A. Students improvise rhythm patterns of four or eight beats by clapping and saying rhythm syllables.
   B. They improvise rhythm patterns of four or eight beats using rhythm instruments.
   C. They improvise a new rhythm to one measure or more of a well-known song written in traditional notation either by clapping or by playing a classroom instrument.
   D. They improvise question-and-answer motives using known rhythm patterns.
   E. They improvise to a given form.
2. Melodic improvisation (based on the melodic building blocks of sung repertoire)
   A. Students improvise melodic patterns of four or eight beats by singing with solfège syllables and hand signs.
   B. They improvise melodic patterns of four or eight beats using barred instruments.
   C. They improvise short musical motives (*la-so-mi*) using hand signs, hand staff, or body signs.
   D. They improvise pentatonic bichord and trichord (*so-mi-la*) melodies to simple four- and eight-beat rhythms using the voice or a barred instrument.
   E. They improvise a melody to one measure or more of a well-known song.
   F. They improvise question-and-answer motives using known melodic patterns.

Students as Informed Audience Members: Listening

Students are surrounded every day by music from a variety of media sources. It is our responsibility as music educators to help our students become critical listeners so that they can identify and understand the purposes of many kinds of music. The music they listen to with their friends (social music) can have a purpose different from that of music repertoire studied in music classes. Of course they must ultimately understand that all music can fall into two categories: good or bad. It is our job as educators to train students to differentiate between good and bad music and allow them to make their own choices in music they listen to. We need to develop students' ability to listen actively to a variety of styles of music and understand the stylistic elements of this repertoire. But the music repertoire we choose to use in our music curriculum should reflect the processes that literature teachers use when they select books to be read in a literature class. Although there can certainly be a disagreement as to what constitutes quality repertoire, there is a general consensus as to what makes great literature.

1. Expand listening repertoire and revisit kindergarten musical concepts.
   A. Students distinguish between singing, inner, whispering, calling, and speaking voices; between low, middle, and high; and between children's, adult male, and adult female voices.
   B. They recognize phrase forms (same and different) in classroom song repertoire, folk music, and masterworks.

C. They recognize known rhythmic features in classroom song repertoire, folk music, and masterworks, including quarter and eighth notes and quarter note rest.
D. They recognize known melodic features in classroom song repertoire, folk music, and masterworks.
E. They develop awareness of expressive controls, that is, dynamics, tempo, and timbre, and their distinctive characteristics in masterworks of various historical periods. Use basic music terminology in describing changes in tempo (including allegro and largo) and dynamics (including forte and piano); students should be able to recognize comparatives (fast and slow, loud and soft).
F. They distinguish same and different between beat and rhythm, higher and lower, louder and softer, and faster and slower in musical performances.
G. They recognize and identify aurally the instrument families.
H. They recognize and identify aurally one instrument from each instrument family.
I. They respond verbally or through movement to short musical examples.
J. They practice appropriate audience behavior during live performances.

Prompt Questions for Constructing a Music Curriculum

These questions will help you tailor the sample curriculum to your own specific needs. It is important that your curriculum reflect your own teaching philosophy and personality, as well as your own content knowledge or expertise. Remember also to reinforce the vision and mission of the school with your music programs, and to review your state standards for music education.

Questions on Where You Are Coming From
1. What is your philosophy of music education?
2. What role does the Kodály concept of music play in the development of your curriculum?
3. What is the mission and vision of your school?
4. How do you reinforce the mission of your school in your music curriculum?
5. How do you and your music students become advocates for music?
6. How do you develop the teaching of music in your school so that music is treated as a core subject area?

Questions on Repertoire in the Classroom
1. How do you select music repertoire for your curriculum?
2. Do you use this repertoire to develop all the students' music skills in performance, playing instruments, literacy, improvisation, and composition as well as prepare them to become critical consumers of music?
3. What melodic, rhythmic, singing, playing, and movement skills do you expect students to master by the end of first grade?
4. How will you encourage students to use the known rhythmic and melodic building blocks to create and build musical compositions, bolstering critical-thinking skills and creativity?
5. How will music benefit a student's overall academic achievement in the first grade?

6. How does your classroom reinforce the core curriculum and the vision of the campus?
7. How do you assess student growth in musicianship skills and music literacy throughout the year?
8. How does your classroom embrace cultural diversity through songs?
9. What is the role of foreign folk, art, and popular music being brought in by students of various cultures, and how do you use it to draw parallels with other genres in your class?

Questions on Music Skills and Content in Grade 1
1. How will you find a balance among the skills of singing, creative movement, playing instruments, reading and writing music, composing and improvising, and listening to music?
2. How do you create music lesson plans that will develop all of a student's music skills?

Questions on Tailoring Your Teaching to Student Populations
1. What are some ways in which you meet the various needs of bilingual and transitioning students to strengthen their primary language and promote acquisition of the English language through repertoire?
2. How do you use a broad range of music genres and styles to reach various populations of your campus and promote a lasting love and respect for all music?
3. How do you use a broad range of learning styles to reach various populations of your campus?
4. What is the place of technology in the music classroom?
5. How do you ensure a safe environment that encourages learning?

Questions on Keeping Your Teaching Relevant
1. How do you incorporate modern styles and genres in the music classroom?

Questions on Embracing Music Learning at Your Campus
1. How do you encourage your faculty, staff, and administration to support your music program?
2. What steps will you take to ensure your philosophy of music learning is supported by your campus?
3. How do you foster relationships with your school's faculty?

Lesson Planning

Now that we have created a sample curriculum, we can develop lesson plan outcomes and lessons for teaching music. We advise that your lesson focus on developing students':

- Knowledge of repertoire: teaching a new song
- Performance skills: learning to sing, play instruments, and move to music
- Critical-thinking skills: teaching music concepts and elements to students according to the frequency of occurrence in the material they are singing

- Creative skills: teaching students how to improvise and compose
- Listening skills: teaching students how to actively listen to music

We address all of these goals in detail throughout the book. Here we begin the process of lesson planning. A primary task for music teachers is to teach basic rhythmic elements. To accomplish this successfully, students need to be guided through a variety of experiential activities (preparation activities) before learning how to identify sounds and label them with rhythmic or melodic syllables or learning the notation of these sounds (practice activities). Once learned, this information (practice) can be applied to expanding their musical skills through reading, writing, and improvisation.

Lesson planning and acquiring music literacy skills are closely intertwined. Teaching a musical element involves eight steps.

Preparation
1. Prepare the learning through kinesthetic activities.
2. Prepare the learning through aural activities.
3. Prepare the learning through visual activities.

Presentation
4. Present the solfège syllable or rhythm label for the new sound.
5. Present the notation for the new sound.

Practice
6. Incorporate the new element (now identified as a familiar element) into the practices of reading
7. Incorporate the new element (now identified as a familiar element) into the practices of writing.
8. Incorporate the new element (now identified as a familiar element) into the practices of improvisation and composition.

This is accomplished throughout a series of lessons.

To undertake these steps, there are two basic lesson plan designs: preparation/practice lessons and presentation lessons.

In a preparation/practice lesson, we prepare one musical element and practice another. For example, when preparing a new element B (steps 1, 2, and 3) we also practice a familiar element A (steps 6, 7, and 8). Once we have taught steps 1, 2, and 3, for element B in a preparation/practice lesson, we address steps 4 and 5 for element B in presentation lessons.

Key Components of Lesson Plan Design

Table 1.1 is the basic preparation/practice lesson plan design we use throughout the book. In each chapter, we add to this basic lesson plan design to incorporate and reflect the information in the chapter. We use a lesson plan structure that divides all lessons into three sections: introduction, core activities, and closure. This design can be modified to accommodate learning objectives for developing students' skills as performers, critical thinkers, improvisers, composers, listeners, and stewards of their cultural and musical heritage.

Table 1.1 Components of the Basic Preparation/Practice Lesson Plan Design

INTRODUCTION	
Performance and demonstration of known musical concepts and elements	
CORE ACTIVITIES	
Acquisition of repertoire:	
Preparation of a rhythmic or melodic element	Element B: this section of the lesson is used for steps 1–3 of preparing a new element
Creative movement	
Practice and performance of musical skills	Element A: this section of the lesson is used for steps 6–8
CLOSURE	
Review and summation	

Table 1.2 explains the segments of a basic preparation/practice lesson plan design.

Table 1.2 Explanation of the Preparation/Practice Lesson Plan

LESSON SECTION ONE: INTRODUCTION	
Demonstration of known musical concepts and elements	This segment of the lesson includes vocal warm-up exercises, singing known songs, developing tuneful singing, and singing known songs with rhythmic or melodic syllables. During this section of the lesson, we address music learning outlined in the music curriculum under the title of "Students as Stewards of Their Cultural Heritage: Repertoire" and "Students as Performers: Performance."
LESSON SECTION TWO: CORE ACTIVITIES	
This section involves acquisition of repertoire and performance of new concepts or elements.	
Acquisition of repertoire	Teaching a new song serves two purposes. First, it expands students' repertoire, and second, the new song should also include rhythmic or melodic concepts or elements that will be addressed in upcoming lessons.
	We present new repertoire for a variety of reasons. Sometimes we wish to teach a song simply to develop students' singing ability. Sometimes a song may be taught because we need to provide a musical context for teaching future musical concepts. The teacher may need to teach repertoire for a future performance or concert.
	During this section of the lesson, we address music learning outlined in the music curriculum under the title "Students as Stewards of Their Cultural Heritage: Repertoire."

(Continued)

Table 1.2 (continued)

Preparation of a new concept or element	Here activities focus on leading students to discover the attributes of a new musical concept or element. The instruction focuses on guiding students through kinesthetic (step 1), aural (step 2), and visual learning (step 3) activities. During this section of the lesson, we address music learning outlined in the music curriculum under the title "Students as Critical Thinkers." Critical thinking is associated with literacy. Through discovery-based learning, children acquire music literacy skills. In this section of the lesson, students are guided to understand the basic rhythmic or melodic building blocks of the song material as well as the formal music structures.
This first period of concentration is followed by a period of relaxation.	
Creative movement	Students learn singing games and folk songs. Activities focus on the sequential development of age-appropriate movement skills through songs and folk games. A sequence for age-appropriate movement skill development is provided in Chapter 3 of *Kodály Today*.
This period of relaxation is followed by a second period of concentration.	
Practice and musical skill development	In this section, the teacher practices the music skills outlined in the music curriculum under the title "Students as Critical Thinkers." This section reinforces known musical elements while focusing on a particular music skill such as reading (step 6), writing (step 7), or improvisation and composition (step 8). (Of course we use these skills as anchors for practicing all other music skills, such as inner hearing, form, memory, part work, and listening.)
LESSON SECTION THREE: CLOSURE	
Review and summation	Review the lesson outcomes. Review the new song. Review the lesson content. Review the new song. Students may review known songs or play a game. The teacher may also perform the next new song that will be taught in a subsequent lesson.

The next four tables elaborate on the basic presentation lesson plan designs we use throughout the book; we use 1.3 (components) and 1.4 (explanation) to label sounds with syllables, and 1.5 (components) and 1.6 (explanation) to present the notation.

Table 1.3   Components of the Basic Presentation Lesson Plan Design for Labeling Sounds with Syllables

INTRODUCTION	
Performance and demonstration of known musical concepts and elements	
CORE ACTIVITIES	
Acquisition of repertoire	
Presentation of a new concept or element	Element B This segment of the lesson is used for step 4
Creative movement	
Presentation of a new concept or element	Element B This segment of the lesson is used for step 4
CLOSURE	
Review and summation	

Table 1.4   Explanation of Presentation Lesson Plan for Labeling Sounds with Syllables

LESSON SECTION ONE: INTRODUCTION	
Demonstration of known musical concepts and elements	
LESSON SECTION TWO: CORE ACTIVITIES	
This section involves acquisition of repertoire and performance of new concepts or elements.	
Acquisition of repertoire	
Presentation of a new concept or element	Using a known song, the teacher presents the label for the new sound with either rhythmic or melodic syllables. Here the teacher will be presenting elements that are outlined in the music curriculum under the title "Students as Critical Thinkers." Students are guided to first label the sound of the new musical element and second to learn the notation of the musical element. They label the sound of the basic rhythmic or melodic building blocks of the song material and subsequently learn the notation.
This first period of concentration is followed by a period of relaxation.	

(Continued)

Table 1.4 (continued)

Movement development Creative movement	
This period of relaxation is followed by a second period of concentration.	
Presentation of a new concept or element	Using another known song, the teacher presents the label for the new sound with either rhythmic or melodic syllables. Here the teacher will be presenting concepts that are outlined in the music curriculum under the title "Students as Critical Thinkers." They label the sound of the basic rhythmic or melodic building blocks of the song material.
LESSON SECTION THREE: CLOSURE	
Review and summation	Review the lesson outcomes. Review the new song. Review the lesson content. Review the new song. Students may review known songs or play a game. The teacher may also perform the next new song that will be taught in a subsequent lesson.

Table 1.5 Components of the Basic Presentation Lesson Plan Design for Notating a New Element

INTRODUCTION	
Performance and demonstration of known musical concepts and elements	
CORE ACTIVITIES	
Acquisition of repertoire	
Presentation of a new concept or element	Element B This segment of the lesson is used for step 5
Creative movement	
Presentation of a new concept or element	Element B This segment of the lesson is used for step 5
CLOSURE	
Review and summation	

Table 1.6 Explanation of the Presentation Lesson Plan Design for Notating New Element

LESSON SECTION ONE: INTRODUCTION	
Demonstration of known musical concepts and elements	
LESSON SECTION TWO: CORE ACTIVITIES	
This section involves acquisition of repertoire and performance of new concepts or elements.	
Acquisition of repertoire	
Presentation of a new concept or element	Element B Using a known song, the teacher presents the notation for the new element. Here the teacher will be presenting concepts that are outlined in the music curriculum under the title "Students as Critical Thinkers."
This first period of concentration is followed by a period of relaxation.	
Movement development Creative movement	
This period of relaxation is followed by a second period of concentration.	
Presentation of a new concept or element	Element B Using another known song, the teacher presents notation for the new element. Here the teacher will be presenting concepts that are outlined in the music curriculum under the title "Students as Critical Thinkers."
LESSON SECTION THREE: CLOSURE	
Review and summation	Review the lesson outcomes. Review the new song. Review the lesson content. Review the new song. Students may review known songs or play a game. The teacher may also perform the next new song that will be taught in a subsequent lesson.

Chapter 2

Developing a Music Repertoire

Students as Stewards of Their Cultural and Musical Heritage

This chapter presents an overview of basic repertoire for teachers to use in developing singing, playing instruments, creative movement, improvisation, and listening. Included in this chapter is an alphabetized list of songs with sources, as well a pedagogical list of songs for teaching rhythmic and melodic elements. It also includes sequenced directions for teaching singing games and movement activities.

Selecting Repertoire

A child's music education should begin with the folk music and rhymes of her own culture:

> It is through the indigenous musics of their cultures that children receive the stories of their people, those that ancestors pass down from generation to generation and others that are contemporary and reflect new customs. Folk music is the treasure trove of children's values, beliefs, cultures, knowledge, games, and stories. The music of children's own cultures must be given respect and status in the classroom, indirectly giving children a sense of their own values and status. Receptivity toward the music of other cultures can be developed from this point of reference, thereby fostering cultural awareness, tolerance and respect.[1]

We use folk music because it belongs to the oral tradition and "draws on the power of repetition and the human urge to generate and create."[2] In the best folk songs, there is a unity between the rhythm and melody; word and musical accents fall together logically.

> The Kodály approach uses games songs that are highly repetitive and melodically simple to help build "inner hearing" (aural) skills and accurate singing (oral) skills. Those music activities could be valuable to the development of social skills and self-confidence in children, including those children with special needs, whereby language experience, aural sensitivity and discrimination, and motor skills are cultivated in enjoyable and purposeful music game settings.[3]

Take time to familiarize yourself with the primary sources for folk music referenced in Chapter 2 of *Kodály Today*. Selecting age-appropriate repertoire for every grade is important. Learning to sing this repertoire from memory will help students "own" this music repertoire. The songs are easy to learn, and they will engage children in the singing process if sung with enjoyment and artistry. Sometimes teachers find it difficult to believe they can keep the imagination of a child engaged by singing simple unaccompanied folk songs. If performed in an aesthetically pleasing manner, the suggested songs will capture the imaginations of children. Of course these songs may also have tasteful piano accompaniments.

The repertoire selected for classroom use should be of high quality and include not only songs that incorporate musical concepts for teaching but also songs to develop the joy found in seasonal songs and multicultural songs. Sometimes music teachers choose song material to help children remember classroom rules; or they can be used as an aid in developing literacy skills or numeracy skills. Although these songs are useful for developing children's social skills, they should not be the primary singing material of the elementary music program. We need to find ways to connect what we are doing in the classroom with the community at large, as well as acknowledge children's own music interests. The *Oxford Handbook of Music Education* proposes that "When children's preferences and tastes in music are acknowledged and incorporated into the music curriculum, they can be helped to understand a wider range of music through active involvement in listening."[4] Asking children to perform a song or a movement they have developed or piece of music they have learned from the web, television, or their parents is important. Finding ways to connect this repertoire to music activities in the classroom can be powerful. Inviting musicians into the classroom to perform live music for children is also a great way to make a musical connection with the community. In so doing, we come to understand "music as an activity to be engaged in and made between people, rather than as a 'thing' to be learned, or set of uniform skills to be imparted, and, moreover, to see how music and musical practices are ever-changing."[5]

We present in this chapter, for the first grade:

- An alphabetical list of repertoire and sources for the songs
- Singing games and directions for playing the games
- A pedagogical list of songs suitable for teaching rhythmic and melodic elements

Grade 1 Song Lists

Alphabetized Song List

Table 2.1 has a core list of game songs for use in the first grade music class.

Table 2.1 Grade 1 Alphabetical Song List

Song	Source
"All Around the Buttercup"	*Let's Sing Together*
"Apple Tree"	*Music in the Preschool*
"Bee, Bee, Bumble Bee"	*Let's Sing Together*
"Bobby Shafto"	*The Kodály Context*

(Continued)

Table 2.1 (continued)

"Bounce High, Bounce Low"	*Sail Away: 155 American Folk Songs*
"Bow Wow Wow"	*150 American Folk Songs*
"Button, You Must Wander"	*The Kodály Method*
"Bye, Baby Bunting"	*150 American Folk Songs*
"Chini, Mini"	*Vamos a Cantar*
"Clap Your Hands Together"	*The Kodály Context*
"The Closet Key"	*150 American Folk Songs*
"Cobbler, Cobbler"	*150 American Folk Songs*
"Doggie, Doggie"	*Music in the Preschool*
"Down Came a Lady"	*150 American Folk Songs*
"Ducks and Geese"	*Enek-zene: Az Altalanos Iskola Szakositott Tantervu, book 1*
"Engine, Engine, Number Nine"	(traditional)
"Farmer in the Dell"	(traditional)
"Frog in the Meadow"	*Sail Away: 155 American Folk Songs*
"Fudge Fudge"	*Let's Slice the Ice*
"Good Night, Sleep Tight"	*Music in the Preschool*
"Here Comes a Bluebird"	*150 American Folk Songs*
"Here We Go 'Round the Mulberry Bush"	*150 American Folk Songs*
"Hot Cross Buns"	*150 American Folk Songs*
"Hush, Baby, Hush"	*150 American Folk Songs*
"In and Out"	*Favorite Nursery Songs*
"It's Raining, It's Pouring"	*An American Methodology*
"Jack and Jill"	*Let's Sing Together*
"Johnny's It"	*Music in the Preschool*
"Johnny Works with One Hammer"	*Music in the Preschool*
"Just from the Kitchen"	*Sail Away: 155 American Folk Songs*
"Lemonade"	*Sail Away: 155 American Folk Songs*
"Let Us Chase the Squirrel"	*150 American Folk Songs*
"Little Rooster" (Pipirigallo)	*Vamos a Cantar*
"Little Sally Water"	*150 American Folk Songs*
"Lucy Locket"	*Sail Away: 155 American Folk Songs*
"Mary Had a Little Lamb"	*Heritage Songster*
"Naughty Kitty Cat"	*Hungarian Folk Song*
"A Nick and a Peck" (Pica Perica)	*Vamos a Cantar*
"No Robbers Out Today"	*Sail Away: 155 American Folk Songs*
"On the Mountain"	*Sail Away: 155 American Folk Songs*

(Continued)

Table 2.1   (continued)

"Pala Palita"	*Vamos a Cantar*
"Pease Porridge Hot"	*Music in the Preschool*
"Pipis y Ganas"	*Vamos a Cantar*
"Que Llueva" (La Virgin de la Cueva)	*El Patio de Mi Casa*
"Queen, Queen Caroline"	*Music in the Preschool*
"Rain, Rain"	*150 American Folk Songs*
"Ring Around the Rosie"	*150 American Folk Songs*
"Round and Round" (A la Ronda, Ronda)	*Vamos a Cantar*
"Seesaw"	*Kodály Today*
"Snail, Snail"	*Sail Away: 155 American Folk Songs*
"Star Light, Star Bright"	*Music in the Preschool*
"Teddy Bear"	*Music in the Preschool*
"This Old Man"	*Heritage Songster*
"A Tisket, a Tasket"	*150 American Folk Songs*
"Tortillitas"	*El Patio de Mi Casa*
"Twinkle, Twinkle Little Star"	*Songs Children Sing*
"Two Four Six Eight"	*Traditional Nursery Rhyme*
"La Vieja Inez"	*El Patio de Mi Casa*
"We Are Dancing in the Forest"	*Music in the Preschool*
"Who Are These People"? (¿Quien es esa gente?)	*Vamos a Cantar*
"Witch Witch"	*Sail Away: 155 American Folk Songs*

References for Table 2.1

Bacon, Denise. *Let's Sing Together!* London: Boosey & Hawkes, 1971.
Choksy, Lois. *The Kodaly Context.* Englewood Cliffs, NJ: Prentice-Hall, 1981.
Dallin, Leon, and Lynn Dallin. *Heritage Songster.* Dubuque, IA: Wm. C. Brown, 1966.
Erdei, Peter, and Katalin Komlós. *150 American Folk Songs.* London: Boosey & Hawkes, 1974.
Forrai, Katalin. *Music in Preschool.* London: Boosey & Hawkes, 1995.
Fulton, Eleanor, and Pat Smith. *Let's Slice the Ice.* St. Louis, MO: Magnamusic, 1978.
Grentzer, Rose Marie, and Marguerite Hood. *Birchard Music Series: Kindergarten.* Evanston, IL: Summy-Birchard, 1959.
Houlahan, Micheál, and Philip Tacka. *Kodály Today.* New York: Oxford University Press, 2008.
Locke, Eleanor G. *Sail Away: 155 American Folk Songs.* London: Boosey & Hawkes, 1988.

Martin, Florence, and Margaret Rose White. *Songs Children Sing*. Minneapolis: Schmitt, Hall & McCreary, 1943. (Originally *The Silver Book of Songs*, 1935, and *Children's Favorite Songs*, 1942.)

Montoya-Stier, Gabriela. *El Patio de Mi Casa*. Chicago: GIA, 2008.

Nemesszeghyne, Marta. *Enek-zene: Az Altalanos Iskola Szakositott Tantervu, book 1*. Budapest, 1962.

O'Hanian, Phyllis Brown. *Favorite Nursery Songs*. New York: Random House, 1956.

Singing Games and Sequenced Directions for Playing

Tables 2.2 and 2.3 list songs and game directions for teaching first grade music concepts and elements. We also recognize that teachers may have better ideas and more creative ways to teach musical games; these game directions are intended to offer helpful guidance.

Table 2.2   Grade 1 Games

Song/Game Title	Source
"All Around the Buttercup"	*Let's Sing Together*
"Bounce High, Bounce Low"	*Sail Away: 155 American Folk Songs*
"Bow Wow Wow"	*150 American Folk Songs*
"Button, You Must Wander"	*The Kodály Method*
"Clap Your Hands Together"	*The Kodály Context*
"Doggie, Doggie"	*Music in the Preschool*
"Down Came a Lady"	*150 American Folk Songs*
"Frog in the Meadow"	*Sail Away: 155 American Folk Songs*
"Fudge Fudge"	*Let's Slice the Ice*
"Here Comes a Bluebird"	*150 American Folk Songs*
"In and Out"	*Favorite Nursery Songs*
"Johnny's It"	*Music in the Preschool*
"Lemonade"	*Sail Away: 155 American Folk Songs*
"Little Sally Water"	*150 American Folk Songs*
"Lucy Locket"	*Sail Away: 155 American Folk Songs*
"Nanny Goat"	*An American Methodology*
"Naughty Kitty Cat"	*An American Methodology*
"No Robbers Out Today"	*Sail Away: 155 American Folk Songs*
"Rain, Rain"	*150 American Folk Songs*
"Ring Around the Rosie"	*150 American Folk Songs*
"Thread Follows the Needle"	*An American Methodology*
"A Tisket, a Tasket"	*150 American Folk Songs*
"We Are Dancing in the Forest"	*Music in the Preschool*

References for Table 2.2

Bacon, Denise. *Let's Sing Together!* London: Boosey & Hawkes, 1971.
Choksy, Lois. *The Kodály Context*. Englewood Cliffs, NJ: Prentice-Hall, 1981.
Choksy, Lois. *Kodály Method*. Englewood Cliffs, NJ: Prentice-Hall, 1998.
Eisen, Ann, and Lamar Robertson. *An American Methodology*. Lake Charles, LA: Sneaky Snake, 1996.
Erdei, Peter (ed.), and Katalin Komlós. *150 American Folk Songs*. London: Boosey & Hawkes, 1974 (7th printing 1985).
Forrai, Katalin. *Music in the Preschool*, 2nd ed. Wooloowin, Queensland, Australia: Clayfield School of Music, 1996.
Fulton, Eleanor, and Pat Smith. *Let's Slice the Ice*. St. Louis, MO: Magnamusic, 1978.
Locke, Eleanor G. *Sail Away: 155 American Folk Songs*. London: Boosey & Hawkes, 1988.
O'Hanian, Phyllis Brown. *Favorite Nursery Songs*. New York: Random House, 1956.

Table 2.3   Grade 1

GAME DIRECTIONS
SUGGESTIONS
Select appropriate games: assess verbal content, game difficulty, content, and the musical concept that will interest students at each age level.
Consider your goal for teaching the game song.
You may want to introduce the song and have the students learn the song prior to teaching the game.
Demonstrate each new step or sequence, and then ask questions about the motions: "Watch me… what did I do?"
You may also want to create lyrics to the song's melody that describe the motions; sing while performing the movement.
GLOSSARY OF MOVEMENT GAME AND DANCE TERMS
These terms often appear in dance and game directions. We thank our student Rebecca Seekatz for contributing this glossary of terms.
Allemande: partners match right hands, touching from hands to elbow. Elbow is bent and hands are up. Partners turn around once to the right so that they return to their original position. The turn may also be done with left hands in the air, turning to the left.
Arch: partners join hands and raise arms to let other students through.
Bottom of the line: in a line or double line, the position furthest away from the head couple, music source, or caller.
Cast off: in a double line, partners turn away from each other and walk toward the bottom on the outside of the line. Other couples may follow.
Circle: students stand side by side in a circle, facing in toward the middle.
Circle left: students move clockwise, with hands joined if desired.
Circle right: students move counterclockwise, with hands joined if desired.
Corner: the person next to you who is not your partner.

(Continued)

Table 2.3 (continued)

Do-si-do: two students face each other, slightly offset. They walk forward, passing right shoulders, and go around each other to move back to their original place. The students should be facing the same direction during the entire movement.
Down: students move toward the bottom of the line, furthest away from the caller or music source.
Double line: students form two parallel lines, with each student facing opposite the partner. *See* Longways set.
Elbow turn: students link arms at the elbow with each other and turn around once. This may be done to the right, linking right arms; or to the left, linking left arms.
Grand right and left: partners face each other, take right hands, and walk forward passing right shoulders. Take left hands with the next person you meet and pass left shoulders. Right to the next, left to the next, and so on. Take two steps forward for each change of hands.
Head couple: in a line dance, the couple closest to the head of the line, the caller, or the music.
Left hand cross: partners face each other, take left hands, and walk forward, passing left shoulders so they have switched places.
Longways set: students form two parallel lines, with each student facing their partner in the opposite line. *See* Double line.
Promenade: partners walk forward side by side, holding each other's hands, right in right and left in left. Teachers should get students into position by saying, "Shake right, shake left, turn forward."
Right hand cross: partners face each other, take right hands, and walk forward, passing right shoulders so they have switched places.
Sashay: partners hold hands and gallop or skip sideways.
Strip the willow: in a line dance, the head couple does a right elbow turn once and a half around so that they are facing the opposite line from which they started. They then each do a left elbow turn once around with the next person in the line (from the line opposite their original line). The head couple meets in the middle for a right elbow turn once around, and then each turns the next person in the opposite line with a left elbow turn; and so on down the line until they reach the bottom. May also be done by holding hands with your partner and pulling inward rather than an elbow turn.
Wring the dishrag: partners face each other, holding hands. With hands held, partners swing their hands forward, up, and over their heads as they turn underneath. Partners should be in their original position, hands still held, at the end of the motion.
GAME DIRECTIONS
"A LA RUEDA DE SAN MIGUEL"
Classroom use—game: circle **Game directions:** Students hold hands and walk in a circle while singing. On the words "que se voltee ____ de burro," teacher calls a student's name. That student turns around and faces outward; the game continues until all students are facing outward.

(Continued)

Table 2.3 (continued)

"ALL AROUND THE BUTTERCUP"
Classroom use—game: circle, choosing, marching on beat
Teaching process version 1: students begin walking to the right. One student is in the middle. That student may tap the beat for the moving students. A simple variation is to have that student spin with eyes shut. On "Just choose me," the student opens eyes and is pointing to a student in the circle. The student who was selected can either walk in the circle crouching down or turn backwards and continue to walk with the group. The game continues until all of the students are selected. The last student left becomes the new "chooser." **Teaching process version 2:** students walk around in a circle holding hands (to the right). Another student is on the outside of the circle tapping the walkers on the head to the beat. On the last beat of the song (a rest), the student who gets tapped steps to the outside of the circle and walks in the opposite direction. The game concludes with a double circle. On "Just choose me," the students make a shape of a flower as directed by the student (a high flower or low flower).

"APPLE, PEACH, PEAR, PLUM"
Classroom use—game: choosing
Teaching process: for a majority of the song, point to a different student to the beat. "Apple, peach, pear, plum. Tell me when your birthday comes." Student answers with the month; for example, "April." Teacher and students chant the months of the year up to April (counting four more students); that student becomes the next to keep the beat around the circle while the class says the rhyme.

"BEE, BEE, BUMBLE BEE"
Classroom use—game: acting out, using fine motor hand movements
Game directions: 　"Bee, bee, bumble bee." 　　Motions: tap up in the air, like conducting four times on the beat; or cross thumbs and make a flying shape. 　"Stung a man upon his knee." 　　Motions: tap knees; four times. 　"Stung a pig upon his snout." 　　Motions: touch nose with both hands (easier); four times. 　"I declare that you are out." 　　Motions: point forward and wag your pointer fingers; four times. **Teaching process: sing and show motions** 　Ask about last lyrics first. 　Sing and show again. 　Ask more about lyrics. 　Ask about what motion teacher did on certain lyrics. 　Ask student to do that motion. 　Add on until they are singing it all. 　Leave out words, audiating the missing portions but doing the movements of the song above.

(Continued)

Table 2.3 (continued)

"BILLY, BILLY"

Classroom use—game: double line game

Game directions: 1   3   5   7   (Line A)
                      ⇕   ⇕   ⇕   ⇕
                       2   4   6   8

Students form two lines; each is facing a partner from the other line.

Verse 1: partners take hands and pull back and forth on the beat.

Verse 2: lines step away from each other and students clap on the weak beat; on the phrase "Walkin' down the alley" student 1 goes down the "alley" improvising a movement (takes the place of student 8… entire line moves down to replace the empty spaces at the front).

Verse 3: on "Here comes the second one" student 2 goes down the "alley" imitating the movement from student 1.

The strutting movements should demonstrate the dotted feeling of the song.

Teaching process: the teacher needs to help students get into two lines (longways set) and teach them how to gently pull their partner's arms back and forth.

"BOBBY SHAFTO"

Classroom use—game: acting out

Game directions:

"Bobby Shafto's gone to sea"
   Motions: put hand up to eye as if searching.
"Silver buckles on his knee"
   Motions: pat knees to the beat.
"He'll come back to marry me,"
   Motions: point to imaginary ring to the beat.
"Pretty, Bobby Shafto."
   Motions: stroke hair to beat to emphasize "pretty."
   Or wave hands in rocking motion. (You may want to substitute another word for "pretty," such as "bonnie" or "little.")

Teaching process: steps: have students sit in a scattered formation or a circle. Ask content questions beginning backwards and working your way to the beginning of the song.

"BOUNCE HIGH, BOUNCE LOW"

Classroom use—game: circle

Teaching process version 1:

Step 1: begin this game in a circle with one or more beach balls. Have the students move the ball up high on the word "high" and down to the ground on the word "low." On "Shiloh," pass the ball to the person on the right.

Step 2: partners have a ball. Toss the ball high and bounce it on the ground during the words "high" and "low." Toss it to the partner on "Shiloh," or bounce it to a partner.

Teaching process version 2:

Materials: bouncy ball and small trash can or laundry basket

(*Continued*)

Table 2.3 (continued)

Steps: begin with all students sitting in a circle. Five students in the circle stand up. The student in position 1 has the ball. Student 1 bounces the ball to student 2, who catches it. Student 2 then bounces it to student 3, continuing until the ball ends up with student 5. The fifth student tries to bounce the ball into the basket in the middle of the circle. The next student in the circle is number 1 for the next five to stand. Continue the process until all the students have had a turn attempting to bounce the ball into the basket.
"BOW WOW WOW"

Classroom use—game: circle, facing partners
 Game directions:
   "Bow wow wow"
     Motions: stomp three times.
   "Whose dog art thou?
     Motions: wave finger at partner.
   "Little Tommy Tucker's dog"
     Motions: grab partner's hands and switch places.
     Or take right hands and switch places.
   "Bow wow wow"
     Motions: stomp three times.
   "Woof!" (This is actually a rest, but you can substitute a word here.)
     Motions: students jump halfway around and face a new partner.

Teaching process: demonstrate the game in a single circle without partners. When the students switch with their imaginary partner, they will step into the circle and turn out. When they jump halfway, they will face back in.   To assign partners, teacher should go around the circle and turn two students toward each other until all students are paired.
"BYE, BYE, BABY"

Classroom use—game: acting out
 Game directions:
   "Bye, Bye Baby, Baby Bye"
   "My Little Baby, Baby Bye"
   Motions: pretend to rock a baby to the beat.
 Teaching process: steps: act out the song, pretending to rock a baby to the beat.

"CHICKA-MA, CHICKA-MA CRANEY CROW"

Classroom use—game: acting out
 Game directions:
   Scattered formation.
   "What time, old witch?"
 Motions: the "witch" rushes out from her hiding place and shouts "One" or the number of victims she seizes as "chicken." That chicken then joins the witch in her hiding place.
 The game goes on until the witch has caught half the group. She then draws a magic line and a tug of war ensues. The first player pulled over to the witch's side becomes the new witch; or the other side, Craney Crow.

(Continued)

Table 2.3 (continued)

Teaching process: one player is chosen to be the "witch," another to be the "Craney Crow." The witch hides, crouching behind a desk, ad lib. The other players line up behind Craney Crow, each with hands on shoulders of the one before, led by Craney Crow. They become the chickens and march around in front of the witch's hiding place, singing the song in a taunting manner.

"CIRCLE 'ROUND THE ZERO"

Classroom use—game: circle, partnering, choosing

Game directions:

"Circle 'round the zero"
   Motions: leader circles around the outside of the circle.
"Find your lovin' zero"
   Motions: leader stops behind a student.
"Back back zero"
   Motions: leader bumps backs with the student she or he stopped behind.
"Side side zero"
   Motions: leader taps hips with that student.
"Front front zero"
   Motions: leader steps in front of the partner and they clap hands.
"Tap your lovin' zero"
   Motions: both partners now tap each other's shoulders.

"CLAP YOUR HANDS TOGETHER" (CUT THE CAKE)

Classroom use—game: circle, one person in middle

Game directions:

"Clap your hands together"
   Motions: clap hands to beat.
"Give yourself a shake"
   Motions: wiggle body.
"Make a happy circle"
   Motions: students grab hands and make a circle.
"And then you cut the cake!"

Note: the final beat of the song is a rest. The student in the middle should "cut" the cake on the rest.

Motions: one person in middle "slices" between two students. The "sliced" students skip or run in opposite directions around the outside of the circle, passing each other. The first one back wins and gets to cut the cake next.

Teaching process: to help ensure that different students get to run, after the game begins the teacher groups the students who have run around the circle all together. All students should get to run, but not all students will get to "cut the cake."

"COBBLER, COBBLER"

Classroom use—game: acting out, steady beat

Game directions version 1: pound (keep the beat gently) on your hand with other fist on the beat. Students can do it with a shoe or other items. "What do you think a cobbler does? Mend a shoe."

(Continued)

Table 2.3 (continued)

Game directions version 2: another option is to have the students sit in a circle with one shoe off, grabbing and passing the shoe to the right on the macrobeat. When it is time to pick the shoes back up, toss the shoes into the middle and call small groups to find their "fixed shoe."   **Game directions version 3:** students sit in a circle with their feet, and teacher can tap the beat on the bottom of the student's foot to the beat.
"DEEDLE, DEEDLE DUMPLING"
Classroom use—game: acting out, circle   **Game directions:** all students (and teacher) take off their left shoe. Keep the strong beat with the right foot, the weak beat with the left foot. Walk in a circle while singing the song. You may start the game by selecting just one student to walk with you. At the end of each repetition, add a student to the train.
"DO, DO, PITY MY CASE"

Classroom use—game: acting out
 Game directions:
     "Do, do pity my case, in some lady's garden"
     "My clothes to wash when I get home, in some lady's garden"
 Motions: act out washing clothes, etc.
 Teaching process: formation: circle
 Have a student choose a chore he or she might perform (dog to walk, lawn to mow, dishes to wash, etc.). Decide what movement will go with that chore. Substitute the chore in the song.

"DOGGIE, DOGGIE"
Classroom use—game: acting out, voice identification, choosing   **Game directions:** class sits in circle, or for a challenge, scattered formation.   Student A is in middle (or at the front of the class for scattered formation) with blindfold on or eyes closed.   Student B has bone. (Teacher can use a rawhide chew bone.)   Class sings first two phrases of song.   Student A sings phrase 3: "Who has my bone?"   Student B sings phrase 4: "I have your bone."   Student A has to guess who has the bone.   Student B then becomes the dog.
"DOWN CAME A LADY"
Classroom use—game: circle, choosing, marching on beat   **Game directions:** students join hands in a small circle with one student in the center. (You may want no more than eight to ten students in the circle.)   All sing, circling around the center student, who at the word "blue" points to one of the other students and then substitutes the color of the chosen student's clothing for the word "blue."   That student steps to the outside the circle and walks in the opposite direction when the singing begins.   This continues until all the students are in the outside circle.   On the last verse, the students in the circle point to the last student left in the center (which was the original circle) and sing the color of his or her clothing.   **Teaching suggestion:** have the students preselect their own color from what they are wearing.

(Continued)

Table 2.3 (continued)

"ENGINE, ENGINE, NUMBER NINE"

Classroom use—game: acting out/windup (or single line)
 Game directions: walking to a steady beat, the teacher leads the students around the room in a line.
 Speaking high or low: walk upright; then walk with knees bent, with the contour of the melody.
 Teaching process: "Yes, no, maybe so"
   Student says which one
     "Y-E-S spells yes..." or "N-O spells no"
 "Laurie goes to the rear, Joseph is our engineer."

"FARMER IN THE DELL"
Classroom use—game: acting out, circle   **Game directions:** students stand in a circle holding hands. One student is in middle as the farmer. Students sing song as they walk around circle. Follow the direction of the verses. "The farmer takes a wife, wife takes a child," etc. Each selected student chooses the next and comes into the center of the circle. At the end, the cheese stands alone.   **Teaching process:** students can walk in circle holding hands, as others are selected for the center of the circle.
"FROG IN THE MEADOW"
Classroom use—game: acting out, line, circle, leaping/jumping   **Game directions version 1:**   1. The players sing and circle around the "frog," pointing menacingly with index fingers.   2. Players in circle close their eyes and sing the song once through "inside their heads." While students in the circle have their eyes closed, the "frog" runs away and hides.   3. As silent singing ends, all hunt the "frog." The finder becomes the next frog.   **Game directions version 2:**   Leapfrog. Groups of five players (four frogs crouched, one jumper/stirrer). "Take a little stick": the stirrer pretends to stir the frog at the back of the line. That frog then leaps over the three frogs in front, and then crouches down at the head of the line. Process repeats until all frogs have leaped.   **Alternate game:** line up four or five students, in a kneeling position, with two steps between each pair. The students sit up to sing the song, and then the front students "duck and cover" while the last student leapfrogs over each student. The line must move back and a new student will be the jumper. Teacher says, "scoot back in 5-4-3-2-1; ready sing."
"HANDY, DANDY"
Classroom use—game: choosing, high-low sounds   **Game directions:** "Handy Dandy, Riddley Roll, which hand will you have, high or low?"   The teacher or another student chants the rhyme while alternating a coin between the right and left hands to the beat. On the words "high or low," place one hand high and the other low. The student selects which hand has the coin, using a high or low voice.

(Continued)

Table 2.3 (continued)

"HERE COMES A BLUEBIRD"
Classroom use—game: acting out, circle, choice, partners **Game directions version 1:** students stand in a circle with hands joined and lifted to create archways. As they sing, one student walks in and out of the arches. On "take a little partner," this student takes a partner, joining hands, and gallops in and out of the opening in the circle or dances around inside the circle. The first student joins the ring, and the partner becomes the new "bluebird." **Game directions version 2:** play as written above, except both the "bluebird" and their partner move in and out of the arches when the song begins again. On "take a little partner," both students select partners to hop in the garden. The circle will shrink as more students become bluebirds.
"HERE WE GO 'ROUND THE MULBERRY BUSH"
Classroom use—game: acting out, improvisation **Game directions:** this works well in a circle. Act out the words "This is the way we wash our clothes so early in the morning." Add everyday tasks that students can do.
"HOP, OLD SQUIRREL"
Classroom use—game: acting out, improvisation (best late in first grade) **Variation:** scattered formation. Students move to the beat. Ask students to improvise other motions for "hop."
"JOHNNY'S IT"
Classroom use—game: voice identification **Teaching steps:** the class can sit in a circle. Choose one student to hide their eyes. Select another student to stand and move to another place in the circle. Class sings the song; the student who is standing sings "Hello, who am I . . ." as a solo. The seated student must guess which classmate is singing.
"JOHNNY WORKS WITH ONE HAMMER"
Classroom use—game: acting out **Teaching steps:** keep the beat in the air with one hand, up and down. Then sing "Johnny works with two hammers. . ." and point with two hands. Let the students decide who the third hammer will be (e.g., a foot, head, etc.). Continue adding "hammers" by moving additional parts of the body.
"JUST FROM THE KITCHEN"
Classroom use—game: acting out **Teaching steps:** move to the beat by flapping your arms like a bird. You may lead students into a line and into a circle, but it should sometimes be free-form. In the circle, one student flies around in the middle and at the end flies over to another student and switches places. At "Miss Mary/Mister Johnny," say the student's name in place of "Miss Mary." Authentic words are "shoo lie loo." Authentic tempo is slow, from the African American tradition. **Alternate simple version:** Students sing the song while seated in the circle and keeping the beat. Make certain there is an empty space in the circle. On the words "Oh Miss 'Susan'" the named student stands, flies across the circle, and sits in the empty space. The game continues in the same manner for as long as it's fun.

(Continued)

Table 2.3 (continued)

"LEMONADE"

Classroom use—game: acting out, guessing game

Game directions version 1: students are in two teams; the song is sung as a call and response.
- Group 1: "Where you from?"
- Group 2: "New York."
- Group 1: "What's your trade?"
- Group 2: "Lemonade."
- Group 1: "Give us some, don't be afraid."
- Group 2 acts out a predetermined action in pantomime (e.g., washing clothes or playing a game).
- Group 1 must guess what group 2 is doing. Then they switch parts.

Game directions version 2: chase game. Divide the class into two sides; each side stands behind their own boundary line. When it's their turn to act out the profession, they go to the middle and act it out. As they sing the first phrases, they link arms and march to the boundary line in formation. When the guessing team guesses correctly, the actors yell "yes" and the guessers chase the actors across their boundary line. If they are tagged they join the opposing team.

Teaching steps: students are in two groups. Each group quietly decides what things they want to act out, and then make two lines facing each other.

Suggestion: to clear up confusion as to when to run, one student from the team acting out needs to whisper the profession to the teacher. The teacher needs to stand between the two lines with arms extended. After the song, the students guessing will begin to say their guesses while the other team performs the charade. When the teacher hears the correct answer, she drops her hands; the guessers chase the actors toward their base.

"LITTLE SALLY WATER"

Classroom use—game: acting out, choosing

Game directions:
- "Little Sally Water, sitting in a saucer"
  - Motions: student in the middle is sitting in the middle.
- "Rise, Sally, rise, Sally"
  - Motions: student in the middle stands up.
- "Wipe away your tears, Sally."
  - Motions: student in the middle wipes away imaginary tears.
- "Turn to the east, Sally."
  - Motions: Student in the middle turns to the designated east.
- "Turn to the West, Sally."
  - Motions: student in the middle turns to the designated west.
- "Turn to the one that you love the best, Sally."
  - Motions: student in the middle closes eyes and spins in a circle with the finger pointed out. At the conclusion of the song the student stops and is pointing to a new student. That student becomes the new "Sally."

Teaching steps: class is sitting in a circle on floor. One student is in the middle ("Sally"). Another option is to have the circle walk counterclockwise while the motions are being acted out. Change the name from Sally to the selected student's name.

(Continued)

Table 2.3 (continued)

"LITTLE SALLY WATER" (WALKER VARIANT)
Classroom use—game: circle, acting out, and choosing   **Game directions:** students join hands in a circle, with one student in the center as "Sally," covering eyes with hands. The circle moves around as they sing the song. The student in the center acts out the song, pointing to another student in the circle at the end of the song, still covering the eyes with one hand so that the choice is accidental. The chosen student becomes "Sally" and goes to the center, and the game starts again.   Alternate words: "Rise Sally, wipe your weepy eyes, Sally."
"LONDON BRIDGE"
Classroom use—game: double line, choosing, partner   Follows "Engine, Engine, Number Nine" well   **Teaching steps:** one set (couple) makes a bridge and the students sing the song and process underneath. At the end of the verse, the bridge pair lowers their hands and catches someone. The student caught picks a person by choosing either "sticks or stones" (or any other choice) and then stands behind the side of the bridge who had chosen the same, creating a line behind each side of the bridge.   Once all students are caught, there can be a tug of war (this is the actual conclusion of the game; it's not great in the classroom).
"LOOBY LOO"
Classroom use—game: acting out, circle   **Game directions:** students put one arm in and then the other one. It is not necessary to distinguish between right and left, as this is difficult in first grade.   Students skip or walk around in a circle holding hands.   Students let go of hands and do motions.   Continue circling in same direction.
"LUCY LOCKET"
Classroom use—game: acting out, circle, loud and soft   **Game directions:** students sit in a circle. One student steps out of the room while teacher hands another student a pocket. Try using a small purse. Student A returns to the room and begins walking around outside the circle as students sing. When student A is close to the person with the pocket, students sing louder; when student A is farther away, they sing more quietly.
"NAUGHTY KITTY CAT"
Classroom use—game: acting out, chase   **Game directions:** students stand in a circle holding hands. One student is in the middle of the circle ("mouse") and another is outside the circle ("cat"). Students can either be stationary or they can walk around the circle while singing the song. On the word "scat," the "windows" open (students hold hands up) and the "cat" chases the "mouse." The teacher may direct the circle to open or close the "windows" as the "cat" chases the "mouse." Both students choose the next person.
"NO ROBBERS OUT TODAY"
Classroom use—game: choosing, chase   **Game directions version 1:** the teacher selects five to six students to be the "travelers." The rest of the class is in a scattered formation (like a forest) in the room.

(Continued)

Table 2.3 (continued)

While the "travelers" hide their eyes, the teacher selects two students to be "robbers," who disguise themselves as trees with the rest of the students. The "travelers" walk through the forest while everyone sings the song. On the teacher's signal, the designated "robbers" rush out and try to catch one "traveler." Those caught become "robbers." Repeat as appropriate. **Game directions version 2**: (like "Sharks and Minnows") One student in the middle of the room on hands and knees is It. All other students are in a line at one end of the room also on hands and knees. Students sing the song several times. After each time the song is sung, the line of students must cross the room, at which time the student in the middle tries to tag them. Those tagged are out and the game continues until all have been tagged. **Game variation**: use this as a movement exploration activity. Students sing the song. A "robber" is designated. The teacher designates how the students and the "robber" are allowed to move. Eventually ask the "robber" how he or she wants the students to walk across the floor. Examples: put hands on knees and walk, march, twirl, skip, hop, jump, crab-walk, bear-crawl, or duck-walk.
"OLIVER TWIST"
Classroom use—game: acting out **Motions and lyrics:** "Oliver Twist, you can't do this, so what's the use of trying?" Motions: one student in middle picks out a motion and everyone copies. "Touch your knees, touch your toes, clap your hands and around you go." Motions: touch knees, touch toes, clap hands, spin around.
"ON THE MOUNTAIN"
Classroom use—game: circle, choosing **Game directions**: students walk in a circle with hands joined. A student in the center calls out the name of whoever is to take his or her place. That student jumps into the center and the other jumps back to the walking circle.
"ONE, TWO, BUCKLE MY SHOE"
Classroom use—game: acting out **Game directions:** Call and response. Students sing numbers and teacher sings the rest of the phrase; then reverse. Or sing numbers and do the motions suggested by the text while teacher sings, acting out music. **Teaching steps**: students act out what teacher sings. Students may sing the numbers and the teacher sings the rest of the phrase. End with all students singing all parts. Additions: eleven, twelve, dig and delve, shoveling the peat; thirteen, fourteen, maids a-courting
"ONE, TWO, THREE, FOUR, FIVE"
Classroom use—game: acting out Game directions: "One, two, three, four, five." Motions: count on fingers.

(*Continued*)

Table 2.3 (continued)

"Once I caught a fish alive."
Motions: act out catching a fish.
    "Six, seven, eight, nine, ten."
Motions: count on fingers.
    "Then I let it go again."
Motions: throw it back.
    "Why did you let it go?"
Motions: hands show "why?"
    "Because it bit my finger so."
Motions: shake finger.
    "Which finger did it bite?"
Motions: hands show "which?"
    "The littlest finger on the right."
Motions: point to pinky.
Teaching steps: this has a similar feel to an elimination chant. You can have the students partner with one another and act out the words. You could also use it for choosing to put them into a line.

"PAIGE'S TRAIN"
Classroom use—game: acting out **Game directions:** teacher sings slowly and class walks slowly; then sings quickly and everyone walks quickly. **Teaching steps:** begin with students patting the beat, hands together with the song slow or fast. Next, have students step in place slow or fast. Then move into stepping slow or fast in a line following a leader. This game often works best when students are scattered in general space.
"PLAINSIES, CLAPSIES"

Classroom use—game: acting out, circle
Game directions version 1:
    "Plainsies"
        Motions: toss a ball in the air and catch it.
    "Clapsies"
        Motions: toss the ball and clap before you catch it.
    "Twirl around to . . ."
        Motions: toss the ball and twirl hands before catching it.
    "Backsies"
        Motions: toss and touch your back before catching it.
    "Right hand, left hand"
        Motions: toss the ball from the right hand and catch with the left. Then left hand tosses back to the right.
    "Toss it high, Toss it low"
        Motions: raise or toss the ball high; raise or toss it low.
    "Touch your knee, touch your toe"
        Motions: touch the ball to the knee and then to the toes.
    "Touch your heel"
        Motions: touch the ball to the heel.

(Continued)

Table 2.3 (continued)

"And through you go"   Motions: bounce the ball under your leg. **Teaching steps version 1:** standing in a circle, with each student holding a ball or beanbag. You may want to let them partner with each other the first couple of times until they have mastered the movements. **Game directions version 2:** Use a class set of bean bags instead of a ball. **Teaching steps version 2:** teacher sings and shows. Teacher explains phrase by phrase each motion. Students sing and do each phrase individually.
"PUMPKIN, PUMPKIN"

Classroom use—game: acting out
Game directions:
"Pumpkin, pumpkin, round and fat"
    Motions: student stands in front of the class with back to the class and hands out like a "fat" pumpkin.
"Turn into a Jack-o-lantern just like that!"
    Motions: student turns around and makes a face at the class.

"QUAKER, QUAKER"

Classroom use—game: singing, pulse
Game directions: students stand and sing in a scatter formation. Shake hands with neighbor throughout the song to the steady beat. On "I don't know; I'll go and see," the student goes to find a new friend to shake hands with. This is a great song for students to get to know one another.
Alternate call-and-response game:
Students stand in a circle and face a partner. Each group takes a turn performing and singing the song as follows:
  Student 1: "Quaker, Quaker how art thee?"
  Student 2 (while taking a bow): "Very well I thank thee."
  Student 1: "How's thy neighbor next to thee?"
  Student 2 (shrugs shoulders): "I don't know I'll go and see!" Student turns around to face the person behind and the game begins again.

"¡QUE LLUEVA!"
Classroom use—game: circle **Game directions:** circle of players. On the last line, "Que si, que no, que caiga un chaparron," students squat down on "chaparron." On the line "Que si, que no, que canta el labrador," students squat down on "labrador."
"RING AROUND THE ROSIE"
Classroom use—game: acting out, circle (stay in place to avoid holding hands) **Leads to:** "Lucy Locket," from "Snail, Snail" (if teacher leads snail line into a circle). **Game directions:** children join hands in a circle and walk around singing the song. At the word "down" they all squat down on their heels, then immediately get up, and the game starts again. Or chant "The cows are in the meadow eating buttercups. A tissue, a tissue, we all stand up!" **Teaching steps:** sequentially easier standing in place in a circle.

(Continued)

Table 2.3 (continued)

"SALLY GO'ROUND THE SUN"
Classroom use—game: circle game
Game directions: students are standing in circle.
"Sally go round de sun, Sally go round de moon. Sally go round de sunshine, every afternoon."
Motions: move in circle holding hands, clockwise.
"Boom!"
Motions: on "Boom!" change directions.
Teaching steps: students in a standing circle step the beat. On "Boom!" they jump and face the other direction.

"SEESAW"
Classroom use—game: acting out, high and low
Teaching steps: on first hearing of song, teacher pretends to be on the high end of a seesaw, holds on to the pretend handle, and seesaws down and up again.
Sing on neutral syllable first time.
Second hearing: teacher seesaws and sings the lyrics.

"SNAIL, SNAIL"
Classroom use—game: follow the teacher, coil
Game directions: teacher leads the students, winding the class around the room, all holding hands (first and last person will have a free hand). Lead the students into the shell shape by winding up, turning out first.
Teaching step: when leading the line, hold left hand but turn right (out) first so the students are looking at each other's backs rather than faces (for discipline reasons).
Say, "Hold on and don't move until your partner pulls you."
This is a good time to ask questions about the lyrics.
"What animal is it about?" (snails)
"Where do they live?" (shells; bring in a shell to show)
To unwind, let go of first student's hand and scoot over to the end of the line; hold hands with the last student and lead them out.

"TEDDY BEAR"
Classroom use—game: steady beat, acting out
Game directions: follow the activities of the verses of the song. All motions should follow the beat.
Teaching steps: to make the game more interesting, add instruments; students play the instruments on the beat as they move.

"THREAD FOLLOWS THE NEEDLE"
Classroom use—game: acting out, circle
Game directions: students stand in a circle without holding hands. The leader makes a weaving pattern in and out of the circle. At the last word, the leader touches a student on the head; the student then follows the leader, as does each one who is touched on the head. The weaving pattern continues until all are chosen or the game ends.

(Continued)

Table 2.3 (continued)

"A TISKET, A TASKET"

Classroom use—game: acting out, circle, choosing

Game directions: students sit in circle. One student skips around circle with an envelope as class sings song. On last word of song, student drops envelope and runs around the circle while being chased by a second student. The student tries to make it back to the empty position before being tagged.

Teaching process: it would help students, when learning this "duck, duck, goose"-like chasing game, to use a class set of bean bags. When students drop the envelope, the teacher places a beanbag to mark the spot for the student being chased to return to. The student who lands on the spot then keeps the beanbag to designate that she has had a turn.

To avoid safety issues, in a smaller classroom, you can tell the students not to run. They could skip or fast-walk.

"TORTILLITAS"

Classroom use—game: stationary, acting out

Game directions: students pretend to make tortillas to the beat. They may add ingredients to their tortillas to make tacos.

"LA VIEJA INEZ"

Classroom use—game: elimination, choosing

Game directions version 1:

Place four color areas—rojo, negro, verde, azul—around the room. A student in the center has the four colors hidden behind his back. Students sing the song and choose a color area. At the end of the song, the student in the center pulls forward a color. Those students standing in that color area are out. The game continues until only one remains.

Game directions version 2:

Students sing the song together while sitting in a circle or any other formation. When they finish singing, the teacher asks one student to "think" a color. Teacher goes down the row, allowing each student to make one guess until someone guesses correctly. The song repeats, and the next time the student who guesses correctly may "think" the new color.

"WE ARE DANCING IN THE FOREST"

Classroom use—game: acting out, circle

Game directions version 1: students are "dancing" in a circle.

A student is appointed the "wolf" and is hiding nearby or is in the center of the circle.

After singing one repetition, the circle asks, "Wolf, are you there?" to which the "wolf" may answer something like, "No, I am putting on my shoes."

The circle continues to ask, "Wolf, are you there?" and the "wolf" may improvise answers. When the "wolf" answers "I'm coming to get you," the students run as the "wolf" chases after them.

The student caught becomes the "wolf" and the game continues.

Game directions version 2: one student is selected to be the "wolf" while the others are children in the forest. While singing the song, the students "dance" around the room; the "wolf" is in a hiding place. Once the song is finished, the students freeze as the "wolf" comes out to search for children. If the "wolf" sees any students move, he or she may tag them and they are out.

Pedagogical Song List for Teaching Rhythmic and Melodic Concepts and Elements

In Table 2.4, we present a list of songs for teaching core rhythmic and melodic concepts and elements for grade one. Note that each element is taught in a basic four-beat pattern. We suggest teaching a variety of patterns that contain any new element.

Table 2.4 Grade 1 Songs Listed in Pedagogical Order

Song Title (* INDICATES FOCUS SONG FOR THIS ELEMENT)
Heartbeat Simple Meter
"Bee, Bee, Bumble Bee"
"Bounce High, Bounce Low"*
"Cobbler Cobbler"
"Engine, Engine, Number Nine"
"Snail, Snail"*
Heartbeat Compound Meter
"Here We Go 'Round the Mulberry Bush"
"No Robbers Out Today"
Singing
Rhythm
"Bounce High, Bounce Low"*
"I Climbed up the Apple Tree"
"Lucy Locket"
"Nanny Goat"
"Rain, Rain"*
"Star Light, Star Bright"
Quarter and Eighth Notes
♩ ♩ ♩ ♩
"Bounce High, Bounce Low"*
"Button, You Must Wander" (phrase 2)
"Good Night"
"Snail, Snail"*
"Star Light, Star Bright"
"Tinker Tailor"
"Two Four Six Eight"
♫ ♫ ♫ ♩
"All Around the Buttercup"

(Continued)

Table 2.4 (continued)

"Bee, Bee, Bumble Bee" (phrases 2, 3, 4)
"Bobby Shafto"
"Bow Wow Wow" (phrase 3)*
"Cobbler, Cobbler"
"Doggie, Doggie"
"Engine, Engine, Number Nine"
"Good Night" (phrase 2)
"I Climbed up the Apple Tree"
"Johnny's It"
"In and Out" (phrase 2)
"Nanny Goat"
"Queen, Queen Caroline"
"Rain, Rain" (phrase 2)*
"Seesaw" (phrase 2)
"Snail, Snail" (phrase 2)
"Star Light, Star Bright" (phrase 4)
"We Are Dancing in the Forest" (phrases 2, 4)
♫ ♫ ♩ ♩
"Bobby Shafto" (phrase 4)
"Bounce High, Bounce Low" (phrase 2)*
"Button, You Must Wander"
"Clap Your Hands Together"
"Frog in the Meadow" (phrase 3)
"Here Comes a Bluebird"
"Little Sally Water"
"Lucy Locket" (phrases 2, 4)
"Ring Around the Rosie"
"Shovel, Little Shovel" (Pala Palita)
♩ ♫ ♩ ♩
"Bye, Baby Bunting"
"Down Came a Lady"
"Frog in the Meadow"
"Here Comes a Bluebird"
so—mi
s m s m
"Good Night"

(*Continued*)

Table 2.4 (continued)

"A Nip and a Peck" (Pica Perica)
"Pipis y Ganas"
"Snail, Snail"*
"Who Are These People?" (¿Quien es esa Gente?)
s m ss m
"Rain, Rain"*
"Seesaw"
"Lemonade"
ss mm ss m
"Doggie, Doggie"
"Good Night"
"Seesaw" (phrase 2)
sm s sm s
"In and Out"
"This Old Man"
Rest
♩ ♩ ♩ 𝄽
"All Around the Buttercup" (phrases 2, 4)
"Bow Wow Wow" (phrase 4)
"Down Came a Lady" (phrase 2)
"Hot Cross Buns"*
"Pease Porridge Hot" (phrase 4)
♩ ♫ ♩ 𝄽
"Frog in the Meadow"
"Pease Porridge Hot"
♫ ♫ ♩ 𝄽
"Clap Your Hands Together" (second and fourth motives)
"Naughty Kitty Cat"
"Who Are These People?" (¿Quien es esa Gente?)
La
s ml s m
"Little Rooster" (Pipirigallo)
s l s m
"Bounce High, Bounce Low"*
"Star Light, Star Bright"

(Continued)

Table 2.4 (continued)

ss ll s m
"Bobby Shafto"
"Bounce High, Bounce Low" (phrase 2)*
"Lucy Locket" (phrases 2, 4)
"Round and Round" (A la Ronda, Ronda)
ss ll ss m
"Bobby Shafto"
"Chini, Mini"
"Snail, Snail" (phrase 2)*
"Star Light, Star Bright" (phrase 4)
"We Are Dancing in the Forest" (phrases 2, 4)
so so la la so so mi mi
"Lucy Locket"
"We Are Dancing in the Forest"
so so la so mi
"Bye, Baby Bunting"
"Here Comes a Bluebird"
so so so la so mi
"A Tisket, a Tasket"
"Bye, Baby Bunting"
"Doggie, Doggie"
"Fudge Fudge"
"Here Comes a Bluebird" (phrase 3)
"Hush, Baby, Hush"
"It's Raining, It's Pouring"
"Johnny's It"
"Little Sally Water"
"Nanny Goat"
"No Robbers Out Today"
"Rain, Rain"*
"Ring Around the Rosie"
Two Beat Meter
"Bounce High, Bounce Low"*
"Button, You Must Wander"
"Nanny Goat"
"Seesaw"

(Continued)

Table 2.4 (continued)

"Star Light, Star Bright"
"This Old Man"
Duple Compound Meter
"Jack and Jill"
"No Robbers Out Today"

Introducing Songs Within a Lesson

Here are suggestions for introducing songs.

Movement

Associate a motion or game with a known song. Perform one motion or action associated with the song; students join in singing when they recognize the song. Once they recognize the song, sing the starting pitch so everyone can join.

Visuals

Create pictures or assemble visuals associated with a particular song; students sing the song once they recognize the visual clue.

Introducing Songs to Students Using a Rhythmic Focus

- Teacher asks students to sing a song.
- Students recognize the song from rhythmic clapping.
- Students read the rhythm of a song written on the board; as soon as they recognize it, they may begin to sing it with text as they clap the rhythm.
- Students write the rhythm of a song but mix up the order of the phrases. Students read the phrases and try to identify the song.
- Students recognize a song, while hearing it performed on a percussion instrument.
- Students sing a song on a neutral syllable, as you perform a rhythm ostinato on a percussion instrument.
- Students recognize a song by hearing an internal phrase (not the first phrase) clapped by the teacher.
- Teacher claps the rhythm of a song and students perform in canon, after two beats.

Introducing Songs to Students Using a Melodic Focus

- Students sing songs.
- Students recognize a song by hearing the teacher sing using a neutral syllable.
- Students read from hand signs with solfège syllables once they recognize the song.
- Students read an internal phrase of music from teacher's hand signs with solfège syllables to recognize a song.

- Students read the teacher's hand signs using inner hearing and recognize a song.
- Students read an internal phrase of song from the teacher's (or another student's) hand signs using inner hearing and recognize a song.
- Students read in canon from teacher's hand signs and recognize a song.
- Students read from the tone ladder using solfège syllables and hand signs and recognize a song.
- Students read an internal phrase of the song from the tone ladder using solfège syllables and hand signs and recognize a song.
- Students read from the tone ladder, using inner hearing with solfège syllables and hand signs and recognize a song.
- Students read an internal phrase of the song from the tone ladder, using inner hearing with solfège syllables and hand signs to recognize a song.
- Students read from traditional rhythmic notation with solfège syllables beneath, using solfège syllables and hand signs to recognize a song.
- Students read an internal phrase from a song written in traditional rhythmic notation with solfège syllables beneath, using solfège syllables and hand signs to recognize a song.
- Students read from traditional notation with solfège syllables beneath, using inner hearing to recognize a song.

Lesson Planning

In the accompanying handbooks for all grades, we have included an alphabetized repertoire list of examples of materials that can be used for teaching singing, music literacy, music skills, and listening. The lesson plans in this chapter and subsequent chapters emphasize the sections of the lesson plan that can be expanded as a result of information presented in the chapter. Our purpose here is to emphasize that everything we do in a music lesson is always related to song material sung by children.

Creating a Preparation/Practice Lesson Plan

Before we label any element in a music lesson, we give children practical experiences that guide them to make a connection with the new element through kinesthetic, aural, and visual activities. This is always done in the context of performance. We call these preparation activities. Once we label an element, we practice it. In other words, we are developing lessons that focus on preparing a new concept as well as practicing known concepts. Generally speaking, we try to address both rhythmic and melodic skills in each lesson. Whenever we are preparing a rhythmic element in the first part of a lesson, we practice a melodic element in the second part of a lesson. Conversely, if we prepare a melodic element in the first part of a lesson, we practice a rhythmic element in the second part of a lesson.

Table 2.5 shows a basic preparation/practice lesson plan template. Note that in the template lesson, we used the wording "Performance and Demonstration of Known Musical Concepts and Elements" as generic terminology for all activities in the introduction. We will continue to use this wording in lesson plan templates so that you can focus on the core activities of the lesson.

Table 2.5 Basic Preparation/Practice Lesson Plan Template

INTRODUCTION	
Performance and demonstration of known musical concepts and elements	Students demonstrate their prior knowledge of known repertoire and musical elements through performance of songs selected from the alphabetized repertoire list.
CORE ACTIVITIES	
Acquisition of repertoire	New song selected from the alphabetized repertoire list that expands students' repertoire and prepares for the learning of a music rhythmic or melodic concept or element. Instructional context: when we are preparing a rhythmic element, the new song should be selected to prepare the next melodic element, and when we are preparing a melodic element, the new song should be selected to prepare the next rhythmic element.
Preparation and presentation of a rhythmic or melodic element	Learning activities in which a new musical concept or element is prepared through known songs found in the alphabetized repertoire list. When preparing a rhythmic element, the second part of the lesson practices a melodic element, and when preparing a melodic element, the second part of the lesson practices a rhythmic element.
Movement development Creative movement	Known song or game found in the alphabetized repertoire list or singing game list. Focus on the sequential development of age-appropriate movement skills through songs and folk games found in the alphabetized repertoire list.
Practice and performance of musical skills	Students reinforce their knowledge of musical concepts and elements working on the skill areas of form, memory, inner hearing, ensemble work, improvisation and composition, and listening through known songs found in the alphabetized repertoire list. When practicing a rhythmic element, the first part of the lesson prepares a melodic element. When practicing a melodic element. the first part of the lesson prepares a rhythmic element.
CLOSURE	
Review and summation Review the lesson outcomes Review the new song	Review of lesson content. Teacher may perform the next new song to be learned in a subsequent lesson found in the alphabetized repertoire list.

In the first section (Preparation of a New Concept) of a lesson, we guide students to discover the concept behind a new element. For example, if we want to teach the musical elements of quarter and eighth notes, students need to be guided to understand the concept of one or two sounds on a beat.

In the second section (Practice) of a lesson, the teacher reinforces and further develops students' understanding of preceding known musical elements through a variety of musical skills. Of course, musical skills may also be practiced during any section of the lesson plan. This section of the lesson may also include assessment activities to help the teacher identify students who require extra help.

Each preparation/practice lesson has an instructional context (preparation) and a reinforcement context (practice). In this type of lesson, we continue to develop singing abilities, teach new repertoire, and enhance movement and listening skills. During the preparation/practice lesson, we do not name the new concept or element but create opportunities for music students to discover the attributes of the new concept or element being studied. This dual structure of the preparation/practice lesson gives students time to process their understanding of the new concept, while promoting further development of their musical skills with the previously learned musical element. This is crucial for positive self-esteem and the enjoyment needed for learning to take place.

Table 2.6 is an example of this type of lesson plan, where the teacher prepares the concept through aural analysis and guides students to practice writing.

The outcomes for this lesson are:

- Preparation: analyzing repertoire
- Practice: writing melodies
- Preparation: analyzing or describing repertoire
- Practice: writing melodies

Table 2.6   Grade 1: $\frac{2}{4}$ Meter, Lesson 2

Outcome	Preparation: analyzing repertoire written in $\frac{2}{4}$ meter Practice: writing melodies which include the solfège syllable *la*
INTRODUCTORY ACTIVITIES	
Warm-up	• Body warm-up • Beat activity *Concerto for Four Harpsichords*, BWV 1065, J. S. Bach (1685–1750) • Breathing: **Ss** practice blowing up a balloon and watch how air is released when deflating the balloon. • Resonance: explore a cow sound using low and high voices. Make sure **Ss** are inhaling and exhaling correctly with the support muscles. • Posture: remind **Ss** of the correct posture for singing.
Sing known songs	"Down Came a Lady" CSP: D • **Ss** sing the song. "The Closet Key" CSP: D • **Ss** sing the song. • **T** adds an ostinato $\frac{2}{4}$ ♩ 𝄽 | ♫ ♩ :|. • **Ss** sing the song with the ostinato.

(Continued)

Table 2.6 (continued)

Develop tuneful singing Tone production Diction Expression	"Cobbler, Cobbler" CSP: A • **Ss** pretend they're falling off a cliff and say "aaaahhhhhhhhh!" • **T** uses a ball. Toss it from one **S** to another, and **Ss** have to follow the movement of the ball with their voices. • **Ss** sing "Cobbler, Cobbler" on "loo" and draw the phrases in the air.	
Review known songs and rhythmic elements	"Pease Porridge Hot" CSP: A • **Ss** sing and keep the beat. • **Ss** sing with rhythm syllables and keep the beat. • **Ss** sing with rhythm syllables and keep the beat. • **T** sings phrases from this song and other known songs; Ss echo-sing with rhythm syllables.	
CORE ACTIVITIES		
Teach a new song	"Plainsies, Clapsies" CSP: A • **T** sings while **Ss** continue the rhythm of the previous song. • **T** sings the song and demonstrates the motions with a scarf or ball. • **T** may select **Ss** to practice the motions while **T** sings. • **Ss** join in the song. • **T** sings the last phrase and "realizes" it sounds like another song (students guess), "Bobby Shafto."	
Develop knowledge of music concepts Describe what you hear	"Bobby Shafto" CSP: A • **Ss** sing song and keep the beat. • Review kinesthetic activities. • **T** and **Ss** sing phrase 1 of the song on "loo" while keeping the beat by patting on beats 1 and 3, snapping or clapping on beats 2 and 4. • **T**: "Andy, how many beats did we tap?" (four) • **T**: "Andy, which beats are stronger?" (1 and 3) • **T**: "Andy, if beats 1 and 3 are strong, beats 2 and 4 are _____?" (weak) • **T** and **Ss** sing and show the strong and weak beats. • **Ss** sing and inner-hear the weak beats.	
Creative movement	"Cut the Cake" CSP: A • **Ss** sing the song. • **T** adds a simple ostinato. • **Ss** sing and play the game with the ostinato.	
Practice and performance of music skills Writing	"Bounce High, Bounce Low" CSP: A • **Ss** sing the song and keep the beat. • **Ss** sing the song with solfège syllables and hand signs.	

(*Continued*)

Table 2.6 (continued)

	· **Ss** fill in the solfège syllables beneath the standard rhythmic notation prepared on the board: ♩ ♩ | ♩ ♩ s l s m ♫ ♫ | ♩ ♩ ss ll s m · **T** erases the solfège on the board and **Ss** complete the *la* writing worksheet.
SUMMARY ACTIVITIES	
Review lesson outcomes Review the new song	"Plainsies, Clapsies" CSP: A

Creating a Presentation Lesson

There are two presentation lessons. In the first we associate solfège or rhythm syllables with the new element, and in the second we present the notation for the new lesson plan. Throughout this book we identify specific songs for teaching specific elements. We refer to these songs as focus songs; they contain core building blocks that we want students to master. Sometimes we target a specific phrase in a focus song; we refer to this phrase as the target phrase for the song.

As mentioned above, in the first presentation lesson, we simply name or label the concept or element studied during the preparation/practice lesson and continue developing singing abilities as well as movement and listening skills, and teach new repertoire. In the second presentation lesson, we show students how to notate target patterns.

Table 2.7 shows a basic presentation lesson plan template for labeling the sound.

Table 2.7 Basic Lesson Plan Template for Presenting Rhythmic or Solfège Syllables

INTRODUCTION	
Performance and demonstration of known musical concepts and elements	Students demonstrate their prior knowledge of repertoire and musical elements, including the new musical element to be presented through performance of songs selected from the alphabetized repertoire list.
CORE ACTIVITIES	
Acquisition of repertoire	New song selected from the alphabetized repertoire list that expands students' repertoire and prepares for the learning of a music rhythmic or melodic concept or element. Instructional context: when we are preparing a rhythmic element, the new song should be selected to prepare the next melodic element; when we are preparing a melodic element, the new song should be selected to prepare the next rhythmic element.

(Continued)

Table 2.7 (continued)

Presentation of a rhythmic or melodic element	Teacher labels the name of the new musical element with rhythm or solfège syllables for the focus pattern.
Creative movement	Known song or game found in the alphabetized repertoire list. Focus on sequential development of age-appropriate movement skills through songs and folk games.
CLOSURE	
Review and summation	Review of lesson content; teacher may perform the next new song to be learned in a subsequent lesson found in the alphabetized repertoire list.

Table 2.8 has a sample presentation for labeling with syllables.

Table 2.8   Grade 1: *la*, Lesson 4

Outcome	Presentation: label the sound of a pitch a step above *so* as *la*.
INTRODUCTORY ACTIVITIES	
Warm-up	• Body warm-up • Beat activity "Fossils," from *Carnival of the Animals*, by Camille Saint-Saens (1835–1921). • Breathing: **Ss** practice blowing up a balloon and watch how air is released when deflating the balloon. • Resonance: explore a cow sound using low and high voices. Make sure **Ss** are inhaling and exhaling correctly with the support muscles. • Posture: remind **Ss** of the correct posture for singing.
Sing known songs	"Snail, Snail" CSP: A • **Ss** sing the song with an ostinato. "Naughty Kitty Cat" CSP: A • **Ss** sing the song. • **T** adds a simple rhythmic ostinato and **Ss** sing the song.
Developing tuneful singing Tone production Diction Expression	"Bobby Shafto" CSP: A • **Ss** sing song and keep the beat. • **Ss** sing text, then sing the song using the syllable "koo," and then "no" and other vowel sounds.

(*Continued*)

Table 2.8 (continued)

Review known songs and melodic elements	"Seesaw" CSP: A • **Ss** sing the song and show the phrases (use several songs that have phrases using *so mi*). • **Ss** sing with solfège syllables and hand signs. • **T** sings phrases with text and **Ss** echo using solfège and hand signs.
CORE ACTIVITIES	
Teaching a new song	"Just from the Kitchen" CSP: E • **T** sings the song while **Ss** continue the ostinato. • On the second listening, **Ss** sing the responses ("shoo-li-loo"). • **T** and **Ss** sing and play the game, clapping on beats 2 and 4.
Presentation of music concepts Describe what you hear with solfège syllables	"Bounce High, Bounce Low" CSP: A • **Ss** sing the song. • Review kinesthetic, aural, and visual awareness activities. • **T**: "When we have a sound that is higher than *so* we call it *la*." • **T** shows the hand sign. • **Ss** discover that *la* is a step above *so*. • **T** sings "*so la so mi*" (phrase 1 of "Bounce High") to individual **Ss** who echo with solfège and hand signs. • **T** sings phrase 1 of the song with text; **Ss** echo using solfège syllables and hand signs. • Repeat with at least six to eight students.
Creative movement	"We Are Dancing in the Forest" CSP: A • **Ss** create accompaniment with rhythmic or melodic elements. • **Ss** sing and play the game.

Presentation of music concepts
 	
Describe what you hear with rhythm or solfège syllables
	"Bobby Shafto"
	CSP: A
	• **Ss** sing the song.
	• **T**: "When we have a sound that is higher than *so* we call it *la*."
	• **Ss** sing the song with solfège syllables and hand signs.
	• **T** labels the sound *la* in related patterns:
	   o "Snail, Snail" (entire song)
	   o "Lucy Locket" (entire song)
	   o "Cobbler, Cobbler" (phrases 1 and 2)
	   o "We Are Dancing in the Forest" (phrases 1, 2, 3, and 4)

SUMMARY ACTIVITIES	
Review the new song Review lesson outcomes	"Just from the Kitchen" CSP: E

Table 2.9 is a basic lesson plan template for notation of rhythmic or melodic elements.

Table 2.9 Basic Lesson Plan Design for Notating Rhythmic or Melodic Elements

INTRODUCTION	
Performance and demonstration of known musical concepts and elements	Students demonstrate their prior knowledge of repertoire and musical elements, including the new musical element to be presented through performance of songs selected from the alphabetized repertoire list.
CORE ACTIVITIES	
Acquisition of repertoire	New song selected from the alphabetized repertoire list that expands students' repertoire and prepares for the learning of a musical rhythmic or melodic concept or element. Instructional context: when we are preparing a rhythmic element, the new song should be selected to prepare the next melodic element; when we are preparing a melodic element, the new song should be selected to prepare the next rhythmic element.
Presentation of a rhythmic or melodic element	Teacher presents the notation in the focus pattern.
Creative movement	Known song or game found in the alphabetized repertoire list. Focus on the sequential development of age-appropriate movement skills through songs and folk games.
Presentation of a rhythmic or melodic element	Teacher presents the notation in related patterns.
CLOSURE	
Review and summation	Review of lesson content; teacher may perform the next new song to be learned in a subsequent lesson found in the alphabetized repertoire list.

Table 2.10 gives an example of a presentation lesson. Note that the lesson still includes many additional musical skills and other learning.

Table 2.10 Grade 1: *so-mi*, Lesson 5

Outcome	Presentation: notate *so-mi*
INTRODUCTORY ACTIVITIES	
Warm-up	• Body warm-up • Beat activity "Stars and Stripes Forever," by John Philip Sousa (1854–1937)

(Continued)

Table 2.10 (continued)

	• Breathing: **Ss** practice blowing up a balloon and watch how air is released when deflating the balloon. • Resonance: explore a cow sound using low and high voices. Make sure **Ss** are inhaling and exhaling correctly with the support muscles. • Posture: remind **Ss** of the correct posture for singing.
Sing known songs	"Bobby Shafto" CSP: A • **Ss** sing the song with the beat in their feet and rhythm in their hands. "Down Came a Lady" CSP: F • **Ss** sing the song with the beat in their feet and rhythm in their hands.
Develop tuneful singing Tone production Diction Expression	"Tortillitas" CSP: A • Sing "Tortillitas" and continue the ostinato. • **Ss** follow a "tortilla" with their voices (**T** may use a poly spot or something round and flat as a prop) up and down as **T** tosses it in the air.

Review known songs and melodic elements	"Doggie, Doggie"
	CSP: A
	• **Ss** sing song and keep the beat.
	• **T** sings the first phrase and **Ss** echo with "s" and "m" and hand signs.
	• **T** sings the second phrase with text and **Ss** echo with "s" and "m" and hand signs.
	• **T** and **Ss** sing these songs, and then **T** sings the first phrase and **Ss** echo with "s" and "m" and hand signs:
	  o "Rain, Rain" (first phrase)
	  o "Good Night, Sleep Tight" (first phrase)
	  o "Seesaw" (first phrase)
	  o "Doggie, Doggie" (first phrase)

	CORE ACTIVITIES
Teach a new song	"Pease Porridge Hot" CSP: A • **T** sings the song while **Ss** pat the beat. • **T** sings the song while **Ss** show the phrases and identify the number of phrases. • **T** sings the song again, pausing after each phrase for **Ss** to label the form (AABC). • **Ss** perform the A phrases; **T** performs B and C. • **Ss** create steady beat motions to accompany each phrase of the song. • **Ss** continue their beat motions into the next song.
Presentation of music literacy concepts Notate what you hear	"Snail, Snail" CSP: A • **Ss** sing the song. • **Ss** sing the first phrase with solfège syllables and hand signs.

(Continued)

Table 2.10 (continued)

	• Review aural presentation:
	  ○ **T**: "We can label pitches with solfège syllables. We call the high sound *so* and the low sound *mi*." Show hand signs spatially, using the whole arm.
	  ○ T sings the first phrase of "Snail, Snail" with solfège syllables and hand signs. **Ss** echo.
	• Introduce the "musical steps":
	  ○ **T**: "*so* and *mi* look like this on our musical steps. From *so* to *mi* is a skip." (Hum *so-fa-mi* to prove that there is something else in the middle.)
	• Introduce the "rhythmic notation with solfège":
	  ○ **T**: "We can write our phrase in traditional notation and put our solfège syllables under the notation."
	  ♩ ♩ | ♩ ♩
	  s m s m
	• Introduce music staff:
	  ○ Five lines and four spaces; **Ss** count the lines and spaces from bottom to top.
	• Rule of placement:
	  ○ **T**: "Sometimes notes are on a line and sometimes notes are in the space." **T** shows a note on a line and a note in a space. (We find it best to place only the note head on the staff.)
	  ○ T chants, "if *so* is on a line then *mi* is on a line below!" **Ss** echo and **T** shows the placement on the staff.
	  ○ T chants, "if *so* is in a space then *mi* is in a space below!" **Ss** echo and **T** shows the placement on the staff.
	• **Ss** read "Snail, Snail" from the staff with solfège syllables and hand signs.
	• Individual **Ss** may read the song with solfège syllables and hand signs.

Creative movement	"All Around the Buttercup" CSP: F-sharp • **Ss** sing and play the game. • **Ss** create an accompaniment with known rhythmic elements. • **Ss** continue their accompaniment into the next song.

Presentation of music literacy concepts
 	
Notate what you hear
	"Rain, Rain"
	CSP: A
	• **Ss** sing song and keep the beat.
	• **Ss** sing song with rhythm syllables and pat the beat.
	• **Ss** sing with solfège syllables and hand signs.
	• **T** reviews the Rule of Placement and **Ss** read "Rain, Rain" from the staff on different staff placements.
	• **T** transforms the melody into other related patterns. **Ss** read with solfège syllables and hand signs:
	  ○ "Tortillitas" (phrase 1)
	  ○ "Doggie, Doggie" (phrase 1)
	  ○ "Cobbler, Cobbler" (phrases 1 and 2)
	• **Ss** may create patterns from other known songs.

(Continued)

Table 2.10 (continued)

	SUMMARY ACTIVITIES
Review lesson outcomes	"Pease Porridge Hot"
Review the new song	

Chapter 3

Teaching Strategies

The goal of this chapter is to present teaching strategies for concepts and elements for first grade. The teaching strategies are presented according to the Houlahan and Tacka model of instruction and learning. In other words, they follow a specified order of instruction. A significant component of the teaching strategies is the guiding questions associated with the cognitive phase of instruction and learning. The questions provide the metacognitive scaffolding that allows students to understand both the process and the product of teaching. Each component of the model of instruction and learning also promotes many opportunities for developing music skills. The teaching strategies are formulaic in structure; ultimately teachers will infuse these strategies with their own creativity to accommodate the changing settings of teaching situations.

Teaching strategies give a narrative as to how to prepare, present, and practice the basic building blocks of music theory.

Teaching Strategies

The teaching strategies in this chapter are a sequence that guides students' understanding of specific musical concepts and elements. We present some of the most important techniques for preparing, presenting, and practicing musical elements. In first grade we teach seven musical concepts. Beat and melodic contour can also be taught in kindergarten. We alternate between rhythmic and melodic concepts throughout the year:

1. Beat
2. Melodic Contour
3. Quarter and Eighth Notes
4. Two-Note Child's Chant
5. Quarter Note Rest
6. Three-Note Child's Chant
7. Duple Meter

Beat

Table 3.1 is an overview of the concept, theory, focus song, and additional songs for teaching beat.

Table 3.1

Element	Concept	Syllables	Theory	Focus Song	Additional Songs
	A level of pulsation used when we listen to music; inner energy			"Snail, Snail"	"Bounce High, Bounce Low," "The Closet Key," "Good Night, Sleep Tight," "Hunt the Slipper," "Star Light, Star Bright"

Cognitive Phase: Preparation

Internalize Music Through Kinesthetic Activities

The teacher should try not to use the word "beat" until the presentation phase.

1. Students sing "Snail, Snail" and perform the "beat" by patting knees, touching the heart, tapping the head, etc. (We do not use the word "beat" but say "point to the snails on your knees" or other language that relates to the song. Later we ask students to pat their knees. Additionally, we suggest that the beat not be clapped.) They should be guided to feel the even pulsation of songs and rhymes and express the pulsation through walking and other movements.
2. Students demonstrate pulsation using motions while performing songs and chants such as "Engine, Engine, Number Nine," demonstrating the motion of wheels turning; "Bee, Bee, Bumble Bee," demonstrating the motion of a bee's wings by flapping their arms; and "Cobbler, Cobbler," using a hammering motion to demonstrate the beat.
3. Students sing and point to a representation of beat (Fig. 3.1). You may also use four snails or four balls or any icon associated with a specific song. The point is that students sing while tracking the beat.
4. If students require assistance, try (1) tapping the beat on their shoulders, (2) tapping the beat on their desks in front of them, or (3) taking their hands and moving them to the beat.
5. The understanding of beat may best be demonstrated by the ability to speed up or slow down when the tempo changes.

FIG. 3.1

Describe What You Hear

1. Assess kinesthetic awareness by allowing the class to perform several of the activities listed above independently.
2. Teacher and students sing phrase 1 of "Snail, Snail" on "loo" and keep the beat on their knees before asking each question.
3. Determine the number of beats in the phrase. T: "Andy, how many times did you tap your knees?" (four)
4. Perform the same activity with different songs. Sing the first four (or eight) beats of a song on a neutral syllable and keep the beat. Ask individual students how many beats they kept. If the students are advanced, change the tempo and ask the questions.

Create a Visual Representation of What You Hear

1. Assess kinesthetic and aural awareness by allowing the class to perform several of the kinesthetic and aural awareness activities.
2. Hum the target phrase with a neutral syllable and ask students to create a visual representation of the target phrase. Students may use manipulatives to create a representation of the four beats. **T:** "How many snails did you tap?" or "How many balls or blocks do you need?"
3. Students share their representations with each other.
4. Invite one student to the board to share a representation with the class. If necessary, corrections to the representation can be made by reviewing the aural awareness questions.
5. Students sing the first phrase of "Snail, Snail" with a neutral syllable and point to the representation.

Associative Phase: Presentation of Beat

Label the Sound

The teacher presents the new element.

1. Assess kinesthetic, aural, and visual awareness with phrase 1 of "Snail, Snail."
2. **T:** "When we tap on our knees we are keeping a *beat* or keeping the *heartbeat*."
3. **T:** "Let's sing 'Snail, Snail' and pat the beat."

Notate What You Hear

The teacher presents notation for the new element.

1. **T:** "We can represent the beat using a heartbeat."

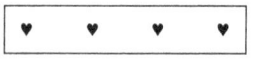

FIG. 3.2

2. **T:** "There are four heartbeats in the first phrase of 'Snail, Snail'; there are four heartbeats in phrase 2 of 'Snail, Snail.'"
3. **T:** "We can read this pattern of beats by pointing as we sing."

Assimilative Phase: Practice Music Skills

Many teachers do not see their classes more than once a week for music. If this is the case, review the focus pattern both aurally and with notation before practicing related patterns.

Aural Practice
Singing
- Teacher sings known melodies with words and students echo-sing while tapping the beat.
- Teacher gives the beat and students sing known songs.

Part Work
- Students sing known repertoire and walk to the beat.
- Groups or individual students sing a different phrase of a song.

Improvisation
- Improvise a question and answer. Teacher supplies the question; students answer.
- Improvise a motion that will demonstrate the beat of a known or unknown song in a fast or slow tempo.

Inner Hearing
- Teacher directs students to sing songs; teacher provides students with action to inner-hear phrases of song.

Visual Practice

Reading
- Practice the focus song and additional songs with the students by pointing to a beat chart and singing known songs. Begin with four-beat phrases and expand to eight and sixteen beats. Consider using the songs "Bounce High, Bounce Low" and "Star Light, Star Bright."

Writing
- Students may place visuals on the board representing the beat. Use any appropriate song in their repertoire.

Improvisation
- Teacher asks a question and students answer, always keeping or pointing to the beat.

Listening
- Students may tap the beat while listening.
- "March," from *The Nutcracker Suite*, by Peter Ilyich Tchaikovsky (1840–1893)
- "Hornpipe," from *Water Music*, by George Frederick Handel (1685–1759)
- "Spring," from *The Four Seasons*, by Antonio Vivaldi (1678–1741)
- "The Ball," from *Children's Games*, by George Bizet (1838–1875)

Teaching Strategy for Melodic Contour

Table 3.2 is an overview of the concept, theory, focus song, and additional songs for teaching melodic contour.

Table 3.2

Element	Concept	Syllables	Theory	Focus Song	Additional Songs
	Demonstrating the shape of a melody		Melodic contour or shape, pitches	"Snail, Snail"	"Doggie, Doggie," "Rain, Rain," "Cobbler, Cobbler," "Snail, Snail," "Bounce High, Bounce Low"

Cognitive Phase: Preparation

Internalize Music Through Kinesthetic Activities

1. Sing and point to a representation of the melodic contour of "Snail, Snail." The contours may be icons or pictures associated with songs. These representations should be four beats in length (Fig. 3.3). Consider using the first four beats of "Bounce High, Bounce Low" as well as the first four beats of "Rain, Rain" or "Snail, Snail." Students show the melodic contour with them arm.

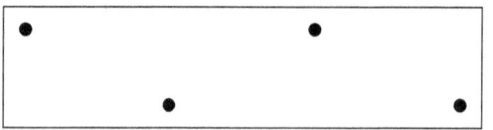

FIG. 3.3

2. Sing "Snail, Snail" and point to the melodic contour with high and low arm motions.
3. Sing "Bounce High, Bounce Low" or "Rain, Rain" and point the melodic contour with high and low arm motions.

Describe What You Hear

1. Assess kinesthetic awareness by allowing the class to perform several of the activities described above independently.
2. The teacher sings the first phrase of one of the songs named above on "loo" but does not show the contour. The task is for the students to individually show the shape of the melody in the air while singing and pointing to imaginary icons. Consider asking students if the snails are in the same place. Sing the phrase beginning on different pitches and ask students to identify the sounds as high or low.
3. Determine whether a student can sing back the phrase and show the correct contour.
4. Teacher sings the first phrase of a song without showing the melodic contour.
5. **T**: "Andy, sing the first phrase of 'Snail, Snail' and pretend to point to the snails." Or for "Bounce High, Bounce Low": "Andy, sing that phrase and pretend to point to the balls as you sing."

Create a Visual Representation of What You Hear

1. Assess kinesthetic and aural awareness by allowing the class to perform several of the kinesthetic and aural awareness activities.
2. Hum the target phrase with a neutral syllable and ask students to create a visual representation of the melody of the target phrase. Students may use manipulatives. You may wish to say, "Show me a picture of the song."
3. Students share their representations with each other.
4. Invite one student to the board to share a representation with the class. If necessary, corrections to the representation can be made by reviewing the aural awareness questions.
5. Students sing the first phrase of "Snail, Snail" with a neutral syllable and point to the representation, and then sing with known elements: "high low high low."

Associative Phase: Presentation

Label the Sound

Teacher presents the new element.

1. Assess the kinesthetic, aural and visual awareness with phrase 1 of "Snail, Snail."
2. **T**: "When we point to the snails, we're pointing to the high and low *pitches* of the melody; these pitches create the musical shape called the melodic contour."

Notate What You Hear
Teacher presents notation for new element.

1. **T**: "We can show music pitches using dots. Our first phrase of 'Snail, Snail' would look like this" (Fig. 3.4).
2. **T**: "We can label these pitches with the words *high* and *low*."

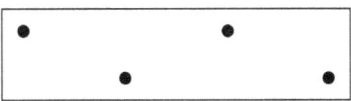

FIG. 3.4

Assimilative Phase: Practice Music Skills
Aural Practice
Singing
- Teacher sings known melodies with words and students say "high" and "low" and point to the melodic contour.

Inner Hearing
- Teacher directs students to sing the focus song, or one of the additional songs, and inner-hear the target phrase.

Improvisation
- Improvise a question and answer.
- Teacher provides the question; students answer. Use only two pitches, one high and the other low.

Visual Practice
Read from Hand Signs
- Transform the target pattern (the first four beats of "Snail, Snail") into basic four-beat melodic patterns found in the students' song material.

Reading
- Practice reading melodic patterns with the students using flash cards; patterns on the flash cards should be derived from well-known songs.

Writing
- Sing patterns from well-known songs and have students place manipulatives showing the pattern.

Improvisation and Composition
- Give the students several icons to arrange.
- Students sing a melody in their heads and arrange the icons to sing their pattern.

Quarter and Eighth Notes

Table 3.3 is an overview of the concept, theory, focus song, and additional songs for teaching quarter and eighth notes.

Table 3.3

Element	Concept	Focus Song	Present Syllables	Theory	Traditional Notation	Practice	Additional Songs
Quarter and eighth notes	One and two sounds on a beat	"Rain, Rain"	*ta, ta-di*	Note head, stem, beam, stick, and traditional notation	Quarter and paired eighth notes ♩ ♫	Tuneful singing Responsorial singing Phrase Same and different	"Bee, Bee, Bumble Bee," "Queen, Queen Caroline," "Seesaw," "Snail, Snail," "Cobbler, Cobbler," "Doggie, Doggie"

Cognitive Phase: Preparation

Internalize Music Through Kinesthetic Activities

1. Students sing "Rain, Rain" and perform the "beat" by patting knees or touching the heart.
2. Students sing "Rain, Rain" and clap the rhythm. **T:** "Put the words in your hands," or "Clap the way the way the words go."
3. Students sing the target phrase (the first four beats) and point to the rhythm. If this task is too simple, ask them to point to a representation of the entire song (Fig. 3.5).

FIG. 3.5 • • •• • •• •• •• •

Note: you may place heart beats or beat bars below the rhythmic representation.

4. Walk the beat and clap the rhythm while singing "Rain, Rain."
5. Have two small groups or two individual students perform the beat and rhythm using two different percussion instruments.

Describe What You Hear

1. Assess kinesthetic awareness by allowing the class to perform several kinesthetic activities.
2. The target phrase for aural awareness is the first phrase of "Rain, Rain."
3. Teacher and students sing phrase 1 on "loo" and keep the beat before asking each question.
4. Determine the number of beats in the phrase. **T:** "Andy, how many beats did we tap?" (four)
5. Determine which beats had more than one sound. **T:** "Andy, on which beat did we sing more than one sound?" (beat 3) **T:** "Andy, how many sounds did we sing on beat 3?" (two)

6. Determine the number of sounds on the other beats in the phrase. **T:** "Andy, if there are two sounds on beat 3, how many sounds did we sing on each of the other beats?" (one) **T:** "Sing the first phrase on 'loo' and keep the beat and hide the beat with two sounds in your head." Teacher may repeat the same process with phrase 2.

Create a Visual Representation of What You Hear
1. Assess kinesthetic and aural awareness by allowing the class to perform several of the kinesthetic and aural awareness activities.
2. Hum the target phrase with a neutral syllable and ask students to create a visual representation of the target phrase. Students may use manipulatives. **T:** "Pick up what you need to recreate what you heard" or "Draw what you heard." Assess students' level of understanding.
3. Students share their representations with each other.
4. Invite one student to the board to share a representation with the class. If necessary, corrections to the representation can be made by reviewing the aural awareness questions.
5. Students sing the first phrase of "Rain, Rain" with a neutral syllable and point to the representation.
6. Teacher may place a heartbeat or beat bar below the rhythmic representation.

Associative Phase: Presentation

Label the Sound
Teacher presents new rhythm syllables.

1. Assess kinesthetic, aural, and visual awareness with phrase 1 of "Rain, Rain."
2. **T:** "When we clap the way the words go, we are clapping the rhythm."
3. **T:** "When we hear one sound on a beat, we call it 'ta'; when we hear two sounds on a beat, we can call them 'tadi'. Both *ta* and *tadi* are called rhythm syllables."
4. Teacher sings "Rain, rain, go away" with rhythm syllables and students echo-sing "*ta ta tadi ta.*"
5. Teacher sings phrase with "loo" and students echo-sing with rhythm syllables.
6. Repeat step 3 with related songs or rhymes.

Notate What You Hear
Teacher presents notation for new sounds.

1. **T:** "When we clap the sounds on the beat, we are clapping the rhythm."
2. **T:** "We can represent one and two sounds on a beat using traditional notation. We can use a quarter note to represent one sound on a beat. A quarter note has a note head and a stem."
3. **T:** "We can use two eighth notes to represent two sounds on a beat. Two eighth notes have two note heads, two stems and a beam."
4. **T:** "Our first phrase of 'Rain, Rain' looks like this:" ♩ ♩ ♫ ♩
5. **T:** "We can read this rhythm pattern using rhythm syllables."

6. Teacher sings rhythm syllables while pointing to the heartbeats; students echo-sing using rhythm syllables while pointing to the heartbeats.
7. Stick notation is an easy way to write rhythmic notation; it is traditional notation without the note heads for quarter and eighth notes. **T:** "Our first phrase of 'Rain, Rain' looks like this in stick notation:" ♩ ♩ ♫ ♩

    T: "Sing 'Rain, Rain' with rhythm syllables." Individual students sing and point to the target phrase (the A phrase) on the board as the class sings the song with rhythm syllables.

Assimilative Phase: Practice Music Skills

Review the focus pattern both aurally and with notation before practicing related patterns.

Aural Practice
Singing
- Teacher sings known melodies with words, and students echo-sing with rhythm syllables.

T: "I say the other words; you say the rhythm names."
T: "Rain, rain, go away."
Ss: "*Ta ta ta di ta.*"
T: "Bee, bee, bumble bee."
Ss: "*Ta ta ta di ta.*"
T: "Queen, queen, Caroline."
Ss: "*Ta ta ta di ta.*"
T: "Seesaw up and down."
Ss: "*Ta ta ta di ta.*"
T: "Snail snail snail snail."
Ss: "*Ta ta ta ta.*"
T: "Doggie, doggie, where's your bone?"
Ss: "*Ta di ta di ta di ta.*"
T: "Cobbler, cobbler, mend my shoe."
Ss: "*Ta di ta di ta di ta.*"

Inner Hearing
- Teacher directs students to inner-hear *ta* in known song material.
- Teacher directs students to inner-hear *ta di* in known song material.
- Teacher directs students to sing focus song, or one of the additional songs, and inner-hear the target phrase.

Improvisation
- Improvise a question and answer. Teacher provides the question; students answer.

Visual Practice
Reading Activities
1. Practice rhythm patterns derived from the focus song and additional songs with the students using flash cards.
2. Name the song: teacher claps the rhythm of a song. Students recognize the song from hearing the rhythm.

3. Matching and inner hearing: match the name of the song with a rhythm written on the board.
4. Flashcard activities may be used with both stick and staff notation.
5. Read the cards in succession. Place the cards on the ledge of the chalkboard and perform them in order. Change the order of the cards to have the students read various patterns, or change the order to move from one song to the next in a lesson. A card may be removed and an individual student may improvise a rhythm to replace the missing pattern.
6. Have a student draw a rhythm card from a box. A classmate may suggest how to perform the rhythm (clapping, jumping, tapping, stamping, blinking, nodding, etc.). The class may echo the rhythm.
7. Perform the rhythm of a known song on an instrument.

Writing Activities
1. Students sing "Snail, Snail" with text and write the rhythm on the board.
2. Students sing "Rain, Rain" with text, and then sing again, clapping the text to compare it with the rhythm of "Snail, Snail" written on the board.
3. Teacher points to the rhythm to help the students determine if both songs have the same rhythm.
4. Students then sing "Rain, Rain" with words. Teacher points to the rhythm and asks whether it fits the song or not.

Improvisation Activities
- Write the rhythm of a four-beat phrase of a known song on the board. Ask students to clap the phrase, but change one or two beats.
- Improvise a new rhythm to one measure or more of a well-known song written on the board. Use "Rain, Rain"; "Bee, Bee, Bumble Bee"; "Cobbler, Cobbler"; "Doggie, Doggie" (the first two phrases); "Engine, Engine, Number Nine"; "Snail, Snail"; and "We Are Dancing in the Forest."
- Write the rhythm of a familiar eight-beat song on the board and leave the last two measures blank. Invite individual students to clap the rhythm while saying the rhythm syllables, and improvise the final two measures.
- Write sixteen beats on the board in four phrases, leaving the last phrase blank. Ask a student to improvise the final four beats. Write the improvised phrase on the board. This type of activity combines improvisation, reading, and writing.
- Question-and-answer rhythmic conversations can continue as a chain around the class. (Teacher claps a rhythmic question and individual students clap an answer.) Have the answer choices on the board.

Listening
- "Andante," from Symphony No. 94, "Surprise," by Franz Joseph Haydn (1732–1809). Do your very best to teach composers' full names and full dates!

♫♫|♫♩ |♫♫|♫♩ |♫♫|♫♩ |♫♫|♩ ♩ ‖

- Prepare the listening activity by having students recognize two-beat patterns found in known songs such as "Bobby Shafto" and "Bounce High, Bounce Low."

Sight Reading
- Houlahan, Mícheál, and Philip Tacka. *Sound Thinking: Music for Sight-Singing and Ear Training*, vol. 1, p. 17. New York: Boosey & Hawkes, 1991.

Listening
- "In the Hall of the Mountain King," movement 4 from *Peer Gynt Suite*, by Edvard Grieg (1843–1907).

Two-Note Child's Chant

Table 3.4 is an overview of the concept, theory, focus song, and additional songs for a two-note child's chant.

Table 3.4

Element	Concept	Focus Song	Present Syllables	Theory	Traditional Notation	Practice	Additional Songs
Bichord of the pentatonic scale	Two pitches, one higher one lower, a skip apart	"Snail, Snail"	so-mi	Music staff, lines and spaces; note head on staff	*so* and *mi* with traditional rhythmic notation	♩ ♫	"Doggie, Doggie," "Rain, Rain," "Cobbler, Cobbler"

Cognitive Phase: Preparation

Internalize Music Through Kinesthetic Activities

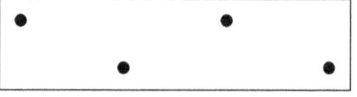

FIG. 3.6

1. Students sing and point to a representation of the melodic contour of "Snail, Snail" (Fig. 3.6).
2. Students sing "Snail, Snail" and show the melodic contour with high and low arm movements.
3. Students sing "Snail, Snail" with rhythm syllables while showing the melodic contour.

Describe What You Hear

1. Assess kinesthetic awareness by allowing the class to perform several of the activities described above independently.
2. The target phrase for aural awareness is the first phrase of "Snail, Snail."
3. Teacher and students sing phrase 1 on "loo" and keep the beat before asking each question.
4. Determine the number of beats in the phrase. T: "Andy, how many beats did we tap?" (four)
5. Determine the number of different pitches. Teacher sings only the first two beats. T: "Andy, how many different pitches did we sing?" (two)

Teaching Strategies

6. Determine whether the students can describe the pitches. **T**: "Andy, describe the pitches." (the first is high and the second is low) **T**: "Andy, I'll sing 'loo', and you echo with high and low." **T**: "Snail snail snail snail." **S**: "High low high low."

Create a Visual Representation of What You Hear
1. Assess kinesthetic and aural awareness by allowing the class to perform several of the kinesthetic and aural awareness activities.
2. Hum the target phrase with a neutral syllable and ask students to create a visual representation of the melody of the target phrase. Students may use manipulatives. **T**: "Pick up what you need to recreate what you heard" or "Draw what you heard." Teacher assesses students' level of understanding.
3. Students share their representations with each other.
4. Invite one student to the board to share a representation with the class. If necessary, corrections to the representation can be made by reviewing the aural awareness questions.
5. Students sing the first phrase of "Snail, Snail" with a neutral syllable and point to the representation, and then sing with known elements: "high low high low."
6. Identify the rhythm of this phrase.

Associative Phase: Presentation

Label the Sound
Teacher will present new solfège syllables.

1. Assess kinesthetic, aural, and visual awareness with phrase 1 of "Snail, Snail."
2. **T**: "We can label pitches with solfège syllables. We call the high sound *so* and the low sound *mi*." Show the hand signs spatially.
3. Sing "*s m s m*" with hand signs, the first phrase of "Snail, Snail":

    ```
    s           s
        m           m
    ```

4. Teacher sings "*s m s m*" with hand signs to individual students, who echo the pattern.
5. **T**: "I'll sing words and you echo solfège names." **T**: "Snail snail snail snail." **Ss**: "*s m s m*."
6. Teacher labels the interval between *so* and *mi* as a skip.

Notate What You Hear
Teacher presents notation for new pitches.

1. Introduce the "musical steps" (Fig. 3.7).
   T: "*so-mi* looks like this on our steps. From *so* to *mi* is a skip."
2. **T**: "We can write our phrase in traditional notation and put our solfège syllables under the notation."

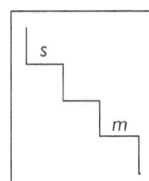

FIG. 3.7

Teacher may direct students to write the stick notation and add the solfège syllables.

3. Introduce the music staff by making students aware of:
   A. Five lines and four spaces
   B. Counting the lines and spaces from the bottom to the top
   C. Distinguishing notes in a space and notes on a line
4. Rule of placement. (Consider using the finger staff for this activity.) T: "If *so* is on a space, *mi* is on the next space down. If *so* is on a line, *mi* is on the next line down." (Note: do not address accidentals until students learn instruments.) "If *so* lives on the fifth line, *mi* lives on the fourth line. . . . If *so* lives on the fourth space, *mi* lives on the third space" (etc.). "*so-mi* looks like this on the music staff" (see Fig. 3.8).

FIG. 3.8

5. Write the first phrase of "Snail, Snail" on the staff using various staff placements.
6. T: "Sing 'Snail, Snail' with solfège syllables." Individual students sing and point to the target phrase (the A phrase) on the board as the class sings the song with solfège syllables and hand signs.
7. Sing "Snail, snail" with rhythm syllables while showing hand signs. (This activity may be difficult for some students at first, but it is an accessible and valuable activity.)

Assimilative Phase: Practice Music Skills

Review the focus pattern before practicing related patterns.

Aural Practice
Singing
- Teacher sings known melodies with words, and students echo-sing with solfège syllables.
  T: "I say the other words; you say the solfège names."
  T: "Snail snail snail snail."
  Ss: "*s m s m.*"
  T: "Doggie, doggie, where's your bone?"
  Ss: "*s s m m s s m.*"
  T: "Cobbler, cobbler, mend my shoe."
  Ss: "*s s m m s s m.*"
  T: "Get it done by half past two."
  Ss: "*s s m m s s m.*"
- Aural dictation
  T: "I'll sing on 'loo', and you echo solfège syllables."

Inner Hearing
- Teacher directs students to sing focus song, or one of the additional songs, and inner-hear the target phrase.

Improvisation
- Improvise a question and answer. Teacher provides the question (using only *so-mi*), and students answer.

- Improvise four-beat *so-mi* motives using hand signs.
- Improvise *so-mi* melodies to simple four- and eight-beat rhythms using a barred instrument.
- Improvise *so-mi* melodies on barred instruments.

Visual Practice
Read from Hand Signs
- Students sing from teacher's hand signs. Transform the target pattern into basic four-beat melodic patterns found in the students' song material. Transform:
  Phrase 1 of "Seesaw" into phrase 1 of "Rain, Rain"
  Phrase 2 of "Seesaw" into phrase 1 of "Doggie, Doggie"
  Phrase 1 of "Doggie, Doggie" into phrase 1 of "Cobbler, Cobbler"

Reading Activities
- Practice melodic patterns with the students using flash cards derived from the focus and additional songs.
- Perform the activity described above on a barred instrument.
- Read *so-mi* ostinati and perform them as an accompaniment on barred instruments using known songs.
- Students sing the first phrase of these songs following the instructor's hand signs: "Rain, Rain"; "Cobbler, Cobbler"; "Doggie, Doggie"; "Snail, Snail"; "This Old Man"; "Apple Tree"; and "Teddy Bear."
- Read four-beat *so-mi* patterns and play on a xylophone or bells.
- Read "Pala palita" and play it on an instrument (Fig. 3.9).

Source: Reprinted from *Vamos a Cantar* with permission of the Kodály Institute at Capital University.

Writing Activities
- Students write the first four beats of "Snail, Snail" using traditional notation and solfège syllables, and then on the staff.

  ♩ ♩ ♩ ♩
  s m s m

- Students write four beats of a known song on a staff using discs on a staff board.
- They label notes written on the staff with solfège syllables.
- Add stems to notes written on the staff. (stem rule)
- Teacher sings "Snail, Snail" on "loo" changing beat 3 from one to two sounds. Students identify the change and write it on the board. They identify the song as "Seesaw" or "Rain, Rain." Consider these examples:
  o Teacher sings the pattern seen above and changes beat 1 from one to two sounds. The pattern is now *s s m s m*. The students identify the change and

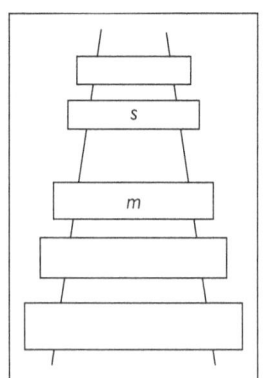

FIG. 3.10

write it on the board. Students identify the song as "Teddy Bear."
  o Teacher sings the pattern and changes beat 2 from one to two sounds. The pattern is now *s s m m s s m*. The students identify the change and write it on the board. They identify the song as "Doggie, Doggie."
- Write four-beat *so-mi* patterns and play on a xylophone or bells).
- Write *so-mi* patterns on the staff using various placements for *so*.

Improvisation Activities
- Improvise question-and-answer motives using known rhythms and *so-mi* melodic patterns. Have the question-and-answer choices written on the board.
- Improvise new words to a known song that uses *so-mi*, such as "This Old Man." Have the song written on the board.

Listening Activities
- "Allegro," from *Toy Symphony*, by Joseph Haydn (1732–1809)

Sight Reading
- Houlahan, Micheál, and Philip Tacka. *Sound Thinking: Music for Sight-Singing and Ear Training*, vol. 1, pp. 24 and 26. New York: Boosey & Hawkes, 1991.

Rest

Table 3.5 is an overview of the concept, theory, focus song, and additional songs for teaching rest.

Table 3.5

Element	Concept	Focus Song	Present Syllables	Theory	Traditional Notation	Practice	Additional Songs
Quarter rest	A beat with no sound	"Hot Cross Buns"		Quarter note rest	𝄽 or a "z"	*so-mi* Reading and writing in C, F, and G *do* positions	"Bow Wow Wow," "All Around the Buttercup," "Pease Porridge Hot," "Zapatitos blanco"

Cognitive Phase: Preparation

Internalize Music Through Kinesthetic Activities
1. Sing "Hot Cross Buns" and keep the beat.
2. Sing "Hot Cross Buns" and perform the rhythm. **T**: "Put the words in your hands."

3. Sing "Hot Cross Buns" and point to a representation of the rhythm. (For the heartbeats with no representation, put the beat on Ss' shoulders; demonstrate this, but do not discuss it.)
4. Divide the class into two groups. Group A performs the beat while group B performs the rhythm.
5. Clap the rhythm and walk the beat, while singing the song.

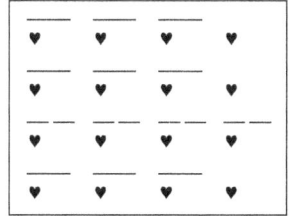

FIG. 3.11

Describe What You Hear
1. Assess kinesthetic awareness by allowing the class to perform several of the activities described above independently.
2. Teacher sings phrase 1 on "loo" while performing the beat before asking each question.
3. Determine the number of beats in the phrase. T: "Andy, how many beats did we tap?" (four)
4. Determine which beat has no sound. T: "Andy, which beat has no sound?" (beat 4) Or "Andy, what can you tell me about beat 4?" (it has no sound)
5. Determine the number of sounds on the other beats. T: "Andy, how many sounds are on each of the other beats?" (one)
6. Students perform "Hot Cross Buns" while tapping the beat and singing the known rhythmic elements. T: "Tap the beat and sing with rhythm names." Ss: "*Ta ta ta __ ta ta ta __ ta di ta di ta di ta di ta ta ta __.*"

Create a Visual Representation of What You Hear
1. Assess kinesthetic and aural awareness by allowing the class to perform several of the kinesthetic and aural awareness activities.
2. Hum the target phrase with a neutral syllable and ask students to create a visual representation of the target phrase. Students may use manipulatives. T: "Pick up what you need to recreate what you heard" or "Draw what you heard. Remember, you are showing four beats and the sounds on these beats." Teacher assesses students' level of understanding.
3. Students share their representations with each other.
4. Invite one student to the board to share a representation with the class. If necessary, corrections to the representation can be made by reviewing the aural awareness questions.
5. Students sing the first phrase of "Hot Cross Buns" with a neutral syllable and point to the representation, and then sing with known elements: "*Ta ta ta __.*"

Associative Phase: Presentation

Label the Sound
Teacher presents new rhythm syllables.

1. Briefly review the kinesthetic, aural, and visual awareness activities.
   A. T: "We call a beat with no sound on it a *rest*."
   B. Immediately sing "Hot Cross Buns." T: "You may say 'shh' every time we encounter a rest."

C. Sing "Hot Cross Buns" and perform the rhythm. **T:** "Put the 'rest' on your shoulders."
D. Teacher sings known songs; students identify the beats with the rest.

Notate What You Hear
Teacher presents notation for new sound.

FIG. 3.12

1. Notate the first phrase of "Hot Cross Buns."
   A. **T:** "We can notate the first phrase of 'Hot Cross Buns'. It looks like this:" ♩ ♩ ♩ 𝄽
   B. Beat 4 has a quarter rest.
2. When writing in stick notation, use a "z" for the quarter rest.

Assimilative Phase: Practice Music Skills

Teacher reviews the known pattern before using related patterns.

Aural Practice
Singing
- Teacher sings known melodies with words, and students echo-sing with rhythm syllables.

   T: "I say the other words; you say the rhythm names."
   T: "Hot Cross Buns."
   Ss: "*Ta ta ta* (rest)."
   T: "Bow wow wow."
   Ss: "*Ta ta ta* (rest)."
   T: "One two three."
   Ss: "*Ta ta ta* (rest)."
   T: "Just choose me."
   Ss: "*Ta ta ta* (rest)."
   T: "Pease porridge hot."
   Ss: "*Ta ta di ta* (rest)."
   T: "Pease porridge cold."
   Ss: "*Ta ta di ta* (rest)."
   T: "Nine days old."
   Ss: "*Ta ta ta* (rest)."
   T: "Zapatitos azúl."
   Ss: "*Ta di ta di ta* (rest)."
   T: "Tienes tú."
   Ss: "*Ta ta ta* (rest)."

Inner Hearing
- Teacher directs students to sing focus song, or one of the additional songs, and inner-hear the target phrase.

Improvisation
- Improvise a question and answer. Teacher provides the question, and students answer. Incorporate use of a rest in the improvisation.

Visual Practice
Read from Hand Signs
- Students sing from teacher's hand signs. Use *so mi* melodies that include a quarter note rest.
- Transform the target pattern into basic four-beat patterns found in the students' song material.

Reading
- Transform the rhythm of one song into another. For example, change the rhythm of "Hot Cross Buns" into "Bow Wow Wow."
- Write the rhythm of "Hot Cross Buns" on the board; students clap the rhythm and sing the song with rhythm syllables.
- Write the rhythm of "Bow Wow Wow" next to that of "Hot Cross Buns"; students clap the rhythm of "Bow Wow Wow" and sing the song with rhythm syllables.
- Students discern that phrases 1 and 4 of both songs are the same.
  - T: "Which beat is different in phrase 2?"
  - T: "Which beat is different in phrase 3?"
  - Read selected phrases and play them on an instrument.
  - Read *Quién es esa gente?* (Fig. 3.13) and play it on an instrument.

FIG. 3.13 "Quién es esa gente?"

Source: Reprinted from *Vamos a Cantar* with permission of the Kodály Institute at Capital University.

Writing
- Place heartbeats over the rhythm of a known song.
- In the early stages of writing, the teacher may furnish a worksheet that has rhythm patterns written with dashes for the students to trace.
- Students sing "All Around the Buttercup" with text and rhythm syllables; select a student to write the rhythm of a phrase on the board.
- Students sing "Cut the Cake" with text; then they sing again, clapping the text to compare it with the rhythm written on the board.
- Students change the rhythm of "All Around the Buttercup" into the rhythm of "Cut the Cake."

- Dictation. Students write a four- or eight-beat rhythm pattern dictated by the teacher.

Improvisation
- Improvise a new rhythm to one measure or more of a well-known song written on the board. Use "Hot Cross Buns"; "All Around the Buttercup"; "Teddy Bear"; "Bow Wow Wow"; "Pease Porridge Hot"; "Here Comes a Bluebird"; "Down Came a Lady"; or "Rocky Mountain." Complete the song using quarter notes, two eighth notes, and/or a rest.
- Improvise using the form of a known composition written on the board. For example, "Hot Cross Buns" is in AABA form. Students could read the song completely and be guided to clap the A phrase but improvise a rhythm for the B phrase after it has been erased.

Listening
- "Allegretto," from Symphony No. 7 in A, Op. 92, by Ludwig van Beethoven (1770–1827)

- "In the Hall of the Mountain King," from *Peer Gynt Suite No. 1*, by Edvard Grieg (1843–1907)

Sight Reading
- Houlahan, Micheál, and Philip Tacka. *Sound Thinking: Music for Sight-Singing and Ear Training*, vol. 1, pp. 18 and 19. New York: Boosey & Hawkes, 1991.

Three-Note Child's Chant

Table 3.6 is an overview of the concept, theory, focus song, and additional songs for three-note child's chant.

Table 3.6

Element	Concept	Focus Song	Present Syllables	Theory	Traditional Notation	Practice	Additional Songs
Trichord of the pentatonic scale	Three pitches; a skip between one of the pitches	"Bounce High, Bounce Low" or "Snail, Snail"	la-so-mi	Staff, lines, spaces, skip between *so* and *mi*; three-note child's chant	*la* with traditional rhythmic notation (add *so* and *mi*)	Practice using the rest with various four-beat rhythm patterns extracted from the students' repertoire that also include quarter and eighth notes	"Snail, Snail," "Bobby Shafto," "Lucy Locket," "We Are Dancing in the Forest"

Cognitive Phase: Preparation

Internalize Music Through Kinesthetic Activities

1. Students sing "Bounce High, Bounce Low" and show the melodic contour.
2. Students sing "Bounce High, Bounce Low" and point to a representation of the melodic contour:

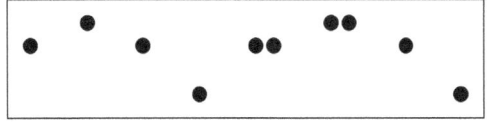
FIG. 3.14

3. Students sing "Bounce High, Bounce Low" with rhythm syllables while showing the melodic contour.
4. Students stand on toes for the high note and bend knees for the low note.

Describe What You Hear

1. Assess kinesthetic awareness by allowing the class to perform several of the activities described above independently.
2. The target phrase for aural awareness is the first phrase of "Bounce High, Bounce Low."
3. Teacher and students sing phrase 1 on "loo" and keep the beat before asking each question.
4. Determine the number of beats in the phrase. T: "Andy, how many beats did we tap?" (four)
5. Determine whether the student can describe the sound on beat 2. T: "Andy, which beat has the highest pitch?" (beat 2)
6. Determine what's known in the phrase. T: "Andy, what hand sign do we use at the beginning of this song?" (*so*) T: "We call the first sound *so*; let's sing *so-high-so-mi* and show the pitches with our hand signs." T: "I'll sing on 'loo,' and you sing with 'so' 'high' 'so' 'mi' and the hand signs."
7. Sing phrase 1 of "Bounce High, Bounce Low" but hide the highest sound in your head."
8. (Optional) T: "Andy, is our new pitch a step or a skip higher than *so*?" (step) If students have trouble with this, the teacher could sing *so-(ti)-so-mi* to determine whether they can hear the difference between a step and a skip.
9. Repeat for phrase 2.

Create a Visual Representation of What You Hear

1. Assess kinesthetic and aural awareness by allowing the class to perform several of the kinesthetic and aural awareness activities.
2. Hum the target phrase with a neutral syllable and ask students to create a visual representation of the melody of the target phrase. Students may use manipulatives. T: "Pick up what you need to recreate what you heard" or "Draw what you heard." Teacher assesses students' level of understanding.
3. Students share their representations with each other.
4. Invite one student to the board to share a representation with the class. If necessary, corrections to the representation can be made by reviewing the aural awareness questions.

5. Students sing the first phrase of "Bounce High, Bounce Low" with a neutral syllable and point to the representation, and then sing with known elements: "*so 'high' so mi.*"
6. Identify known rhythmic elements.
7. Sing the phrase with rhythm syllables and clap the rhythm.

Associative Phase: Presentation

Label the Sound
Teacher presents new solfège syllables.

1. Assess kinesthetic, aural, and visual awareness with phrase 1 of "Bounce High."
2. Present the syllables and hand signs for the new note. **T:** "We can label the high pitch with the solfège syllable *la*." Sing and show the hand signs for the phrase spatially.
3. Sing the phrase with solfège syllables and hand signs.
4. Teacher sings text; students echo with solfège syllables and hand signs.
5. Teacher identifies the interval between *so* and *la* as a step.

Notate What You Hear
Teacher presents notation for new pitch.

1. Show the steps, stick notation, and staff, and write *so-mi-la* on the steps and beneath the notation.

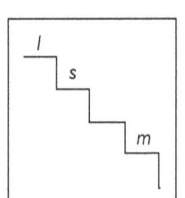

FIG. 3.15

2. **T:** "*la* looks like this on our steps:" (Fig. 3.15)
3. Teacher sings "*la so* that's a step, *so mi* that's a skip" for students. Students echo.
4. **T:** "We can write our phrase using traditional rhythm notation and put our solfège syllables under the stick notation."

♩ ♩ ♩ ♩
s l s m

5. Rule of Placement. **T:** "If *so* is on a line, *la* is in the space above and *mi* is on the next line down. If *so* is in a space, *la* is on the line above and *mi* is in the space below."
6. Teacher notates first four beats of "Bounce High, Bounce Low" and students read with solfège syllables and hand signs:

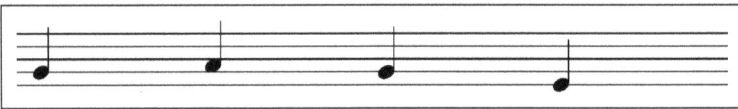

FIG. 3.16

7. Working from the (presentation) phrase above, change the rhythm to another song having the melodic same pattern.

Assimilative Phase: Practice

Many teachers do not see their classes more than once a week for music. If this is your case, review the focus pattern both aurally and with notation before practicing related patterns.

Aural Practice
Singing
- Teacher sings known melodies with words and students echo-sing with solfège syllables.
    T: "I say the other words; you say the solfège names."
    T: "Bounce high bounce low."
    Ss: "*so la so mi.*"
    T: "Bounce the ball to Shiloh."
    Ss: "*so so la la so mi.*"
    T: "Goes around around around."
    Ss: "*so so la la so so mi.*"
    T: "Bobby Shafto's gone to sea."
    Ss: "*so so la la so so mi.*"
    T: "Silver buckles on his knee."
    Ss: "*so so la la so so mi.*"
    T: "Lucy Locket lost her pocket."
    Ss: "*so so la la so so mi.*"
    T: "Kitty Fischer found it."
    Ss: "*so so la la so mi.*"
    T: "We are dancing in the forest."
    Ss: "*so so la la so so mi.*"
    T: "While the wolf is far away."
    Ss: "*so so la la so so mi.*"
- Students read from teacher's model. **T:** "I'll sing on 'loo', and you echo solfège syllables."

Inner Hearing
- Teacher directs students to sing "Bounce High, Bounce Low" with solfège syllables and inner-hear the *la*.
- Teacher directs students to sing focus song, or one of the additional songs, and inner-hear the high pitch, *la*.

Improvisation
- Improvise a question and answer. Teacher supplies the question, and students answer.
- Improvise short musical motives (*la-so-mi*) using hand signs, hand staff, or body signs.
- Improvise *so-mi-la* melodies to simple four- to eight-beat rhythms using the voice or a barred instrument.

Visual Practice
Read from Hand Signs
- Students sing from teacher's hand signs.

- Transform the target pattern into basic four-beat patterns found in the students' song material.
- Teacher may sing these phrases, with students echo-singing solfège syllables and using hand signs:

| s ♥ | l ♥ | s ♥ | m ♥ | "Bounce High, Bounce Low" |

| s s ♥ | l l ♥ | s ♥ | m ♥ | Bounce the ball to Shiloh
Kitty Fisher found it
Only ribbon round it |

| s s ♥ | l l ♥ | s s ♥ | m m ♥ | Lucy Locket lost her pocket
Not a penny was there in it
We are dancing in the forest |

| s ♥ | s l ♥ | s ♥ | m ♥ | Here comes a bluebird
Through my win-dow |

(Optional:)

| s s ♥ | m l ♥ | s ♥ | m ♥ | "Little Sally Water"
"Bye, Baby Bunting"
"Rain, Rain" (phrase 2)
"Doggie, Doggie" (phrase 2) |

- The last four songs need careful preparation. If necessary, follow the same strategy used to teach the *s l s m* pattern.

Reading

- Using any of the songs and melodic patterns shown above, read well-known melodic patterns from hand signs, traditional notation, or staff notation. The patterns here illustrate the fact that the melodic contour of all phrases is related. *la* occurs on beat 2.
- Read a new song from staff notation.
- Read a new song or known patterns on a barred instrument.
- Practice part singing. The teacher may use the right hand and left hand to show two *so-mi-la* patterns. Group A sings from the teacher's right hand and group B from the left.
- Matching and inner hearing: match the name of the song with the solfège syllables and a rhythm written on the board.
- Read a *la-so-mi* song from hand signs.
- Perform a *la-so-mi* song on a xylophone or tone bells.
- Have students read the rhythm of "Lucy Locket," changing the rhythm one beat at a time to "We Are Dancing in the Forest" or "Bobby Shafto."
- Read "A la ronda ronda" and play it on an instrument.

FIG. 3.17 "A la Ronda Ronda"

A la ron - da ron - da, so - pla - ra el zon - da,
en la huer - ta de Pa - lan las ci - rue - las ca - e - ran

Source: Reprinted from *Vamos a cantar* with permission of the Kodály Institute at Capital University.

Writing
- Write the first eight beats of the song "We Are Dancing in the Forest" in staff notation.
  - After students write and sing the two phrases with solfège syllables and hand signs, teacher sings it changing beat 7 to one sound instead of two. Students identify the change on beat 7. They then sing the song with the change and recognize that the melody has now become "Lucy Locket."
- Add rhythm to melody notes written on a staff.
- Write four-beat *la-so-mi* patterns and play on the xylophone; use the pattern to create an accompaniment for known songs (Fig. 3.18).

FIG. 3.18

Improvisation
- Improvise a new rhythm and melody to one measure or more of a well-known song.
- Improvise question-and-answer motives using known rhythm and melodic patterns.
- Create a melodic ostinato for a barred instrument; write it on the board.

Listening
- "Rain, Rain," recording by Ella Jenkins (1924–). (This recommendation is related to the text of "Rain Rain," not the melody.)
- "A Tisket, a Tasket," recording by Ella Jenkins (1924–).

Sight-Reading Materials
- Houlahan, Micheál, and Philip Tacka. *Sound Thinking: Music for Sight-Singing and Ear Training*, vol. 1, pp. 28–32. New York: Boosey & Hawkes, 1991.

Two-Part Reading
- Denise Bacon, *50 Easy Two-Part Exercises: First Steps in A cappella Part Singing Using Sol-fa and Staff Notation*, 3rd ed. (Clifton, NJ: European American Music, 1980). (Originally published 1977.)

Duple Meter

Table 3.7 is an overview of the concept, theory, focus song, and additional songs for teaching duple meter.

Table 3.7

Element	Concept	Focus Song	Present Syllables	Theory	Traditional Notation	Practice	Additional Songs
2/4 meter	Organization of strong and weak beats	"Bounce High, Bounce Low"		Accent; bar lines, measures; double bar line, time signature, strong and weak beats	2/4	*la-so-mi* Reading and writing in C, F, and G *do* positions	"Cobbler, Cobbler," "Bye, Baby Bunting," "Little Sally Water"

Cognitive Phase: Preparation

Internalize Music Through Kinesthetic Activities

1. T: "Let's sing 'Bounce High, Bounce Low' and pretend to push your little brother on a swing." (Use the motion of pushing a swing.)
2. Teacher and students sing the first four beats with these motions: pat, shoulders, pat, shoulders.
3. Students point to a representation of strong and weak beats:

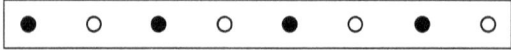

FIG. 3.19

4. Sing "Bounce High, Bounce Low" with rhythm syllables for the motions pat, shoulders, pat, shoulders.

Describe What You Hear

1. Assess kinesthetic awareness by allowing the class to perform several of the activities described above independently.
2. Teacher and students sing the first four beats of "Bounce High, Bounce Low" on "loo" and keep the beat before asking each question. Teacher should perform loud and quiet taps as students sing; try not to disturb the singing but make a distinction between the loud and soft beats. Do not make the distinction when singing.
3. Determine the number of beats in the phrase. T: "Andy, how many beats did we tap?" (four)
4. Determine whether students feel the stress in the strong beats. T: "Andy, do all of the beats feel the same?" (some beats are stronger)
5. Determine which beats are strong and which are weak. T: "Andy, which beats are stronger?" (beats 1 and 3) T: "If beats 1 and 3 are strong, beats 2 and 4 are _____." (weak) T: "Let's sing and show our strong and weak beats." Teacher and students sing the first four beats with the motions pat, shoulders, pat, shoulders.

Create a Representation of What You Hear

1. Assess kinesthetic and aural awareness by allowing the class to perform several of the kinesthetic and aural awareness activities.

2. Hum the target phrase with a neutral syllable and ask students to create a visual representation of the target phrase. Students may use manipulatives. **T:** "Pick up what you need to recreate the strong and weak beats you heard" or "Draw what you heard." (The students could show four or eight beats using Unifix cubes. The strong and weak beats might be distinguished using colors.) Teacher assesses students' level of understanding.
3. Students share their representations with each other.
4. Invite one student to the board to share a representation with the class. If necessary, corrections to the representation can be made by reviewing the aural awareness questions.
5. Students sing the first phrase of "Bounce High, Bounce Low" with a neutral syllable and point to their representation.
6. Students sing all of "Bounce High, Bounce Low" with rhythm or solfège syllables while pointing to the representation of strong and weak beats.

Associative Phase: Presentation

Label the Sound
Teacher presents the new rhythm element.

1. Assess kinesthetic, aural, and visual awareness with phrase 1 of "Bounce High, Bounce Low."
2. **T:** "In music we call the strong beats accents. We can show the strong beats by conducting" (Fig. 3.20).
3. Sing "Bounce High, Bounce Low" and conduct.

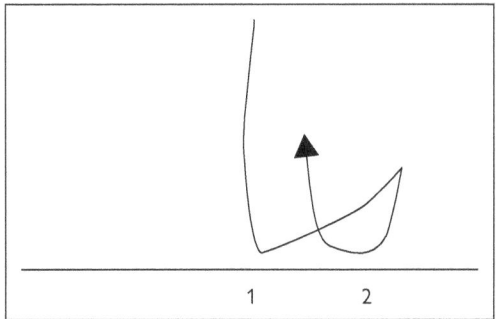

FIG. 3.20

Notate What You Hear
Teacher presents the notation for 2/4 time signature.

1. **T:** "We can show strong beats in two ways: using an accent or writing bar lines."
2. **T:** "In music, we call > 'accent.'"
3. **T:** "Instead of drawing accents, musicians use another method. They put a line before each strong beat. This is called a bar line." (Accent defines bar line.)
4. **T:** "At the end we draw a double bar line. A double bar line is like a musical stop sign."
5. **T:** "Andy, how many beats are between the bar lines?" (two)
6. **T:** "Musicians call the distance between bar lines a 'measure.'"
7. **T:** "Musicians show the number of beats in each measure by erasing the first bar line and writing a 'time signature.' When there are two beats in a measure, the time signature is 2/4 time signature. Initially you might want to write a 2 over a heartbeat, and then a 2 over a quarter note, and finally":

Assimilative Phase: Practice Music Skills

Aural Practice
Singing
- Teacher sings known melodies with words, and students echo-sing with conducting: "Bounce High, Bounce Low"; "Cobbler, Cobbler"; "Bye, Baby Bunting"; and "Little Sally Water."

Inner Hearing
- Teacher directs students to sing focus song, or one of the additional songs, and inner-hear the target phrase.

Improvisation
- Improvise a question and answer. Teacher provides the question, and students answer.
- Improvise a melody to a four- or eight-beat rhythm pattern. Students must conduct a two-beat pattern as they are improvising.

Visual Practice
Reading
- Read these songs with time signatures and bar lines: "Rain, Rain"; "Seesaw"; "Snail, Snail"; and "Lucy Locket." A subsequent activity is to number the measures and instruct the students to perform the rhythm in a specified order.
- Read "Doggie, Doggie" from traditional rhythmic notation written without bar lines on the board. Select individual students to sing while the other students put strong beats on their imaginary tambourines, or play on real instruments (for example, louder instrumentation on the first beat and softer instrument on the second beat).
- Read "Doggie, Doggie" on the board. **T:** "Andy, circle the strong beats." **T:** "Sara, please add in the bar lines for us."
- Read selected patterns and play them on an instrument.

Writing
- Teacher and students sing "Rain, Rain" on "loo." **T:** "Andy, come and place eight heart beats on the board as we sing."
♥ ♥ ♥ ♥ ♥ ♥ ♥ ♥
Teacher and students sing "Rain, Rain" on "loo." **T:** "Andy, which beats are strong beats?" **T:** "How can we show strong and weak beats?" Write > over the strong beats, after writing heartbeats on the board for "Rain, Rain":
>   >   >   >
♥ ♥ ♥ ♥ ♥ ♥ ♥ ♥
- Students add bar lines, a double bar line at the end and a time signature at the beginning.
- Teacher dictates the rhythm of "Lucy Locket." Students write the rhythm on the board one phrase at a time and add bar lines and time signature. They determine the solfège syllables and write them beneath the rhythm.

- Students write any of the aforementioned songs in staff notation with bar lines. They practice writing in relative positions.

Improvisation
- Individual students improvise a four-beat phrase between pairs of phrases in "Pease Porridge Hot." (Have a diagram of the phrases written on the board, including the improvised "blank" sections.)

Listening
- "Allegro assai," from *Brandenburg Concerto No. 2,* by J. S. Bach (1685–1750)
- "Finale," from Symphony No. 4 by Peter Ilyich Tchaikovsky (1840–1893)

Sight Reading
- Houlahan, Micheál, and Philip Tacka. *Sound Thinking: Music for Sight-Singing and Ear Training*, vol. 1, p. 17. New York: Boosey & Hawkes, 1991.

Developing a Lesson Plan Design Based on the Teaching Strategies

The goal of this section is to show how our model of instruction and learning incorporates information for developing musical literacy into the preparation/practice and presentation lesson plan designs.

In the cognitive phase of learning, students explore a music concept moving through three stages of learning: in stage one students learn to internalize music and construct kinesthetic awareness, in stage two they learn to describe the characteristics of the new concept by constructing aural awareness, and in stage three they construct a representation of the new concept. Each of these three stages of learning is explored in three lesson plans.

In the associative phase of learning, students learn how to describe the sounds of music with rhythm or solfège syllables and how to translate these sounds into music notation. Stage one is aural presentation of the new rhythmic or melodic syllables and hand signs using known song material that contains the target pattern (the most frequent pattern having the new element) and related patterns. Stage two is visual presentation of the target pattern using traditional notation. Each stage of learning is explored in two lesson plans.

In the assimilative phase of learning, students practice and gain fluency in integrating the new element into their vocabulary of other known rhythmic and melodic elements. In stage one, students aurally practice the rhythm or solfège syllables and hand signs for the new element with music skills. In stage two, students visually practice the new element with musical skills. Aural practice should take place independently from visual practice, but visual practice should never take place without recourse to aural practice. These stages of learning take place in a concentrated manner over three lessons and may be practiced independently or combined.

Table 3.8a demonstrates how the phases of learning are reflected in a number of lesson types.

Table 3.8a Connecting Lessons Plans to Phases of Learning and Instruction

Phase 1: Cognitive Phase (Preparation)
Lesson 1 Stage 1: internalizing music through kinesthetic activities: developing kinesthetic awareness **Ss** listen to **T** sing the new song. **Ss** perform the new song with movement. Rationale: to match patterns of experience to patterns of music.
Lesson 2 Stage 2: describing what you hear: constructing aural awareness by responding to questions **Ss** aurally analyze the characteristics of the new musical element with **T**'s help. **Ss** describe the characteristics of the new element. Rationale: to verbalize what they perceive.
Lesson 3 Stage 3: developing a representation from memory: constructing visual awareness **Ss** create a visual representation based on their aural understanding. Rationale: to visually represent what they have heard and verbalized.
Phase 2: Associative Phase (Presentation)
Lesson 4 Stage 1: associate the sound of the new element with solfège or rhythmic syllables.
Lesson 5 Stage 2: associate traditional notation with the sound of the new musical element.
After lesson 5, the new element is now referred to as a *known* element. Phase 3: Assimilative Phase (Practice) After the fifth lesson, **T** begins with introducing another new element in preparation/practice and presentation lesson plan cycle. During the practice segments of these lessons, **T** assimilates the known element. Stage 1: **Ss** aurally practice music skills, assimilating the new element in familiar songs and new ones. Stage 2: **Ss** visually practice music skills, assimilating the new element in familiar songs and new ones.

The lesson plan designs and lesson plans that follow represent how students begin the process of understanding the sounds of a new element before learning how to notate it. These plans show where the various phases and the stages of learning take place. We include after each plan design a segment from an actual lesson plan so you can see how these ideas translate into practical applications in the classroom. For the purposes of showing you examples of lesson plans, we use these elements:

New element	Grade 1, Unit 2, Teaching quarter and eighth notes
Known element	Grade 1, Unit 2, Melodic contour

(Continued)

Table 3.8a (continued)

New element	Grade 1, Unit 3, Teaching *s-m*
Known element	Grade 1, Unit 2, Teaching quarter and eighth notes

Lesson 1: Kinesthetic

The lesson plan template in Table 3.8b is for developing a preparation/practice lesson plan framework for the cognitive phase of learning, stage one.

Table 3.8b

Outcome	
INTRODUCTORY ACTIVITIES	
Warm-up	
Sing known songs	
Develop tuneful singing Tone production Diction Expression	
Review known songs and elements	
CORE ACTIVITIES	
Teach a new song	
Preparation of new concept **Develop knowledge of music literacy concepts** Internalize music through kinesthetic activities	**Cognitive phase, stage 1** **Ss** listen to **T** sing the focus song. **Ss** perform the focus song with a movement that demonstrates the concept. Rationale: to match patterns of experience to patterns of music.
Creative movement	
Practice music performance and literacy skills Reading and listening	
SUMMARY ACTIVITIES	
Review lesson outcomes Review the new song	

Table 3.9 shows a lesson plan for developing a preparation/practice lesson plan framework for the cognitive phase of learning, stage one, teaching one and two sounds on a beat.

Table 3.9   Grade 1, Unit 2, Lesson 1: Teaching One and Two Sounds on a Beat

Outcome	
INTRODUCTORY ACTIVITIES	
Warm-up	
Sing known songs	
Develop tuneful singing Tone production Diction Expression	
Review known songs and elements	
CORE ACTIVITIES	
Teach a new song	
Develop knowledge of music literacy concepts Internalize music through kinesthetic activities	"Rain, Rain" CSP: A • **Ss** sing "Rain, Rain" and pat the beat. • **Ss** sing "Rain, Rain" and clap the rhythm. • **Ss** sing and point to a representation of phrase 1 on the board. ♦ ♦ ♦ ♦ ♦ • **Ss** sing "Rain, Rain" while one **S** taps the representation. Line up several **Ss** and have them sing and tap the phrase. • Divide class in half and have one group walk the beat while the other claps the rhythm. Switch roles. • Choose one **S** to walk the beat and clap the rhythm. • **Ss** inner-hear the song while performing beat against rhythm.
Creative movement	
Practice music performance and literacy skills Reading	
SUMMARY ACTIVITIES	
Review lesson outcomes Review the new song	

Lesson 2: Aural

Table 3.10 is a lesson plan template for developing a preparation/practice lesson plan for the cognitive phase of learning, stage two.

Table 3.10

Outcome	
INTRODUCTORY ACTIVITIES	
Warm-up	
Sing known songs	
Develop tuneful singing Tone production Diction Expression	
Review known songs and elements	
CORE ACTIVITIES	
Teach a new song	
Preparation of new concept **Develop knowledge of music literacy concepts** Describe what you hear	Cognitive phase, stage 2 Describe what you hear. **Ss** aurally analyze the characteristics of the new musical element with **T's** help. **Ss** describe the characteristics of the new element by answering a series of carefully sequenced questions from **T**. In this way, they can develop their audiation skills during the process of answering questions. They must inner-hear the focus phrase in order to be able to answer **T's** questions.
Creative movement	
Practice music performance and literacy skills Writing	
SUMMARY ACTIVITIES	
Review lesson outcomes Review the new song	

Table 3.11 presents a lesson plan for developing a preparation/practice lesson plan for the cognitive phase of learning, stage two, teaching one and two sounds on a beat.

Table 3.11 Grade 1, Unit 2, Lesson 2: Teaching One and Two Sounds on a Beat

Outcome	
INTRODUCTORY ACTIVITIES	
Warm-up	
Sing known songs	
Develop tuneful singing Tone production Diction Expression	
Review known songs and elements	
CORE ACTIVITIES	
Teach a new song	
Develop knowledge of music literacy concepts Describe what you hear	"Rain, Rain" CSP: A • Sing "Rain, Rain." • Review kinesthetic awareness activities. • **Ss** and **T** sing the first phrase of "Rain, Rain" on "loo" and tap the beat before asking each question. • **T**: "Andy, how many beats did we tap?" (four) • **T**: "Andy, which beat had the most sounds?" (beat 3) • **T**: "Andy, how many sounds did we sing on beat 3?" (two) • **T**: "If we sang two sounds on beat 3, how many sounds did we sing on each of the other beats?" (one) • **Ss** sing "Rain, Rain" with text and inner-hear the beat with two sounds. • **Ss** sing "Rain, Rain" while **T** softly sings "Doggie, Doggie" as a partner song. Switch.
Creative movement	
Practice music performance and literacy skills Writing	

(Continued)

Table 3.11 (continued)

SUMMARY ACTIVITIES	
Review lesson outcomes	"Sail Away, Ladies"
Review the new song	

Lesson 3: Visual

In Table 3.12 we see a lesson plan template for developing a preparation/practice lesson plan framework for the cognitive phase of learning, stage three.

Table 3.12

Outcome	
INTRODUCTORY ACTIVITIES	
Warm-ups	
Sing known songs	
Develop tuneful singing Tone production Diction Expression	
Review known songs and elements	
CORE ACTIVITIES	
Teach a new song	
Preparation of new concept **Develop knowledge of music literacy concepts** Create a representation of what you hear	Cognitive phase Stage 3: developing a representation from memory; constructing visual awareness **Ss** create a visual representation of the focus phrase based on their aural understanding. Rationale: to visually represent what they have heard and verbalized.
Creative movement	

(Continued)

Table 3.12 (continued)

Practice music performance and literacy skills Improvisation	
SUMMARY ACTIVITIES	
Review lesson outcomes Review the new song	

Table 3.13 shows a lesson plan for developing a preparation/practice lesson plan framework for the cognitive phase of learning, stage three, teaching one and two sounds on a beat.

Table 3.13 Grade 1, Unit 2, Lesson 3: Teaching One and Two Sounds on a Beat

Outcome	
INTRODUCTORY ACTIVITIES	
Warm-ups	
Sing known songs	
Develop tuneful singing Tone production Diction Expression	
Review known songs and melodic elements	
CORE ACTIVITIES	
Teach a new song	
Develop knowledge of music literacy concepts Create a representation of what you hear	"Rain, Rain" CSP: A • Sing "Rain, Rain." • Review and assess kinesthetic and aural awareness activities; ask the same questions from the previous lesson. • **T** sings the first phrase of "Rain, Rain" while **Ss** create a visual representation with Unifix cubes, demonstrating the number of sounds on a beat. • **Ss** share representations with each other and discuss similarities and differences.

(continued)

Table 3.13 (continued)

	• One **S** shares a representation on the board. If necessary, corrections to the representation can be made by reviewing the aural awareness questions. • **Ss** sing the first phrase of "Rain, Rain" on "loo" and point to the representation.
Creative movement	
Practice music performance and literacy skills Improvisation	
SUMMARY ACTIVITIES	
Review lesson outcomes Review the new song	

Lesson 4: Presentation

Table 3.14 presents a lesson plan template for the associative phase of learning, stage one, presentation, labeling the sound.

Table 3.14

Outcome	
INTRODUCTORY ACTIVITIES	
Warm-ups	
Sing known songs	
Develop tuneful singing Tone production Diction Expression	
Review known songs and elements	

(*Continued*)

Table 3.14 (continued)

	CORE ACTIVITIES
Teach a new song	
Presentation of music literacy concepts Describe what you hear with solfège or rhythm syllables	Phase 2: the associative phase: presentation Stage 1: associate the sound of the new element with solfège or rhythmic syllables with a focus pattern.
Creative movement	
Presentation of music literacy concepts Describe what you hear with solfège or rhythm syllables	Phase 2: the associative phase: presentation Stage 1: associate the sound of the new element with solfège or rhythmic syllables with a related pattern.
	SUMMARY ACTIVITIES
Review lesson outcomes Review the new song	

Table 3.15 shows a presentation lesson plan for the associative phase of learning, stage one, presentation, labeling the sound of one and two sounds on a beat with the rhythm syllables *ta* and *tadi*.

Table 3.15 Grade 1, Unit 2, Lesson 4, Presentation: Label the Sound of One and Two Sounds on a Beat with *ta* and *tadi*

Outcome	
	INTRODUCTORY ACTIVITIES
Warm-ups	
Sing known songs	
Develop tuneful singing Tone production Diction Expression	

(Continued)

Table 3.15 (continued)

Review known songs and melodic elements	
CORE ACTIVITIES	
Teach a new song	
Presentation of music literacy concepts Describe what you hear with solfège or rhythm syllables	"Rain, Rain" CSP: A • **Ss** sing first phrase of "Rain, Rain" and **T** reviews and assesses kinesthetic, aural, and visual awareness activities and questions. • **T**: "When we hear one sound on a beat we call it '*ta*,' and when we hear two sounds on a beat we can call it '*tadi*.'" • **T** writes the words "*ta*" and "*tadi*" on the board (*not* the notation). • **T** sings first phrase of "Rain, Rain" with rhythm syllables and **Ss** echo-sing "*ta ta ta di ta*" while clapping the rhythm. • **T** sings first phrase of "Rain, Rain" with rhythm syllables and **Ss** echo-sing "*ta ta ta di ta*" clapping the beat. • **T** performs the same echo activity as a class and with individual **Ss**.
Creative movement	

Presentation of music literacy concepts
 	
Describe what you hear with solfège or rhythm syllables
	"Bee, Bee, Bumble Bee"
	• **Ss** chant the rhyme.
	• **T** reviews aural presentation. **T**: "When we hear one sound on a beat we call it '*ta*,' and when we hear two sounds on a beat we can call it '*tadi*.'"
	• **T** sings four-beat patterns from related songs with text and **Ss** echo with rhythm syllables:
	  o "Seesaw" (phrase 1)
	  o "Bee, Bee, Bumble Bee" (phrase 1)

	o "Queen, Queen Caroline" (entire chant) o "Engine, Engine, Number Nine" (entire chant) o "Cobbler, Cobbler" (phrase 1) • **Ss** echo as a class and individually.
SUMMARY ACTIVITIES	
Review lesson outcomes Review the new song	

Lesson 5: Presentation

Table 3.16 has a lesson plan template for a presentation lesson plan for the associative phase of learning, stage two, a new element.

Table 3.16

Outcome	
INTRODUCTORY ACTIVITIES	
Warm-up	
Sing known songs	
Develop tuneful singing Tone production Diction Expression	
Review known songs and elements	
CORE ACTIVITIES	
Teach a new song	
Presentation of music literacy concepts Notate what you hear	Phase 2: the associative phase: presentation Stage 2: associate traditional notation with the sound of the new musical element in a focus pattern.
Creative movement	
Presentation of music literacy concepts Notate what you hear	Phase 2: the associative phase: presentation Stage 2: associate traditional notation with the sound of the new musical element in a related pattern.
SUMMARY ACTIVITIES	
Review lesson outcomes Review the new song	

Table 3.17 shows a presentation lesson plan for the associative phase of learning, stage two, presenting the notation of one and two sounds on a beat with quarter note and two eighth notes.

Table 3.17 Grade 1, Unit 2, Lesson 5: Present the Notation of One and Two Sounds on a Beat with Quarter and Eighth Notes

Outcome	
INTRODUCTORY ACTIVITIES	
Warm-up	

(*Continued*)

Table 3.17 (continued)

Sing known songs	
Develop tuneful singing Tone production Diction Expression	
Review known songs and melodic elements	
CORE ACTIVITIES	
Teach a new song	
Presentation of music literacy concepts Notate what you hear	"Rain, Rain" CSP: A • **Ss** sing "Rain, Rain" with rhythm syllables and keep the beat. • **T**: "We can represent one and two sounds on a beat using traditional notation. We can use a quarter note to represent one sound on a beat. A quarter note has a note head and a stem." Show on the board. • **T**: "We can use two eighth notes to represent two sounds on a beat. Two eighth notes have two note heads, two stems, and a beam." Show on the board. • **T**: "Our first phrase of 'Rain, Rain' looks like this": ♩ ♩ ♫ ♩ • **T**: "We can read this rhythm pattern using rhythm syllables." **T** sings rhythm syllables while pointing to heartbeats, and **Ss** echo-sing and point.
	• **T**: "Stick notation is an easy way to write rhythmic notation. Stick notation is traditional notation without the note heads for quarter and eighth notes." ♩ ♩ ♫ ♩ • Sing "Rain, Rain" with rhythm syllables while pointing to the phrase written on the board. Individual Ss sing and point while class sings song with rhythm syllables. • **T** switches the pattern to represent phrase 1 of "Lemonade." • **Ss** read and identify the song.
Creative movement	
Presentation of music literacy concepts Notate what you hear	"Bee, Bee, Bumble Bee" • **Ss** chant the rhyme. • **Ss** chant with rhythm syllables and pat the beat. • **Ss** chant while pointing to standard rhythm notation.

(Continued)

Table 3.17 (continued)

	• **T** changes the rhythm into these songs, in this order: "Rain, Rain" "Doggie, Doggie" (entire song) "Engine, Engine, Number Nine" (entire chant) "Queen, Queen Caroline" • **Ss** sing the rhythm syllables while pointing to the standard notation of each. • Several **Ss** go up and write the rhythm notation for a four-beat phrase from any of the previous songs or chants. • Review answers and call on more **Ss** until everyone has a turn.
SUMMARY ACTIVITIES	
Review lesson outcomes Review the new song	

The assimilative phase, stages one and two, takes place during the next units. Stage one and stage two are integrated into various sections of lessons. In our lesson plan structure, we focus on the skills of reading, writing, and improvisation during the next three lessons, at the same time as we prepare another new element to be mastered.

Lesson Segment for Practicing Reading

We use the preparation/practice lesson plan framework in Table 3.18, but note how we focus on practicing reading while preparing the next new element.

Table 3.18 Grade 1, Unit 3, Lesson 1: Preparing *so-mi*; Practicing Reading Quarter and Two Eighth Note Patterns

Outcome	
INTRODUCTORY ACTIVITIES	
Warm-up	
Sing known songs	
Develop tuneful singing Tone production Diction Expression	

(Continued)

Table 3.18 (continued)

Review known songs and rhythmic elements	
CORE ACTIVITIES	
Teach a new song	
Develop knowledge of musical literacy concepts	
Internalize music through kinesthetic activities	
Creative movement	
Practice music performance and literacy skills Reading	"Rain, Rain" CSP: A • **Ss** sing the song. • **T** sings phrase 1 of "Rain, Rain" on "loo" and **Ss** identify the song. • **Ss** read the rhythm of "Rain, Rain" from the board and keep the beat. • **T** gradually adds additional phrases, turning "Rain, Rain" into "Queen, Queen Caroline." • **T** changes the rhythm into "Allegretto" from Symphony No. 94, *Surprise*, by Josef Haydn (1732–1809). ♫ ♫ | ♫ ♩ ♫ ♫ | ♫ ♩ ♫ ♫ | ♫ ♩ ♫ ♫ | ♩ ♩
SUMMARY ACTIVITIES	
Review lesson outcomes	
Review the new song	

Lesson Segment for Practicing Writing

We use the preparation/practice lesson plan framework in Table 3.19, but note how we focus on practicing writing while preparing the next new element.

Table 3.19 Grade 1, Unit 3, Lesson 2: Preparing *so-mi*; Practicing Writing Quarter and Two Eighth Note Combinations

Outcome	
INTRODUCTORY ACTIVITIES	
Warm-up	

(Continued)

Table 3.19 (continued)

Sing known songs	
Develop tuneful singing Tone production Diction Expression	
Review known songs and rhythmic elements	
CORE ACTIVITIES	
Teach a new song	
Develop knowledge of musical literacy concepts Describe what you hear	
Creative movement	
Practice music performance and literacy skills Writing	"Rain, Rain" CSP: A • Sing "Rain, Rain" with words. • Sing "Rain, Rain" with rhythm syllables and keep the beat; **Ss** draw eight beat bars on the board. • Determine the number of sounds on each beat for phrase 1. • Ask **Ss** how we notate these sounds. • One **S** writes it on the board above the beat bars. • **Ss** sing phrase 1 with rhythm syllables while clapping the rhythm. • Repeat for phrase 2. • **Ss** sing "Rain, Rain" with rhythm syllables while clapping the rhythm. "Doggie, Doggie" CSP: A
	• Repeat the process described above with the first two phrases of "Doggie, Doggie." • Each **S** completes a writing activity.

(Continued)

Table 3.19 (continued)

SUMMARY ACTIVITIES	
Review lesson outcomes	"Alleluia"
Review the new song	

Lesson Segment for Practicing Improvisation

We use the preparation/practice lesson plan framework in Table 3.20, but note how we focus on practicing improvisation while preparing the next new element.

Table 3.20 Grade 1, Unit 3, Lesson 3: Preparation of *so-mi*; Practice Improvisation Using Quarter and Two Eighth Notes

Outcome	
INTRODUCTORY ACTIVITIES	
Warm-up	
Sing known songs	
Develop tuneful singing Tone production Diction Expression	
Review known songs and rhythmic elements	
CORE ACTIVITIES	
Teach a new song	
Develop knowledge of musical literacy concepts Create a visual representation of what you heard	
Creative movement	

(*Continued*)

Table 3.20 (continued)

Practice music performance and literacy skills
 	
Improvisation
	"Rain, Rain"
	CSP: A
	• **T** has the first phrase of "Rain, Rain" and four distinct rhythm patterns of quarter notes and eighth notes prepared on board in standard notation.
	• **Ss** sing "Rain, Rain" with words.
	• **Ss** sing "Rain, Rain" with rhythm syllables.
	• **Ss** clap the first phrase of "Rain, Rain" as a "question."
	• Revealing only one at a time, **T** chooses one of four quarter-eighth-note rhythms as an "answer."
	• Perform several times with each of the responses.
	• **T** claps the first phrase of "Rain, Rain" and chooses one **S** to perform an answer; or **Ss** can create their own.
	
	  <u>Teacher</u> <u>Student</u>
	  ♩ ♩ ♫ ♩ ♫ ♫ ♫ ♩
	                ♫ ♫ ♩ ♩
	                ♩ ♫ ♩ ♫
	                ♩ ♫ ♫ ♩

SUMMARY ACTIVITIES	
Review lesson outcomes Review the new song	

Chapter 4

Students as Performers

Developing Music Skills and Creative Expression

The goal of this chapter is to give a quick overview of techniques for developing tuneful singing, reading, inner hearing, writing, improvisation, playing instruments, creative movement, and listening skills. You will find more detailed activities in Chapter 3 of *Kodály Today*. Here we also present listening examples that can be used for development of movement as well as music literacy skills. Where possible, music skills should practice all of the rhythmic and melodic elements outlined in the curriculum for each grade. Grade one elements include quarter notes, eighth notes, quarter note rests, and melodies composed of a three-note child's chant.

Tuneful Singing Skills

Posture

1. Teacher explains to students the correct head position:
   Face should look straight ahead.
   Try several exercises, such as moving the head up and down and sideways to relax the head and neck muscles.
   Stand with your back against a wall and make sure that your head and the heels of your feet are touching the wall. The head should feel suspended as if you are a puppet or a balloon.
   Keep the spine straight.
2. Teacher explains to them the correct seated position:
   Shoulders should be relaxed and rotated toward the back.
   Neck muscles should be relaxed.
   Tongue should be relaxed in the bottom of the mouth.
   Spine should be extended.
   Rib cage is lifted.
   Be at the edge of your chair when singing.
   Feet are on the floor.

Hands are on the legs.
Eyes are on the conductor.

3. Teacher explains the correct standing position:
   Shoulders should be relaxed and rotated toward the back.
   Neck muscles should be relaxed.
   Tongue should be relaxed in the bottom of the mouth.
   Spine should be extended.
   Rib cage is lifted.
   Arms should dangle freely at the sides. Hands should be relaxed at the sides.
   Knees should be relaxed and very slightly bent.
   Feet should be firmly placed on the ground and roughly ten to twelve inches apart. Feet should be slightly apart, less than the width of the shoulders. Make sure the body is resting on the balls of the feet.
   Eyes are on the conductor.

Body Warm-up

1. *Body stretches.* Teacher explains that students' shoulders should be kept down, and they should reach for the stars; each hand should alternate with the other.
2. *Shaking arms.* Extend arms in front of the body and shake each arm separately.
3. *Shoulder roll.* Roll each shoulder separately, making a circle.
4. *Shrugging shoulders.* Shrug your shoulders, hold the position for several counts, and then release.
5. *Head rolls.* Drop head to left shoulder and trace a half circle, moving chin toward chest and right shoulder.
6. *Neck stretch.* Drop the right ear to the right shoulder and the left ear to the left shoulder. Move the neck, making a yes-or-no motion.
7. *Facial stretch.* Ask students to act surprised. Try to drop your jaw and say *mah, mah, mah* several times.
9. *Knee flex.* Arms should be extended forward and hands should be relaxed; bounce the body by flexing the knees.
10. *Wiggle toes.* Wiggle toes inside your shoes.

Breathing

1. *Correct breathing posture.* Students lie on the floor with a book placed on their abdominal muscles. When inhaling, the book rises, and when exhaling, the book lowers. Students should stand and place a hand on the abdominal muscles. They then exhale and inhale, paying attention to abdominal muscle and not raising their shoulders. They need to be encouraged to take in a deep breath through their nose and mouth, not a shallow one. Sometimes it is useful for students to exhale air against the palm of the hand.
2. *Awareness of the diaphragm and other abdominal muscles for breathing.* These exercises will help students understand the use of the abdominal muscles for breathing:
   Show students how to sip through a straw correctly and expand their waist.
   Show students how to release air using a "sss" or hissing sound.

Show students how to release air using the word "ha."
Guide the students to yawn, as this opens up the back of the throat and relaxes the voice.
3. *Sighing*. This is a gentle way of using a higher voice than students usually speak with. Try having them sigh a few times, starting each sigh a little higher than the last.
4. *Practice breathing*. Breathe in through the nose for four counts and exhale through the mouth for four counts.
5. *Consonants*. Students echo four-beat patterns of consonants (k-k-k-k, ss-ss-ss-ss, p-p-p-p, zz-zz-zz-zz, etc.).

Resonance

1. *Pitch exploration using a story*. When you tell your class a story, modulate your voice to include high, medium, and low voice for characters in the story or high, medium, and low sounds for events in the story. Repeat the story and ask students to make the sounds.
2. *Flashlight*. As you move a flashlight beam projected onto the blackboard, ask students to follow the contour of the moving beam of light.
3. *Use of sirens*. Imitate the sound of a siren with the voice. Challenge the students to make soft and loud, high and low, long and short sirens, and sirens that just go up, just come down, or do both.
4. *Voice modulation*. Select songs and rhymes that can be used to develop a student's singing voice. As young children say chants, they may be guided to speak using a "baby bird's voice" (high) or a "grandfather's voice" (low). Chanting using these voice types will teach a young learner how to modulate the voice. Guide young students to perform the chant "Bee, Bee, Bumble Bee" using a high voice; then perform the chant using a low voice.
5. *Slinky*. Explore the upper and lower ranges of the voice by using a Slinky toy.
6. *Animal and bird sounds in upper range*. Students are asked to imitate animal and bird sounds in the upper range such as owls, cats, and cuckoos. Pretend to be an owl and make a high-pitched "whoooo" sound. Repeat this several times, each time try to make the "whoooo" a little higher than the last.
7. *Falling off a cliff*. The teacher asks students to pretend they are falling off a cliff and say "aaaahhhhhhhhhh!"
8. *Use a ball*. Throw a ball from one student to another; students have to follow the movement of the ball with their voices.
9. *Use a balloon*. This can help demonstrate correct breathing and control of the breath.

Tone Production

1. *Humming or singing on a neutral syllable*. Students sing but follow the direction of a ball thrown up in the air, to move from chest to head voice.
2. *Humming or singing melodic patterns from folk songs using a neutral syllable*. Students hum a pattern from a song, but the last note should be shortened to take a breath and repeat the pattern.

3. *Humming or singing two patterns using a neutral syllable.* Students sing two melodic patterns together without taking a breadth.
4. *Vocally exploring pure vowel sounds.* Sing with known solfège syllables and hand signs.
5. *Vocally exploring pure vowel sounds via colors.* Sing a song using a number of colors to practice pure vowel sounds. For example, students can sing "Here comes a bluebird" but use a word for another color. "Blue" allows students to experience the correct vowel formation for its vowel sound, *oo*. "Gold" (singing "gold bird") allows them to experience the correct vowel formation for *oh*. "Green" works for *ee*. "Aqua" illustrates *ah*.
6. *"Loo" sound.* Students sing known melodies on "loo," using upper, lower, or middle voice.

Diction

1. *Tongue twisters or articulators sung on one note.* Students gain flexibility by reciting. For example, "Mummy made me mash my M&M" involves the lips, teeth, and tip of the tongue.
2. *Tongue twisters on two notes.* They can be sung by two groups using two notes at the interval of a fourth or fifth.
3. *Unvoiced consonants.* Students say the unvoiced consonants *p*, *t*, and *k* using known rhythm patterns of songs that are four to eight beats in length.

Tuneful Singing

1. *so-mi.* It is important to practice the *so-mi* minor third as well as patterns formed with *so-la-so-mi* combinations. Patterns formed with *mi-so* and *la* should also be practiced, paying particular attention to *mi-la*, the perfect fourth interval.
2. *Singing phrases of songs using different vowel sounds.* Students sing phrases of songs using different vowel sounds such as *ah, eh, ee, oh,* and *oo*, making sure that the tone is very light and relaxed.
3. *Singing softly.* Teacher and students sing a known song. Then students sing the known song softly as they listen to each other.
4. *Singing with dynamic markings.* Students should sing known melodies using the correct dynamic names and terms:

pp	pianissimo
p	piano
mp	mezzo-piano
mf	mezzo-forte
f	forte
ff	fortissimo

    It is best to sing songs using two contrasting dynamics, as with *f* and *p*.

Reading Skills

Rhythmic Reading Activities

Read traditional rhythmic notation from flash cards, the interactive SMART board, or worksheets. Read a known song from rhythmic notation that includes grade one elements. The process:

1. Sing the song and tap the beat.
2. Sing the song with rhythm syllables.
3. Tap the beat as the students keep the beat and read the rhythm of the complete song, or the rhythm of a specific phrase, using inner hearing or singing aloud.

Transforming Rhythm of a Known Song into an Unknown Song
Transform a known song into an unknown song by sequentially changing rhythms that include grade one elements. The process:

1. Students sing a known song.
2. Teacher erases parts of the song and replaces with new rhythms.
3. Students clap the rhythm and say the new rhythm syllables.
4. Teacher transforms to a new rhythm entirely and sings a new song.

Form
Present mixed-up phrases of the rhythm of a known song to have students correctly rearrange the form. The process:

1. Teacher presents the phrases out of order.
2. Students identify the song.
3. They arrange the phrases in the proper order.
4. Students sing the song.

Inner Hearing
Students can practice inner hearing using both aural and visual activities.

Aural Inner-Hearing Exercises
Students can chant the rhythm of a known melody and inner-hear specific rhythmic motifs signaled or indicated by the teacher. The process:

1. Sing the song with text.
2. Sing the song with rhythm syllables and keep the beat.
3. Sing the song with rhythm syllables; teacher signals which measures to chant silently.

Visual Inner-Hearing Exercises
Students read the rhythmic notation of a known melody and inner-hear certain motifs indicated by the teacher on the reading exercises. The process:

1. Sing the song with text.
2. Sing the song with rhythm syllables and keep the beat.
3. Sing the song with rhythm syllables from notation; teacher indicates which measures to chant silently.

Students can also read the rhythmic notation of an unknown melody and inner-hear certain motifs indicated by the teacher on the reading exercises. The process:

1. Sing the song with text.
2. Sing the song with rhythm syllables and keep the beat.
3. Sing the song with rhythm syllables from notation; teacher indicates which measures to chant silently.

Matching

Match song titles to written rhythms that include grade one elements. The process:

1. List the titles of four songs on the board.
2. Write a phrase from each song in rhythmic notation.
3. Students match the rhythm to the title of the song.

Error Identification

Students read the rhythm of a known song and identify rhythmic errors that are made by the teacher. The process:

1. Teacher or a student writes a sixteen-beat rhythm pattern.
2. Teacher or the student claps a slightly different pattern.
3. Another student must identify the phrases and the beats where the changes occur.

Retrograde

Read a rhythm of a known song in retrograde that includes grade one elements. The process:

1. Sing the song with text.
2. Sing the song with rhythm syllables and keep the beat.
3. Sing the song with rhythm syllables from notation.
4. Sing the song backward with rhythm syllables from notation.

Melodic Reading Activities

Hand Signs

Sing a known melodic pattern or song and an unknown melodic pattern or song from the teacher's hand signs to include grade one concepts. The process:

1. Teacher gives the starting pitch and shows hand signs for a phrase of music.
2. Students sing with solfège and hand signs.

Tone Ladder

Teacher points to a pattern on the tone ladder that includes grade one concepts.

1. Teacher points to notes of a known song on the tone ladder.
2. Students can sing each note or wait to sing the melodic motif.
3. They sing with solfège syllables and hand signs.

Traditional Rhythmic Notation with Solfège Syllables

Students read known melodies from flash cards or from the board that include grade one elements. They sing using solfège syllables and hand signs. The process:

1. Students sing the known song with rhythm syllables.
2. Students sing the known song with solfège syllables and hand signs.
3. Teacher points to the notation, keeping the beat while the students read with rhythm syllables and clap the rhythm or conduct.
4. Teacher points to the notation, keeping the beat while the students sing with solfège syllables and hand signs.
8. Students perform the exercise aloud, singing on a neutral syllable as they conduct.

Reading from Finger Staff
Sing a song while showing placement on the finger staff to include grade one concepts. The process:

1. Students sing song with solfège and hand signs.
2. Teacher reviews the rule of placement for solfège syllables on the finger staff.
3. Students sing with solfège syllables and show placement on the finger staff.

Reading from the Staff
Students read known melodies with solfège syllables from the staff to include grade one elements. Students sing using solfège syllables and hand signs.

Students can also read unknown melodies with solfège syllables from the staff to include grade one elements. Students sing using solfège syllables and hand signs. The process:

1. Students sing the known song with rhythm syllables.
2. Students sing the known songs with solfège syllables and hand signs.
3. Teacher points to the notation, keeping the beat while the students read the rhythm syllables and clap the rhythm.
4. Teacher reviews the rule of placement for the students, gives students the starting pitch, and has them read the notes of the melody from the tone set written on the staff.
5. Students read the known song from the staff aloud, singing with solfège syllables and hand signs. The teacher might begin this activity by first asking the students to inner-hear the melody and then read aloud.
6. The students perform the exercise aloud, singing on a neutral syllable.

Transform a Melody
Transform a known song into an unknown song by sequentially changing rhythms and pitches. This can be accomplished using traditional rhythmic notation and solfège syllables or from the staff. The process:

1. Sing the known song.
2. Teacher transforms parts of the song.
3. Students clap the rhythm while saying the rhythm syllables; they may then sing with solfège syllables and hand signs.
4. Teacher transforms additional parts of a new melody, and the students sing the new song.

Form
Present mixed-up phrases of a known song written with traditional rhythmic notation and solfège, or on the staff, and students correctly rearrange the song. The process:

1. Teacher presents the phrases out of order.
2. Students identify the song.
3. Students arrange the phrases in the proper order.
4. Students sing the song.

Inner Hearing
Aural Activities
Students read a known song from the teacher's hand signs with solfège syllables and "hide" (sing inside their head) a specific melodic motif that is indicated by the teacher. Melodic notes include those from the grade one curriculum.

Students then read an unknown song from the teacher's hand signs and hide a specific melodic motif that is indicated by the teacher. Melodic notes include those from the grade one curriculum. The process:

1. Sing the song with text.
2. Sing the song with solfège syllables and hand signs.
3. Sing the song with solfège syllables; teacher signals which measures to sing silently.

Visual Activities
Students read a known song from rhythmic notation and solfège, or staff, and hide a specific motif that includes notes of the grade one curriculum. Students read from the staff and sing on solfège with hand signs.

Students then read an unknown song from rhythmic notation and solfège, or staff, and hide a specific motif that include notes of the grade one curriculum. Students read from the staff and sing on solfège with hand signs. The process:

1. Sing the song with text.
2. Sing the song with rhythm syllables and solfège syllables and hand signs.
3. Sing the song with syllables from notation; teacher indicates which measures to sing silently.

Matching
Match song titles to written melodies that include notes of the grade one curriculum. The process:

1. Teacher write phrases on the board.
2. Students identify sections from known songs.

Error Identification
Students read a known song and identify rhythmic or melodic errors that include notes of the grade one curriculum. The process:

1. Teacher or a student writes a sixteen-beat melody on the board.
2. Teacher or students sings, changing the notes.

Another student must identify the phrases and the beats where the changes occur.

Inner-Hearing Skills

Hand Signs

1. Students follow teacher's hand signs of known songs and inner-hear solfège syllables.

2. Students follow and sing teacher's hand signs and inner-hear specified solfège syllables.
3. Teacher shows hand signs for an entire known song, and students inner-hear and recognize the song.
4. Students "sing" the indicated measures of a song using inner hearing.

Tone Ladder

1. Students follow teacher's pointing to tone ladder and inner-hear solfège syllables.
2. Students follow and sing from the tone ladder and inner-hear specific solfège syllables.
3. Teacher points out a whole song on the tone ladder, and students inner-hear and recognize the song.

Rhythmic Notation or Staff Notation

1. Students recognize a song from inner hearing rhythmic or staff notation.
2. Sight-read and memorize a simple melodic pattern without hearing it aloud.

Rhythm Activities

1. Teacher claps rhythm for a known song and students inner-hear and recognize the song.
2. Teacher sings part of a known song and students inner-hear solfège syllables and clap the rhythm for the second phrase.

Melodic Activities

1. Students inner-hear solfège written out without rhythmic notation and recognize the song.
2. Students inner-hear a song written with traditional notation and solfège syllables.
3. Students inner-hear a song written on the staff.

Additional Inner-Hearing Activities

1. Students sing a melody with solfège syllables, and teacher indicates where students should sing the melody silently.
2. Students read from a score, but the teacher indicates where they should sing silently with inner hearing.
3. Teacher sings or plays a melody and students have to remember the first note of the melody played. This exercise can be extended from short to longer melodic motives.
4. Students sing a well-known song and teacher claps a four-beat ostinato. Students must clap and sing known song. This activity can be extended to an eight-beat ostinato.
5. Students sing a series of notes and teacher plays a series of notes above or below these. Students must identify the intervals of the solfège of the melody sung or performed by the teacher.

Writing Skills

Rhythm

Manipulatives
Students use manipulatives to create a visual representation of a new concept. The process:

1. Teacher sings focus pattern on neutral syllable.
2. Students use Unifix cubes or SMART boards to create representation.

Fill in the Blank
Students fill in the blanks of a known song. The process:

1. Teacher and students sing a song.
2. Teacher sings the song on "loo" and students echo-sing with rhythm syllables.
3. Teacher has written the song with missing measure or measures; students fill in what is missing.

Traditional Rhythmic Notation
Students write the rhythmic notation of known and unknown motives that include notes of the grade one curriculum. The process:

1. Sing the song and keep the beat.
2. Students sing the phrase to be notated and draw a representation of the rhythm.
6. Teacher reviews how to write different sounds on the beat.
7. Students write the phrase with stick notation.
8. They add note heads.
9. They read notation with rhythm syllables.

Writing Melody

Manipulatives
Students use manipulatives to create a visual representation of a new concept. The process:

1. Teacher sings focus pattern on neutral syllable.
2. Students use Unifix cubes or SMART boards to create representation.

Tone Set
Write the tone set of a song on the board as it is being performed, to include elements of the grade one curriculum. The process:

1. Sing the song with text.
2. Sing the song with solfège syllables.
3. One student goes to the board and writes down the tone set with highest to lowest pitch in the song.

Traditional Rhythmic Notation with Solfège Syllables
Students write the rhythmic notation with solfège syllables of a known or unknown song, to include elements of the grade one curriculum. The process:

1. Students sing the song and keep the beat.
2. They sing the phrase and clap the beat.
3. They sing the phrase and clap the rhythm.
4. They sing the phrase with rhythm syllables.
5. Teacher reviews how to write different sounds on the beat.
6. Students write the phrase with stick notation.
7. They add note heads.
9. They read notation with rhythm syllables.
10. They sing the known phrase with solfège syllables.
11. They sing the example and add solfège syllables.

Fill in the Blank

Students complete the empty measures of a known song with traditional notation and solfège or on the staff. The process:

1. Teacher and students sing a song.
2. Teacher sings the song on "loo" and students echo-sing with rhythm while conducting; repeat, having students sing with solfège syllables and hand signs.
3. Teacher has written the song with missing measure or measures; students fill in what is missing.

Fill in the Blank: Staff Notation

Fill in the blanks of a known song, with students completing the empty measures of a known song in staff notation. The process:

1. Teacher and students sing a song.
2. Teacher sings the song on "loo" and students echo-sing with rhythm while conducting and then with solfège syllables and hand signs.
3. Teacher has written the song with missing measure or measures on the staff; students fill in what is missing.

Staff Notation

Students write known song or unknown song using staff notation where *do* = F, G, C. The process:

1. Students echo-sing and keep the beat.
2. Students echo-sing with rhythm syllables.
3. Teacher guides students to determine the solfège syllables through questioning:
    o T: "What is the solfège syllable for the last pitch?"
    o T: "What is the solfège syllable for the first pitch?"
4. Students sing with solfège syllables and hand signs.
5. Teacher guides students with hand signs to determine placement of pitches on the staff.
6. Students write the melody on the staff.

Writing a Memorized Melody from Hand Signs Using Staff Notation

1. Teacher writes rhythm of known song on the board.
2. Teacher performs melody with hand signs and students memorize.

3. Teacher provides students with the melody on the staff but with incomplete measures. Students complete the missing measures.

Improvisation Skills

Actions

Improvise actions to a known chant. The process:

1. Teacher and students sing a known song.
2. Teacher chooses students to improvise actions on the beat or to text.

Choose Alternate Ending

Students clap the rhythm of a known song and choose an alternate ending from four options containing the musical element being practiced in a four-beat pattern. The process:

1. Students sing a known song.
2. They identify the form.
3. They sing the song with rhythm syllables.
4. They sing the song with rhythm syllables but choose an alternative rhythmic ending from four options.

Rhythm Chain

Students improvise rhythm patterns. The process:

1. Students clap a four-beat rhythm pattern, one after the other, without pause, using know rhythmic patterns.
2. In another version, students clap a four-beat rhythm pattern, one after the other, without pause, using know rhythmic patterns; but they must repeat the four beats of the previous student.

Improvise Rhythmic Ostinato

Students create a rhythmic ostinato to known songs. The process:

1. Students sing a known song.
2. Teacher demonstrates an improvised rhythmic ostinato.
3. Students create their own rhythmic ostinato base.
4. A student performs rhythmic ostinato on a classroom percussion instrument while class sings known song.

Improvise Rhythmic Variation on a Known Songs

Students are challenged to fill in the missing measures of known songs with improvised rhythms. The process:

1. Students are given the rhythmic notation of a known song. (Some of the measures contain only "heartbeats" or beat bars.)
2. They sing the song, performing the rhythm where it is notated and patting the beat elsewhere.
3. They perform the rhythm where it is notated and improvise elsewhere.

Question and Answer
Students create a rhythmic question and answer. The process:

1. Clap a four-beat rhythmic question to a student; he or she must respond by clapping back a four-beat answer.
2. Students may do this exercise without naming any of the rhythms. Later, they can clap their answer and say rhythm syllables. Question-and-answer conversations can continue as a chain around the class.

Improvise New Rhythms for Phrases of Known Form
Improvise new rhythmic phrases to a known form. The process:

1. Teacher assigns each student a phrase of the form ABA'C.
2. Student 1 claps the rhythm of the A phrase.
3. Student 2 improvises phrase B.
4. Student 3 improvises a variant for phrase A'.
5. Student 4 improvises phrase C.

Melody

Actions
Improvise actions to a known chant. The process:

1. Teacher and students sing a known song.
2. Teacher chooses students to improvise actions on the beat or to text.

Improvise Melodic Ostinato
Students create a four- or eight-beat melodic ostinato with known melodic elements. The process:

1. Students sing known song with text.
2. They sing known song with solfège syllables and hand signs.
3. Teacher sings a melodic ostinato, and students sing known song with solfège and hand signs.
4. Teacher sings song and students improvise a new melodic ostinato.

Choose Alternate Ending
Students sing a known song and choose an alternate ending from four options that contain the musical element being practiced in a four-beat pattern. Teacher gives students a series of choices with just the beginning note and ending note. The process:

1. Students sing known song with text.
2. They sing known song with solfège syllables and hand signs.
3. They sing known song with solfège syllables and hand signs but only tap beats for the last phrase.
4. They sing known song with solfège syllables and hand signs but choose to complete the ending for the song from four options provided by teacher.

Improvise New Phrases to Known Form
Improvise phrases in a known song. The process:

1. Teacher assigns each student a phrase of the form ABA'C.
2. Student 1 sings phrase A.
3. Student 2 improvises phrase B.
4. Student 3 improvises a variant for phrase A'.
5. Student 4 improvises phrase C.

Improvise New Form
Improvise a new form for a known song. The process:

1. Students sing known song.
2. They analyze the form of the known song.
3. They change the form by improvising new melodies.
4. They perform the song with a different form.

Question and Answer
Students create an answer to a question. The process:

1. Teacher establishes the beat and sings a four-beat melody; students respond with a different four-beat melody.
2. Sing a pattern and ask the students to change one beat. (This can also be done visually and may be easier for some students.)
3. As students become more proficient, teacher lengthens the phrase or changes the tempo. This leads to performance of melodic conversations. Question-and-answer conversations can continue as a chain around the class.

Movement

Create Movement to Form
Create movements that correlate to the form of a song or piece of music. The process:

1. Students sing known song.
2. Discuss the form.
3. Students create movements for each section of the song (i.e., verse, refrain).
4. Students perform the song with movements.

Musical Memory

Memorizing by Reading Hand Signs

Show typical melodic and rhythmic patterns and ask the students to sing patterns back that include elements of the grade one curriculum. The process:

1. Select a melody and show it with hand signs.

2. Students sing from hand signs in solfège syllables.
3. Students sing in canon with hand signs with solfège syllables.
4. Students write the melody from memory.

Memorization from Rhythmic Notation

Students look at a rhythmic score and memorize it. The process:

1. Students inner-hear the notation with rhythm syllables.
2. They identify the form.
3. They chant the rhythm syllables out loud.
4. They chant the example with rhythm syllables from memory.
5. They may write the rhythm using rhythmic notation.

Memorization from Rhythmic Notation with Solfège Syllables

Students memorize a new piece of music from notation. The process:

1. Students look at a score and memorize a phrase of the musical example by silently singing in their head using hand signs.
2. They identify the form.
3. They sing the example with hand signs from memory.
4. They may write the melody using rhythmic notation and solfège syllables.

Memorizing from Staff Notation

Students memorize a new piece of music from staff notation. The process:

1. Students look at a score and memorize a phrase of the musical example by silently singing in their head using hand signs.
2. If some phrases of the musical example are known and others unknown, the students may sing the known phrases and the teacher may sing the unknown phrases. They listen and learn the unfamiliar phrases.
3. They may write the melody using rhythmic notation and solfège syllables.

Inner-Hearing Memorization

Students are given an unknown piece that contains known elements to learn without singing aloud. The process:

1. Students inner-hear the example with rhythm syllables and keep the beat.
2. They inner-hear the example with solfège syllables and hand signs.
3. They identify the form of the example.
4. They write down the example from memory.

Memorizing by Ear

Teacher plays a musical phrase on the piano, and students memorize by ear by following this process:

1. Students identify the meter.
2. They sing the example with rhythm syllables.
3. They identify the solfège syllables for the ending and starting pitches.
4. They sing the example with solfège syllables and hand signs.
5. They sing the example with absolute pitch names and hand signs.
6. They write the exercise or play it back on the xylophone.

Understanding Form

Aural

Aurally recognizing same, similar, or different phrases in a song. The process:

1. Teacher sings first phrase.
2. Students sing second phrase alternating phrase by phrase until song is complete.
3. Students verbally identify the form.

Aurally Identify the Form of a Known Folk Song

Teacher or another student performs a known folk song and students identify the form.

Aurally Identify the Form of an Unknown Folk Song

Teacher or another student performs unknown folk song and students identify the form.

Students Demonstrate Knowledge of Form Through Aural Improvisation

1. Teacher assigns individual students form letter names (A, A', B, C, etc.).
2. Student 1 begins exercise by singing the A phrase.
3. Other students sing phrase variants in the order chosen by teacher (AA'BA; AAA'A; ABA'C).

Rhythmic Question and Answer

1. Teacher claps a four-beat rhythmic question and students answer with a different four-beat pattern.
2. Students create a chain of four-beat rhythmic questions and answers.
3. Teacher sings one phrase from a song and students sing an answer to the phrase with rhythm syllables.

Melodic Question and Answer

1. Teacher sings one phrase from a song and students sing an answer to the phrase with solfège syllables and hand signs.
2. Students create a chain of four-beat melodic questions and answers.

Changing the Rhythmic Form of a Folk Song

1. Students label the rhythmic form of a folk song and create a different rhythm for a phrase. If the form is ABAC, teacher erases the C and has students create a new rhythmic pattern for C.
2. Students label the form of a folk song and change the song to reflect a new form.

Part-Work Skills

As you begin to implement these activities into your lessons, follow this teaching sequence.

1. Teacher and class.
2. Class and teacher.
3. Divide the class into two groups, each performing its own part. Switch.
4. Two small ensembles, each performing its own part.
5. Two students, each performing their own part.

This section gives techniques and activities that are divided between simpler and more advanced part work. The activities are useful for helping students learn simpler repertoire. Once they have mastered these activities with easier repertoire, the transition to performing more complex musical examples will occur more quickly.

Keep a Beat

Sing a folk song while marching, walking, or in some way moving to the beat. Performing a song while keeping the beat requires students to concentrate on two tasks at the same time. This activity is valuable in both the classroom and the choral rehearsal.

Keep a Beat and Demonstrate Music Comparatives

Once students can sing and perform the beat both accurately and musically, add the task of altering tempo and dynamics. To accomplish this, the students will need a strong foundation in being able to demonstrate music comparatives such as slow and fast, high and low, loud and soft, duple meter beat (marching), and compound meter beat.

Call-and-Response or Antiphonal Singing

Although students perform only one phrase of music in a call-and-response song, they must eventually learn to sing both phrases if they are going to be able to sing rhythmically and musically. Developing this ability requires audiation practice (using inner hearing). Call-and-response singing may be applied to folk songs (you may also think of call and response as responsorial singing). Some simple examples of call-and-response songs are "Skin and Bones," "Charlie over the Ocean," and "Pizza, Pizza."

Pointing to a Beat

Perform or point to a visual of the beat in a song while singing. This "tracking" ability promotes more fluent music reading and reading in general. Students may also keep the beat by performing it on a percussion instrument.

Clapping the Rhythm

Sing a song while clapping the rhythm. This can be accomplished in a number of ways. Students need to perform this activity musically, and always according to the phrase. They may sing while clapping (we suggest clapping with two fingers) the rhythm or performing the rhythm on a percussion instrument. Two students may perform a simple folk song, one performing the beat while the other does the rhythm; use different timbres for beat and rhythm. The teacher may write the rhythm of a known song on the board and place the beat below the rhythmic notation. Two students can go to the board and perform the song, with one pointing to the beat and the other to the rhythm.

Tapping on Specified Beat

When students are singing familiar melodies, ask them to tap on the strong beats while singing. Or they might tap on the rests in a known song or the beginning of each phrase. This activity may also be done with a musical instrument.

Singing the Final Note of a Composition

The teacher sings a known melody but does not sing the final note; students must fill it in. This activity helps them understand the tonal strength of each note. An interesting activity is to have students explore alternative endings to known compositions. This strengthens their understanding of harmonic functions and voice leading.

Rhythmic Ostinato

An ostinato is a repeated rhythmic or melodic motive used to accompany a song. Here we offer a procedure for performing a rhythmic ostinato. Singing songs with hand-clapping movements can also be included in this category. For example, the singing game "Four White Horses" has specified hand-clapping movements to perform while singing the song. Depending on the age of the students, you may use several ostinatos together.

The students sing the melody while the teacher claps a rhythmic ostinato or sings a melodic ostinato. (It is important, when teaching students rhythm, that the students do not develop their knowledge of rhythm on the basis of visual clues. The teacher should always make sure the students hear the new rhythm pattern being clapped, as opposed to being seen.)

1. The students sing the melody while the teacher claps a rhythmic ostinato or sings a melodic ostinato.
2. The students and the teacher exchange parts.
3. Divide the students into two groups, one group to sing and the other to perform the ostinato. Switch tasks.
4. Two students perform the work.
5. One student sings while performing the second part. More advanced students can perform the ostinato on percussion.

Performing Rhythm Canons Based on Simple Rhythms

These canons are based on simple rhymes or rhythms of very simple melodies. Rhythm syllables can be used to perform the canons. Begin the canon after two or four beats. Practice this technique with familiar repertoire. Although the rhythm of many folk songs can work well when performed in canon, the best songs for this type of activity are those that have a rest at the end of every phrase. A good example is "Bow Wow Wow." Perform the canon with two timbres. The process:

1. Teacher and class.
2. Class and teacher.
3. Divide the class into two groups; each performs its own part. Switch.
4. Two small ensembles, each performing its own part.
5. Two students, each performing one part.
6. Have the students begin to clap the rhythm of a simple song; the teacher can clap in canon. Once they are comfortable with hearing the canon, the teacher and students can reverse roles. Canons maybe performed kinesthetically, aurally, and visually, or using a combination of techniques.

Performing a Kinesthetic Canon

The teacher performs a rhyme with a beat motion for every four beats. The students follow in canon, performing the rhythm as well as the beat motion. For example, say "Ali Baba forty thieves" while tapping four beats. Now say it and tap the beats on different parts of your body, and have students imitate. Once students are proficient at this activity, perform it in canon after four beats with text. You could also perform a rhythm and have students clap it back after two or four beats.

Performing a Visual Rhythm Canon with Rhythm Syllables

The goal of this activity is for students to read a rhythm in canon. The canon can be performed with the teacher and students, or just the students. To perform a rhythm canon visually, have students read rhythm flash cards of the rhyme or melody to be used for the canon. The teacher should keep a steady pulse but show the card quickly and move on to the next card while the students are still performing the rhythm of the first card. In other words, give the students a brief look at every card in succession. The speed of this process may be increased so that the students are always saying something different from what they are seeing. Students should perform the canon by reading with rhythm syllables.

Performing an Aural Rhythm Canon with Rhythm Syllables

Performing aural canons can be more challenging than visual canons. Aural rhythm canons are performed without the aid of notation. If a motion is attached to a phrase, the exercise is simple to perform. Echo clapping is a preliminary preparation for aural canon work. This task can be made more complex by having students clap back the rhythm while chanting or singing the rhythm syllables.

Performing Simple Rhythm Canons Based on Simple Folk Songs

These canons are based on the rhythms of very simple melodies. Rhythm syllables can be used to perform the canons. Here is a procedure for performing a rhythmic canon.

1. Perform the song with actions and words.
2. Sing the song with rhythm syllables and keep the beat.
3. Say rhythm syllables while clapping the rhythm.
4. Think the rhythm syllables and clap the rhythm.
5. Teacher taps the rhythm using a drum or wood block; students clap and say the rhythm syllables beginning after four beats.
6. Teacher writes the canonic part below the notation of the song. T: "Where should we begin writing the second part? What should be written in the empty measures?"
7. Teacher and students may perform in canon after two beats.
8. Challenge a student to sing while pointing to the notation in canon.

Melodic Ostinato

Students accompany known songs with melodic ostinatos. Melodic ostinati should be based on the melodic building blocks of known song repertoire. This activity is only appropriate for classes that have a good number of independent, strong singers.

Combining Drones and Melodic Ostinatos

Divide the class into three groups. One group sings the folk song. A second group accompanies the folk song with a drone composed of the tonic note or tonic and dominant notes, and a third group sings a melodic ostinato.

Instrumental Performance Skills

Students should be guided to recognize the timbre of all pitched instruments (xylophones, wood instruments, metallophones, and glockenspiels) as well as nonpitched instruments (tambourine, wood blocks, guiro, cowbell, triangle) both aurally and visually. Students should be made aware of the wood versus metal nonpitched percussion instruments. As always, instruments should complement singing rather than be an additive element.

Appropriate Instruments

Xylophone: for playing a moving drone, ostinato, and melodies; two mallets striking
Recorder: more extended range
Claves: rhythmic ostinatos
Rhythm sticks: rhythmic ostinatos
Guitar: for playing chords
Keyboard: accompaniment
Drums: emphasize the beat
Tambourine: beat and rhythm

Teaching Progression

1. Beginning music examples should be derived from known singing material. Sing the song with text.
2. Perform the music with rhythm syllables and conduct.
3. Perform the music with solfège syllables and hand signs.
4. Connect the fingering to solfège syllables and perform.
5. Read the music with rhythm syllables and conduct.
6. Read the music solfège syllables and hand signs.
7. Sing the music with letter names and hand signs
8. Perform the example but inner-hear the solfège syllables.

Reinforce Concepts Using Instruments

- *Beat.* Use simple percussion instruments to keep the beat of a rhyme or folk song.
- *Beat and rhythm.* Use simple rhythm instruments to perform first the beat and then the rhythm of a folk song; then use them to perform the beat and rhythm of a folk song simultaneously.
- *Rhythmic ostinati.* Use simple rhythmic instruments to perform a rhythmic ostinato (a repeated rhythmic pattern) to a folk song. Then use them to perform two simultaneous sounding ostinati to a folk song.
- *Melodic ostinati.* Use glockenspiels, xylophone, metallophones, and melody bells to perform a melodic ostinato to a folk song.

Canons

Instruments may be used for playing canons in the classroom.

Rhythmic Canons
1. Teacher performs a known rhythmic pattern in canon with students clapping the rhythmic pattern. Use simple rhythmic instruments.

Melodic Canons

1. Teacher performs a folk song in canon with students on a pitched percussion instrument.
2. Teacher performs a folk song in canon with students on a piano.
3. Teacher performs a folk song in canon with students on a guitar.
4. Teacher performs known melodic pattern on a guitar and students echo with solfège syllables.

Listening

These activities may be used with instruments for developing listening:

1. Teacher performs or introduces a new song on a pitched percussion instrument.
2. Teacher performs an excerpt from a listening example on a nonpitched instrument before playing the recording for the students.
3. Teacher performs an excerpt from a listening example on the recorder before playing the recording for the students.
4. Teacher performs or introduces a new song on the recorder.
5. Teacher performs an excerpt from a listening example on an instrument before playing the recording for the students.

Transitions

These activities put instruments to use in transitioning from one segment of a lesson to another:

1. Teacher performs a rhythmic ostinato on a classroom instrument to accompany a folk song and maintains the ostinato to transition to the next song in the lesson.
2. Teacher performs a melodic ostinato on a classroom instrument to accompany a folk song and maintains the ostinato to transition to the next song in the lesson.

Aural Rhythmic Practice

Teacher performs known rhythmic pattern on a nonpitched percussion instrument and students echo with rhythm syllables.

Aural Melodic Practice

1. Teacher performs known melodic pattern on a pitched percussion instrument and students echo with solfège syllables.
2. Teacher performs known melodic pattern on recorder and students echo with solfège syllables.
3. Teacher performs known melodic pattern on piano and students echo with solfège syllables.

Writing Rhythmic Practice

1. Teacher performs the focus pattern or related pattern of a rhythmic concept on a nonpitched percussion instrument and students write missing beats or whole pattern on the board.
2. Teacher performs the focus pattern or related pattern of the concept on piano and students write missing beats or whole pattern on the board.

Writing Melodic Practice

1. Teacher performs the focus pattern or related pattern of a melodic concept on a pitched percussion instrument and students write missing beats or the whole pattern on the board.
2. Teacher performs the focus pattern or related pattern of a melodic concept on a recorder and students write missing beats or the whole pattern on the board.
3. Teacher performs the focus pattern or related pattern of a melodic concept on guitar and students write missing beats or the whole pattern on the board.

Creative Movement Skills

Beat Motions

1. Students create beat motions to accompany a folk song.
2. They borrow beat motions from another song.
3. They create motions that act out the story of a folk song.
4. Some play charades and act out a song while others try to guess the song.
5. Students perform beat motions in a canon.

Form

1. Students create beat motions that reflect the form of a folk song.
2. They create motions for each phrase of a song, and then shuffle the motions to change the order of the phrases in a folk song.
3. They create motions to reflect forms (for example, binary) in a listening example of classical music.
4. They show cadences by freezing at the point of the cadence.

Instruments

1. Students create a rhythmic or melodic ostinato on instruments.
2. They become a pentatonic piano and the teacher chooses a conductor to point to each student to create a melodic pattern.
3. Students use instruments to create sound effects to accompany a folk song (e.g., train sounds).

Rhythmic Concepts

1. Students create motions to reflect the tempo of various folk songs or classical listening examples.
2. They create motions that reflect a rhythmic ostinato.

3. They demonstrate the difference between simple meter and compound meter by skipping or marching.

Singing

1. Students create alternate text for a folk song.
2. They conduct each other in different styles.

Melodic Concepts

1. Students create motions that reflect the melodic contour of a folk song.

Ostinati

1. Students demonstrate creative movement through ostinato (body percussion).
2. They create simple four-beat ostinato using two levels of body percussion (snap, clap, pat, stomp).

Props

1. Students use props to show creative movement.
2. They move to sung or recorded music using props, such as scarves or ribbons, matching the mood of the piece.

Movement and Listening

The movement examples in Table 4.1 can be used as an introductory activity for every lesson and are part of the body warm-up for students. We recommend choosing a movement piece that connects to the next singing activity in the lesson. Look for examples that are in the same meter, tempo, tonality, key, and dynamics as the next song in the lesson. Recorded examples for movement may also include some of the listening repertoire that students will later read and listen to in the music lesson. The table has a sample developed by teachers in the Kodály Certification Program at Texas State University in 2014.

Table 4.1

Title	Composer/Performer	Key, Style, Features
CLASSICAL		
"Dance of the Sugar Plum Fairy," from *Nutcracker Suite*	Peter Ilyich Tchaikovsky (1840–1893)	Duple meter
"Kangaroos," from *Carnival of the Animals*	Camille Saint Saëns (1835–1931)	Contrasting movements
"Anvil Chorus," from *Il Trovatore*	Giuseppe Verdi (1813–1901)	Major, contrasting styles, dynamic contrast
"Liberty Bell March"	John Philip Sousa (1854–1932)	Major, upbeat, march

(continued)

Table 4.1 (continued)

Title	Composer/Performer	Key, Style, Features
"In the Hall of the Mountain King"	Edvard Grieg (1843–1907)	Minor, accelerando
"Stars and Stripes"	John Philip Sousa (1854–1932)	Movements for piccolo, marching, themes, "solo" sections, form
"Spring," from *Four Seasons*	Antonio Vivaldi (1678–1741)	Steady beat, texture, major tonality, *do*
"Semper Fidelis"	John Philip Sousa (1854–1932)	Major tonality, quadruple meter, syncopation, *mi re low do*
"March of the Toy Soldiers," from *Nutcracker Suite*	Peter Ilyich Tchaikovsky (1840–1893)	Major, steady beat, orchestra families
"Radetsky March"	Johann Strauss, 1825–1899	Movement, $\frac{4}{4}$ march, form, dynamics
"Flight of the Bumble Bee"	Nikolai Rimsky-Korsakov (1844–1908)	Tempo, introduction
JAZZ		
"Sing, Sing, Sing (with a Swing)"	Benny Goodman (1909–1986)	Minor, form, fast
"A Tisket, a Tasket"	Folk song; Ella Fitzgerald (1917–1996)	Major and minor tonalities, form
"Sonando"	Pancho Sanchez (b. 1951)	Movement, Cuban jazz, variation on instruments and vocals
"Jumpin' with Symphony Sid"	Tito Puente and His Orchestra (1923–2000)	Major tonality, phrases, body movement, Latin
"Boogie Woogie Bugle Boy of Company B"	Andrews Sisters (released 1941)	Dance moves, $\frac{2}{2}$ C major, upbeat swing
"Jump Jive an' Wail"	Louis Prima, 1910–1978	Movement, major, $\frac{4}{4}$, walking bass, chord progress
"Nutcracker Suite"	adapted by Brian Setzer (b. 1959)	Movement, medley, tempo changes, major and minor sections, classical turned into jazz
"I Wanna Be Like You," from Disney's *Jungle Book*	Big Bad Voodoo Daddy (released 1996)	Moderato, minor-major contrasting sections

(continued)

Table 4.1   (continued)

Title	Composer/Performer	Key, Style, Features
"Trickle Trickle"	Manhattan Transfer (released 1979)	Moderato, contrasting solo and ensemble
"Rhumba de Burros"	Ignatius Jones (b. 1957)	Rhumba beat, Spanish, big band, percussion, major vocal and instrumental sections
"My Favorite Things"	John Coltrane (1926–1967)	Dynamics, $\frac{3}{4}$
POPULAR		
"Charlie Brown"	The Coasters (released 1959)	Form, $\frac{4}{4}$ meter, fast
"Apache" (Jump on It)	Sugarhill Gang, from *8th Wonder* (released 1981)	Steady beat, rap, strong-and-weak beat
"Louie, Louie"	Richard Berry (1935–1997)	Strong beat, dance movements
"I Like to Move It, Move It," from Dreamworks' *Madagascar*	Dreamworks Film 2005; Reel 2 Real (released 1993)	Fast tempo throughout, high energy
"Good Feeling"	Flo Rida, from *Good Feeling* (released 2012)	Strong beat, contrasting sections, fast tempo, rap
"Jailhouse Rock"	Elvis Presley (1935–1977)	Swing feeling, dance
"Tribal Dance"	2 Unlimited, from *No Limit* (released 1993)	Rhythmic elements, strong beat, rap, high energy
"Under the Sea," from Disney's *The Little Mermaid*	1989; sung by Samuel E. Wright (b. 1946)	Form, $\frac{4}{4}$, beat, Caribbean style
"Shine Bright Like a Diamond"	Sia Furler/Rihanna (released 2012)	Movements, minor
"Shout"	Isley Brothers (released 1959)	Movements, F major, $\frac{2}{2}$
"Hand Jive"	Sha Na Na (released 1978)	Hand movements, call and response to singer during verse
"Thank God I'm a Country Boy"	John Denver (1943–1997)	Major, $\frac{2}{4}$, $\frac{3}{4}$ (mixed meter), allegro, folk style
"Roar"	Katy Perry (released 2013)	Body movement, major, syncopation, $\frac{4}{4}$, dynamics

(Continued)

Table 4.1 (continued)

Title	Composer/Performer	Key, Style, Features
"Singin' in the Rain"	Gene Kelly (1912–1996)	Body movements, 4/4, F major, swing,
"Good Morning"	Debbie Reynolds, in film *Singin' in the Rain* (released 1952)	Body movements, form, 4/4, B♭ major, upbeat
"Ghostbusters"	Ray Parker, Jr. (b. 1954)	Halloween, pop/rock, major, instrumental and vocal
"Frozen Heart," from Disney's *Frozen*	Robert and Kristen Lopez (released 2014)	
"G.T.O."	Ronny and the Daytonas (1964)	50s rock, twelve-bar R&B progression, t = 140, major
FOLK		
"Chilili"	Bolivian folk song	Good for form, fast-paced
"Carnavalito"	Brazilian folk song	Good for form or beat, skip game
"Henehene Kou'Aka"	Performed by Israel Kamakawiwo'ole (1959–1997)	Hawaiian dance movements
"Down on the Danforth"	New England Dance Masters	Modal, largo, mezzo-piano, folk dance song
"La Charreada"	Linda Ronstadt (b. 1946)	Mariachi, movement, call and response, major, *do-mi-so–high do*
"The Fox"	Folk song; Nickel Creek (released 2000)	Folk orchestration, major

Listening Examples for Grade 1 Concepts and Elements

Listening examples will also include songs that the teacher sings to children and will not include new element.

Quarter and Eighth Note

Live Performance Sung by the Teacher
    "When I First Came to This Land"
    "Ser Come el Aire Libre"
    "Go Tell Aunt Rhody"
    "Little Dappled Cow"

Chosen from *Sail Away: 155 American Folk Songs to Sing, Read, and Play*; and *150 American Folk Songs to Sing, Read, and Play*.

Recorded Performance
Students learn to read the rhythm of the "Andante" from Symphony No. 94 in G, *Surprise*, by Joseph Haydn (1732–1809). It is best for the teacher to write the rhythms on the board and have students perform them as they listen to the work.

so-mi

Live Performance (sung by the teacher)
"Doney Gal"
"Johnson Boys"
"Wondrous Love"
"Bought Me a Cat"

Chosen from *Sail Away: 155 American Folk Songs to Sing, Read, and Play*; and *150 American Folk Songs to Sing, Read, and Play*.

Recorded Performance
"Allegro," from *Toy Symphony*, by Leopold Mozart (1719–1787)

Rest

Live Performance
"A Frog He Would A-Wooing Go"
"Oh, No, John"
"The Old Sow"
"When I Was a Young Girl"

Chosen from *Sail Away: 155 American Folk Songs to Sing, Read, and Play*; and *150 American Folk Songs to Sing, Read, and Play*.

Recorded Performance
"Allegretto," from Symphony No. 7 in A, Op. 92, by Ludwig van Beethoven (1770–1827)
"In the Hall of the Mountain King," movement 4 from *Peter Gynt Suite*, by Edvard Grieg (1843–1907)
"Children's Song," from *For Children*, vol. 1, no. 2, by Béla Bartók (1881–1945)

la

Live Performance
"Little Mohee"
"Mama, Buy Me a Chiney Doll"
"There Was a Man"
"Who Killed Cock Robin?"

Chosen from *Sail Away: 155 American Folk Songs to Sing, Read, and Play*; and *150 American Folk Songs to Sing, Read, and Play*.

Recorded Performance
  "Rain, Rain, Go Away," by Ella Jenkins (1924–)

Duple Meter

Live Performance
  "Old Blue"
  "Riding in the Buggy"
  "The Riddle Song"
  "Mister Frog Went a-Courting"

Chosen from *Sail Away: 155 American Folk Songs to Sing, Read, and Play*; and *150 American Folk Songs to Sing, Read, and Play.*

Recorded Performance
  "Allegro Assai," from Brandenburg Concerto No. 2, by J. S. Bach (1685–1750)
  "Finale," from Symphony No. 4, by Peter Ilyich Tchaikovsky (1840–1893)

Lesson Planning

Designing a Preparation/Practice Lesson Plan That Includes Music Skills

In this chapter, we have presented activities for developing a student's singing voice, movement skills, and instrumental skills, as well as how the teacher can develop music literacy skills. As a result of the information contained in this chapter, we can make certain modifications to our basic preparation/practice lesson plan by developing appropriate

- Creative movement activities for students
- Instrumental activities for them
- Reading, writing, and improvisation activities
- Inner-hearing activities
- Listening activities
- Part-work skills

Table 4.2 presents a Preparation/Practice Lesson Plan Template showing how the information for this chapter can now be used to modify a lesson plan design. We have bolded the sections of the lesson plan that can be modified to incorporate material from Chapter 4.

Table 4.2   Preparation/Practice Lesson Plan Design

Introduction	
Demonstration of known musical concepts and elements	Body warm-ups and breathing exercises Students demonstrate their prior knowledge of repertoire and musical elements through performance of songs selected from the alphabetized repertoire list. These songs may be accompanied by rhythmic or melodic instruments.

(Continued)

Table 4.2 (continued)

	CORE ACTIVITIES
Acquisition of repertoire	Teach a new song by rote using an appropriate technique.
Preparation of a new concept	Learning activities in which students are taught a new musical concept through known songs found in the alphabetized repertoire list
Movement development	Focus on sequential development of age-appropriate movement skills through songs and folk games.
Practice and musical skill development	Students reinforce their knowledge of musical concepts and elements, working on the skill areas of reading and writing, form, memory, inner hearing, ensemble work, instrumental work, improvisation and composition, and listening through known songs found in the alphabetized repertoire list.
	CLOSURE
Review and summation	Review of lesson content; teacher may perform the next new song to be learned in a subsequent lesson found in the alphabetized repertoire list

When repertoire and selected activities are applied to the preparation/practice lesson framework, the lesson itself becomes more visible. The lesson plan in Table 4.3 includes repertoire and several activities; some procedural portions of this lesson have been removed.

Table 4.3 Grade 1, Unit 4, Rest, Lesson 2

Outcome	Prepare: analyze repertoire that contains a beat with no sound
	Practice: writing music with *so-mi*
	INTRODUCTORY ACTIVITIES
Warm-up	• Body warm-up
	• Beat activity
	William Tell Overture, Gioachino Rossini (1792–1868)
	• Breathing: **Ss** practice blowing up a balloon and watch how air is released when deflating the balloon.
	• Resonance: explore a cow sound using low and high voices. Make sure **Ss** are inhaling and exhaling correctly with the support muscles.
	• Posture: remind **Ss** of the correct posture for singing.
Sing known songs	"Rain, Rain"
	CSP: A
	• **Ss** sing the song with an ostinato.
	"Nanny Goat"
	CSP: A
	• **Ss** sing the song.
	• Add an ostinato using either body percussion or instruments.

(Continued)

Table 4.3 (continued)

Develop tuneful singing Tone production Diction Expression	"All Around the Buttercup" CSP: F-sharp • **Ss** hum the song. • **Ss** "sing" the song on a hiss. • **Ss** sing the song on a unified pure vowel ("nee," "neh," "nah," "noh," or "noo").
Review known songs and rhythm elements	"Doggie, Doggie" and "Snail, Snail" CSP: A • **Ss** read from the board and identify each song. • **Ss** sing each song and pat the beat. • **Ss** sing with rhythm syllables and pat the beat. • **T** hums motifs from songs and **Ss** echo with rhythm syllables and pat the beat.
CORE ACTIVITIES	
Teach a new song	"A Tisket, a Tasket" CSP: A • **T** sings the song. • **T** sings again and asks **Ss** to figure out how to play the game on the basis of the lyrics of the song. • **T** and **Ss** sing and play the game. • **T** may transfer the accompaniment to instruments. • **Ss** continue their accompaniment into the next song.
Develop knowledge of music concepts Describe what you hear	"Hot Cross Buns" CSP: A • **Ss** sing the song. • Review kinesthetic awareness activities. • **T** and **Ss** sing first phrase of song on "loo" while performing the beat before asking each of these questions: • **T**: "Andy, how many beats did we tap?" (four) • **T**: "Andy, which beat has no sound?" (the last one, beat 4) • **T**: "Andy, if beat 4 has no sound, how many sounds are on each of the other beats?" (one) • **Ss** sing the song and put the rest on their shoulders.
Creative movement	"Cut the Cake" CSP: A • *Note: this will be a new song.* • **T** sings while demonstrating the game. • After two or three cycles, **Ss** join the singing and **T** drops out.
Practice and performance of music skills Writing	"Snail, Snail" CSP: A • **Ss** sing the song and pat the beat. • **Ss** sing with rhythm syllables and pat the beat. • Sing first phrase with solfège syllables and hand signs.

(Continued)

Table 4.3 (continued)

	<ul><li>One **S** writes solfège syllables under the rhythmic notation on a worksheet. ♩ ♩ | ♫ ♩ s m ss m ♫ ♫ | ♫ ♩ ss mm ss m</li><li>**T** reviews rules of placement.</li><li>**Ss** fill in the blanks on the staff for "Snail, Snail" on their worksheet.</li><li>**T** explains rules for adding stems to note heads.</li></ul>
SUMMARY ACTIVITIES	
Review the new song Review lesson outcomes	"A Tisket, a Tasket" CSP: A

Designing a Presentation Lesson Plan Template That Includes Music Skills

Table 4.4 is an example of a Presentation Lesson Plan Template. We want to show how the information in this chapter can be incorporated into this lesson.

Table 4.4 Presentation Lesson Plan Design for Labeling Sounds with Syllables

INTRODUCTION	
Demonstration of known musical concepts and elements	Body warm-ups and breathing exercises **Ss** demonstrate their prior knowledge of repertoire and musical elements through performance of songs selected from the alphabetized repertoire list. These songs may be accompanied by rhythmic or melodic instruments.
CORE ACTIVITIES	
Acquisition of repertoire	Teach a new song by rote using an appropriate technique.
Presentation of new element	**T** presents the syllables for the new musical element in the focus pattern of a known song.
Movement development	Known song or game found in the alphabetized repertoire list; CSP. Focus on the sequential development of age-appropriate movement skills through songs and folk games.
Presentation of new element	**T** presents the syllables for the new musical element in a related pattern of a known song.
CLOSURE	
Review and summation	Review of lesson content; **T** may perform the next new song to be learned in a subsequent lesson found in the alphabetized repertoire list.

(Continued)

Again, when repertoire and selected activities are applied to in a lesson, the lesson planning process itself becomes more evident. The lesson plan in Table 4.5 includes activities appropriate to a presentation lesson.

Table 4.5   Grade 1, Unit 4, Rest, Lesson 5

Outcome	Present: notate the quarter rest
INTRODUCTORY ACTIVITIES	
Warm-up	• Body warm-up • Beat activity "Hall of the Mountain King," Edvard Grieg (1843–1907) • Breathing: **Ss** practice blowing up a balloon and watch how air is released when deflating the balloon. • Resonance: explore a cow sound using low and high voices. Make sure **Ss** are inhaling and exhaling correctly with the support muscles. • Posture: remind **Ss** of the correct posture for singing.
Sing known songs	"We Are Dancing in the Forest" CSP: A • **Ss** sing the song and briefly play the game.
Develop tuneful singing Tone production Diction Expression	"Tortillitas" CSP: A • **Ss** sing the song. • Sing song on "loo." • **Ss** sing the song and keep the beat.
Review known songs and rhythm elements	"Down Came a Lady" CSP: A • **Ss** sing the song and pat the beat. • **Ss** read the rhythm syllables from the board. • **T** sings individual phrases of the song and **Ss** echo-sing with rhythm syllables while keeping the beat.
CORE ACTIVITIES	
Teach a new song	"La Vieja Inez" CSP: B • **T** sings the song and **Ss** identify three rests in it. • **T** writes names of colors in English and Spanish on board. • **T** sings song while acting out the call and response between La Vieja Inez and **Ss**. • **T** introduces the color guessing game. • **T** and **Ss** sing the song and play the game. • **Ss** play the game, singing the responses.

(Continued)

Table 4.5 (continued)

Presentation of music concepts Notate what you hear	"Hot Cross Buns" CSP: A - Sing song with text and keep the beat. - Review awareness activities and aural presentation. - **T**: "Our first phrase of 'Hot Cross Buns' looks like this." **T** shows the traditional rhythmic notation for quarter notes and quarter rests. - Point to notation and sing first phrase of "Hot Cross Buns." - **T**: "We represent a *rest* on a beat with traditional notation." **T** points to the *rest*. "This is what it looks like when we read *rest*." - **T**: "We represent a *rest* in stick notation with a 'Z' when we are writing." - **T**: "Let's sing 'Hot Cross Buns' and draw the rhythm in the air as we sing."
Creative movement	"Lucy Locket" CSP: A - **Ss** sing the song. - Play and sing the circle game. - **Ss** create a rhythmic accompaniment with known elements.

Presentation of music concepts
 	
Notate what you hear
	"Bow Wow Wow"
	
	CSP: D
	
	- **Ss** sing the song and pat the beat.
	- **Ss** sing with rhythm syllables and pat the beat.
	- **T** writes the rhythm on the board; **Ss** clap it, sing the song with rhythm syllables, and pat the beat.
	- **T** transforms the rhythm into other related song material:
	  o "Bow Wow Wow"
	  o "All Around the Buttercup"
	  o "Pease Porridge Hot"
	  o "Down Came a Lady"
	  o "Naughty Kitty Cat"

SUMMARY ACTIVITIES	
Review lesson outcomes Review the new song	"La Vieja Inez" CSP: B

Chapter 5

Unit Plans and Lesson Plans

A primary objective of this text is to present teachers with a sequential series of lesson plans to inspire the artistry inherent in every student. As is evident in all of our publications, we are also involved with developing cognition, the "thinking" abilities that lead to a deeper understanding and appreciation of music through performing, critical thinking, listening, literacy, composing, and improvising. Kodály offers us a timely reminder concerning the importance of excellent teaching techniques to enable the student to engage with music as a true artist: "It is not technique that is the essence of art, but the soul. As soon as the soul can communicate freely, without obstacles, a complete musical effect is created. Technique sufficient for a free manifestation of the child's soul can easily be mastered under a good leader in any school."[1]

This chapter furnishes teachers with a detailed series of lesson plans arranged according to concept. With the exception of Unit 1 (review lessons), each unit is divided into three sections:

Section 1. A summary overview of the repertoire used to prepare, present, and practice a particular music element
Section 2. A brief outline of the music skills that are to be developed in the unit plan
Section 3. Five sequential lesson plans for preparing, presenting, and practicing a music element

Consult *Kodály Today* for a more comprehensive overview of lesson planning.
These are the lesson plan units presented in this chapter:

Unit 1, Kindergarten Review
Unit 2, Teaching Quarter and Eighth Notes
Unit 3, Teaching a Two-Note Child's Chant *so-mi*
Unit 4, Teaching Quarter Note Rest
Unit 5, Teaching a Three-Note Child's Chant *la*
Unit 6, Teaching Duple Meter

Remember that these lesson plans are only sketches of what can be accomplished in the lesson. We have not included transitions between the sections of the lessons as we want teachers to get an idea of the flow of the lesson plan. Teachers should infuse these lessons with their own musicianship and creativity.

Our suggested five-lesson sequence allows students to engage and explore concepts through music literature. Building on the numerous performance experiences within these lessons, the teacher can guide students toward an understanding of musical elements and concepts.

The five sequenced lessons are divided as follows. The first three are preparation/practice lesson plans.

> Lesson one is a plan for developing the *kinesthetic* awareness of a new melodic or rhythmic concept and concentrated practice of known melodic or rhythmic elements through *reading*. (Reading is normally connected to listening.)
> Lesson two is a plan for developing *aural* awareness of a new melodic or rhythmic concept and concentrated practice of known melodic or rhythmic elements through *writing*.
> Lesson three is a plan for developing *visual* awareness of a new melodic or rhythmic concept and concentrated practice of known melodic or rhythmic elements through *improvisation and composition*.

There are two presentation lessons in the associative phase.

> Lesson four is the first presentation lesson; the goal is to *label* the new sound with rhythm or solfège syllables.
> Lesson five is the second presentation lesson; the goal is to *present the notation* for the new element.

The objectives for each type of lesson are derived from activities proposed in the teaching strategies (see Chapter 4). Although the lessons will differ across the three phases of learning, all preparation/practice lessons, regardless of the element being prepared, are similar in structure. The same is true for all presentation lessons. You will note that lessons one, two, and three focus on kinesthetic, aural, and visual preparation of a new element respectively and practice of a familiar element through reading, writing, and improvisation activities. Lessons four and five focus on presenting and initial practice of the newly learned element. Chapter 10 of *Kodály Today* describes the types of lesson plan structure as well as information on adapting these lesson plans for the inclusive classroom.

Transitions in Lesson Plans

Transitions are the cement that holds the segments of a lesson together. Transitioning between songs and activities can become an interesting means to help tie and often hold the lesson together. They can be used to move students from one activity to another in a music lesson. Here we present some sample transition activities that can be used to enliven a creative music lesson plan. Transitions may be thought of as conscious and unconscious: with the former, the students are aware that they are moving between songs or activities, and with the latter, the teacher guides students to different activities. Spend time analyzing all of the repertoire and materials you will be using in the lesson. This will allow you to see possible connections in the suggested repertoire. Transitions should be logical. When they are properly planned, they add the elements of surprise, creativity, and magic to a lesson. Many of the best transitions are musical. If you are transitioning into a segment of a lesson where the focus is on rhythm, use a rhythmic activity such as an ostinato to move to the next segment. If you are transitioning into a melodic segment of the lesson, you could use a melodic ostinato to move to the next section.

Chapter 10 of *Kodály Today* includes many ideas for creating transitions in lesson plans.

Tables 5.1 and 5.2 show two versions of the same lesson plan: Table 5.1 is a lesson plan with no transitions, and Table 5.2 has the same lesson plan with transitions. Transitions should not detract from the lesson but should allow the teacher to move smoothly from one segment of the lesson to another.

Table 5.1   Grade 1, Unit 3, *so-mi*, Lesson 1

Outcome	Preparation: internalizing *so-mi* through kinesthetic activities Practice: reading quarter note and eighth note patterns in known songs
INTRODUCTORY ACTIVITIES	
Warm-up	• Body warm-up • Beat activity "Stars and Stripes Forever," by John Philip Sousa (1854–1937) • Breathing: **Ss** practice blowing up a balloon and watch how air is released when deflating the balloon. • Resonance: explore a cow sound using low and high voices. Make sure **Ss** are inhaling and exhaling correctly with the support muscles. • Posture: remind **Ss** of the correct posture for singing.
Sing known songs	"Doggie, Doggie" CSP: A • **Ss** sing "Doggie, Doggie." • **Ss** sing with a simple ostinato (pat, clap, pat, clap).
Develop tuneful singing Tone production Diction Expression	"Good Night, Sleep Tight" CSP: A • **Ss** sing "Good Night, Sleep Tight" with words. • **T** may choose **Ss** to sing alone or in small groups. • Sing "Good Night, Sleep Tight" on "loo," "boo," "zoo."
Review known songs and melodic elements	"Seesaw" CSP: A • **Ss** sing "Seesaw." • **T** sings phrase by phrase; **Ss** echo-sing using high and low. "Cobbler, Cobbler" CSP: A • **Ss** sing "Cobbler, Cobbler." • **T** sings phrases 1 and 2; **Ss** echo-sing using high and low while showing the melodic contour.

(Continued)

Table 5.1 (continued)

	CORE ACTIVITIES
Teach a new song	"Bow Wow Wow" CSP: D • **T** sings "Bow Wow Wow" while **Ss** step the beat. • **T** sings "Bow Wow Wow" while **Ss** show the phrases in the air. • **Ss** identify the number of phrases. • **T** sings phrase by phrase demonstrating game motions. **Ss** echo. • **T** and **Ss** sing and play.
Develop knowledge of musical concepts Internalize music through kinesthetic activities	"Snail, Snail" CSP: A • **Ss** sing "Snail, Snail." • **Ss** sing "Snail, Snail" and keep the beat. • **Ss** sing "Snail, Snail" and point to a representation of focus phrase. • **Ss** sing "Snail, Snail" and clap the melodic contour. • **Ss** sing "Snail, Snail" with rhythm syllables while showing contour. • **Ss** sing and pat the beat.

Creative movement	"Witch, Witch" CSP: A • **Ss** sing and play the game. • **Ss** sing and step the beat.
Practice and performance of music skills Reading	"Rain, Rain" CSP: A • **Ss** sing the song. • **T** sings phrase 1 of "Rain, Rain" on "loo" and **Ss** identify the song. • **Ss** read the rhythm of "Rain, Rain" from the board and keep the beat.
	SUMMARY ACTIVITIES
Review lesson outcomes Review the new song	"Bow Wow Wow" CSP: D

Table 5.2 Grade 1, Unit 3, *so-mi*, Lesson 1

Outcome	Preparation: internalizing *so-mi* through kinesthetic activities Practice: reading quarter note and eighth note patterns in known songs
	INTRODUCTORY ACTIVITIES
Warm-up	• Body warm-up • Beat activity

(continued)

Table 5.2 (continued)

	"Stars and Stripes Forever," by John Philip Sousa (1854–1937) • Breathing: **Ss** practice blowing up a balloon and watch how air is released when deflating the balloon. • Resonance: explore a cow sound using low and high voices. Make sure **Ss** are inhaling and exhaling correctly with the support muscles. • Posture: remind **Ss** of the correct posture for singing.
Sing known songs	"Doggie, Doggie" CSP: A • **Ss** sing "Doggie, Doggie." • **Ss** sing with a simple ostinato (pat, clap, pat, clap). • Keep ostinato going and change the song to "Cobbler, Cobbler." • Keep ostinato going as **T** sings "Good Night, Sleep Tight" on "loo"; **Ss** identify the song.
Develop tuneful singing Tone production Diction Expression	"Good Night, Sleep Tight" CSP: A • **Ss** sing "Good Night, Sleep Tight" with words. • **T** may choose **Ss** to sing alone or in small groups. • **Ss** sing "Good Night, Sleep Tight" on "loo," "boo," "zoo." • **T** asks **Ss** to pretend to be owls and sing the song on "loo." • **T** asks **Ss** to pretend to be ghosts and sing slowly on "boo." • **T** asks **Ss** to pretend they want to go to the "zoo!" • **T**: "The zoo has a playground, and you'll never believe what I saw. I saw a seesaw."

Review known songs and melodic elements	"Seesaw"
	CSP: A
	• **Ss** sing "Seesaw."
	• **T** sings phrase by phrase; **Ss** echo-sing high and low.
	"Cobbler, Cobbler"
	CSP: A
	• **Ss** sing "Cobbler, Cobbler."
	• **T** sings phrase by phrase; **Ss** echo and show the melodic contour for phrases 1 and 2.
	• **T** sings phrase 1 of "Rain, Rain" with text; **Ss** echo and sing with high and low. Repeat the same activity with these songs:
	  o "Snail, Snail" (phrase 1)
	  o "Good Night, Sleep Tight" (phrase 1)
	  o "Tortillitas" (phrases 1 and 3)
	  o "Doggie, Doggie" (phrase 1)
	  o "Teddy Bear" (phrase 1)

CORE ACTIVITIES	
Teach a new song	"Bow Wow Wow" CSP: D • **T** sings "Bow Wow Wow" while **Ss** step the beat. • **T** sings "Bow Wow Wow" while **Ss** show the phrases in the air.

(continued)

Table 5.2 (continued)

	• **Ss** identify the number of phrases. • **T** sings phrase by phrase demonstrating game motions. **Ss** echo. • **T** and **Ss** sing and play. • **Ss** sing the song with a simple ostinato (pat, pat, clap, clap). • **Ss** continue the ostinato while **T** sings the next song. • Little Tommy Tucker had another pet!" **T** sings "Snail, Snail" on "loo" and **Ss** guess the song.
Develop knowledge of musical concepts Internalize music through kinesthetic activities	"Snail, Snail" CSP: A • **Ss** sing "Snail, Snail." • **Ss** sing "Snail, Snail" and keep the beat. • **Ss** sing "Snail, Snail" and point to a representation of focus phrase. ○ ○ ○ ○ • **Ss** sing "Snail, Snail" and clap the melodic contour. • **Ss** sing "Snail, Snail" with rhythm syllables while showing contour. • **Ss** sing and pat the beat. • **T** performs the activity, changing the representation to the first phrase of "Seesaw." • **Ss** continue the beat into the next song.
Creative movement	"Witch, Witch" CSP: A • **Ss** sing and play the game. • **Ss** sing and step the beat. • **Ss** continue the beat as **T** sings the next song on "loo."
Practice and performance of music skills Reading	"Rain, Rain" CSP: A • **Ss** sing the song. • **T** sings phrase 1 of "Rain, Rain" on "loo" and **Ss** identify the song. • **Ss** read the rhythm of "Rain, Rain" from the board and keep the beat. **T** gradually adds additional phrases, turning "Rain, Rain" into "Queen, Queen Caroline." • **T** changes the rhythm into "Allegretto," from Symphony No. 94, *Surprise*, by Joseph Haydn (1732–1809): ♫♫ | ♫♩ ♫♫ | ♫♩ ♫♫ | ♫♩ ♫♫ | ♩ ♩
SUMMARY ACTIVITIES	
Review lesson outcomes Review the new song	"Bow Wow Wow" CSP: D

General Points for Planning Lessons

1. Goals for each lesson should come from the outcomes listed in the concept plans; but singing in tune should always be a primary goal of each lesson.
2. Work to select the best song material for each class and make sure you enjoy this repertoire. We suggest three to eight songs in a thirty-to-forty-minute lesson. Memorize all of the song material you are going to use. Be able to sing this material with the correct tempo, dynamics and character.
3. Every new song you teach should be introduced appropriately. Sometimes we review a familiar song as we would a new song. This is an opportunity for the teacher to spend more time polishing the song and making sure that students are able to sing artfully.
4. When teaching a new element, is it surrounded by known rhythmic or melodic patterns?
5. Our lessons contain both rhythmic and melodic elements, one for preparation and the other for practice. Remember that when you abstract a pattern or motif from a song, always sing the song again to put it back in context and to give students the experience of enjoying the performance of the song.
6. There should be a focus to each section of the lesson that you can assess informally and formally.
7. Know your repertoire. Be able to analyze the materials for each lesson from an analytical, performance perspective and from a pedagogical one.
8. Try to find variety in the song material for the lesson.
9. Our lessons include periods of relaxation and concentration. The pace of a lesson is critical. Veteran teachers always tell us that it is better to teach faster than slower. Students will follow you if you're moving.
10. Give the students plenty of individual experience in the classroom. It is important to work from the group toward individual activities. You'll notice that students are attentive to their peers when they do things like go to the board or perform on their own.
11. We have suggested a comfortable starting pitch for each song. Feel free to experiment with what works best for your classroom.

Evaluating a Lesson

1. Learning should stem from the enjoyment of singing songs, chanting rhymes, and playing games. The overarching goals of a music lesson should be singing, listening, and enjoyment of music. Musical concepts and elements are taught to enhance this enjoyment.
2. We believe that reading and/or writing should be addressed during each lesson. Even if students simply read or write a small motive from a song, they develop a deeper understanding and appreciation of the song.
3. Include opportunities for both review and reinforcement of musical elements and concepts.
4. A good lesson plan should reveal clear answers to these questions:
    A. Was the lesson presented musically?
    B. What were the primary and secondary goals of the lesson?

C. How were the goals of the lesson achieved?
D. How many songs and games were used in the lesson?
E. What activities used in conjunction with the song material led students to an understanding of the goals of the lesson?
F. Was there an emphasis on singing and making music?
G. Did the lesson use a variety of songs?
H. Were the goals of the lesson achieved?
I. Was new material prepared and presented in the lesson? What exercises were used in the lesson? Did the musical exercises planned for the lesson help the students achieve the goals?
J. Was there a logical sequence and pacing in the lesson?
K. Was the culmination of the lesson clear?
L. Were there periods of relaxation and concentration in the lesson?
M. What musical skills were developed in the lesson?
N. Were the students active collectively and individually during the lesson?
O. Did the lesson plan offer an opportunity to assess student progress?
P. Was the lesson enjoyable for the students?
Q. Did the lesson begin and end with singing?

Unit Plans

The units presented here give teachers lesson plans arranged according to concept.

Kindergarten Review Lessons Unit Plan

Song Repertoire							
	Known Songs	Songs for Tuneful Singing	Songs to Review Known Elements	Songs to Prepare Next New Concepts	Songs to Review Known Elements	Creative movement	Songs to Review Known Elements
Lesson 1	"We Are Dancing in the Forest"	"Bow Wow Wow"	"Engine, Engine, Number Nine" (review high and low chant)	"Doggie, Doggie"	"Snail, Snail" (review presentation of high and low melody)	"A la Rueda de San Miguel"	"Rain, Rain" (review notation of high and low melody)
Lesson 2	"Lucy Locket"	"London Bridge"	"Hey, Hey, Look at Me" (review fast and slow)	"We Are Dancing in the Forest"	"Snail, Snail" (review reading high and low melody)	"A la Rueda de San Miguel"	"Rain, Rain" (review writing high and low melody), "Doggie, Doggie"

Song Repertoire							
Lesson 3	"Bobby Shafto"	"Doggie, Doggie"	"Snail, Snail" (review high and low melody)	"Queen, Queen Caroline"	"Rain, Rain" (review kinesthetic and aural awareness of rhythm)	"Bow Wow Wow"	"Snail, Snail" (review improvising high and low melody)
Lesson 4	"Down Came a Lady"	"Lucy Locket"	"Snail, Snail" (review rhythm)	"Closet Key"	"Rain Rain" (review visual awareness of rhythm)	"We Are Dancing in the Forest"	"Bounce High, Bounce Low"(review presentation of rhythm)
Lesson 5	"Lucy Locket"	"Queen, Queen Caroline"	"Bobby Shafto" (review rhythm)	"On a Mountain"	"Rain, Rain" (review presentation of rhythm)	"Bee, Bee, Bumble Bee"	"Bounce High, Bounce Low" (review notation of rhythm)

Unit 1: Kindergarten Review

Grade 1, Unit 1, Kindergarten Review, Lesson 1

Outcome	Review performing and reading of high and low chant, and high and low melody
INTRODUCTORY ACTIVITIES	
Warm-up	• Body Warm-up • Beat activity "Fossils," from *Carnival of the Animals*, by Camille Saint-Saëns (1835–1921) • Breathing: **Ss** practice blowing up a balloon and watch how air is released when deflating the balloon. • Resonance: explore a cow sound using low and high voices. Make sure **Ss** are inhaling and exhaling correctly with the support muscles. • Posture: remind **Ss** of the correct posture for singing.
Sing known songs	"We Are Dancing in the Forest" CSP: A • **T** and **Ss** sing the song. • **Ss** sing and pat the beat. • **Ss** continue the beat while **T** sings the next song.

Develop tuneful singing Tone production Diction Expression	"Bow Wow Wow" CSP: D • **T** sings song and **Ss** draw each phrase with their arms and breathe. • **T** and **Ss** sing "Bow Wow Wow" while performing the phrase motions and focusing on breathing. • **T**: "Little Tommy Tucker just *loved* to travel! And his favorite city was Chicago. So Tommy packed his bags and went and jumped on…"
Review known songs and elements	"Engine, Engine, Number Nine" • **T** and **Ss** chant the rhyme and keep the beat. • **T** chants with a high voice. **T**: "That was not my normal voice, was it? What kind of voice did I just use?" (high voice) • **Ss** chant with their high voices and keep the beat. • **T** chants with a low voice. **T**: "That wasn't my normal voice or high voice. What kind of voice did I just use?" (low) • **Ss** chant with their low voices and keep the beat. • **T** reviews how to spell "high" and "low." • **T** points to "high" or "low" on the board, and **Ss** perform accordingly while keeping the beat. o **Ss** continue the beat while **T** sings the next song.
CORE ACTIVITIES	
Teach a new song	"Doggie, Doggie" CSP: A • **T** sings the song while **Ss** keep the beat. • **T**: "What was stolen from the doggie?" (his bone) • **T** dramatically sings the song, playing the part of the "doggie" and the "thief." • **T** gives the bone to three to four **Ss** who will sing the part of the "thief." • **T** demonstrates how to play the game. • **T** and **Ss** sing and play the game.
Review presentation of music literacy concepts Label what you hear High and low melody	"Snail, Snail" CSP: A • **Ss** sing "Snail, Snail" and keep the beat. • **Ss** sing "Snail, Snail" and briefly play the game. • Review kinesthetic, aural, and visual awareness activities. • **T**: "In music, a phrase in a song is made up of notes that we call pitches. Pitches can be high or low, and this creates the shape of a melody or melodic contour." • **T**: "Let's sing 'Snail, Snail' and show the shape of the melody (highs and lows) with our bodies." • **Ss** sing phrase 1 of "Snail, Snail" while showing the melodic contour with body movements but use the words *high* and *low*. • **T** and **Ss** sing and play the game.

Creative movement	"A la Rueda de San Miguel" CSP: C • T and Ss sing and play the game. • Ss perform the song with various beat motions. • Ss continue marching in a circle while singing the next song.
Review presentation of music literacy concepts Notate what you hear High and low melody	"Rain, Rain" CSP: A • Ss begin with a quick review of "Snail, Snail"; sing the song. • Ss sing phrase 1 using the words *high* and *low* and keep beat for phrase 2. • T gives one S four snails; S places the snails above or below a line on board to represent the melodic contour composed of pitches. • T: "Where are the music pitches? Describe the music contour of the song." (high, low, high, low) • Ss sing and point to representation using "high" and "low." • T transforms the pattern into "Rain, Rain." • Ss read the new pattern and identify the song. • T transforms the pattern into "Apple Tree." • Ss read the new pattern and identify the song.
SUMMARY ACTIVITIES	
Review lesson outcomes Review the new song	"Doggie, Doggie" CSP: A

Grade 1, Unit 1, Kindergarten Review, Lesson 2

Outcome	Review performing fast and slow Review reading and writing high and low melody
INTRODUCTORY ACTIVITIES	
Warm-up	• Body warm-up • Beat activity "Fossils," from *Carnival of the Animals*, by Camille Saint-Saëns (1835–1921) • Breathing: Ss practice blowing up a balloon and watch how air is released when deflating the balloon. • Resonance: explore a cow sound using low and high voices. Make sure Ss are inhaling and exhaling correctly with the support muscles. • Posture: remind Ss of the correct posture for singing.

Sing known songs	"Lucy Locket" CSP: A • **T** and **Ss** sing the song. • **Ss** sing and pat the beat. • **Ss** continue the beat while **T** sings the next song.
Develop tuneful singing Tone production Diction Expression	"London Bridge" CSP: A • **T** and **Ss** sing the song while performing the beat. • **Ss** sing song on "loo" while performing the beat; focus on breath control and expression.
Review known songs and elements	"Hey, Hey, Look at Me" CSP: A • **Ss** sing the song. • **Ss** may suggest various beat motions to perform in the song. • **T** sings and performs the beat at a slow tempo. **T**: "What just happened to our tempo?" (we used a slow tempo) • **T** reviews how to spell *slow*. • **T** sings and performs the beat at a fast tempo. **T**: "What just happened to our tempo?" (we used a fast tempo) • **T** reviews how to spell *fast*. • **T** points at either "slow" or "fast" on the board and **Ss** perform additional songs accordingly. • **Ss** continue the beat while **T** sings the next song.
CORE ACTIVITIES	

Teach a new song	"We Are Dancing in the Forest"
	CSP: A
	• **T** sings the song while **Ss** keep the beat.
	• **T**: "What are we doing in the forest?" (dancing)
	• **Ss** create a new beat motion while **T** sings the song.
	• **T**: "Who are we hiding from?" (the wolf)
	• **T** sings the song and traces the phrases in the air. **Ss** copy.
	• **T** sings the song and traces the phrases on the board.
	• Three or four **Ss** trace the phrases on the board while **T** sings.
	• **T** and **Ss** sing the song and keep the beat.
	  o **Ss** sing the song while **T** performs the motions for "Snail, Snail."
	  o **Ss** identify and sing the song.

Review known songs and elements	"Snail, Snail" CSP: A • **Ss** sing and play game. • **Ss** sing phrase 1 on a neutral syllable and identify that there are two pitches. • **Ss** label the two pitches as "high" and "low." • **Ss** sing phrase 1 using the words *high* and *low* and sing and "clap the way the words go" for phrase 2. • **T** places melodic contour flash cards of "Snail, Snail" on the board.

	• **Ss** sing the contour with "high" and "low."
	• **T** places flash cards with the melodic contour of other known songs on the board.
	• **Ss** sing the contour with "high" and "low" and identify the name of the song.
	• **T** asks **Ss** to move their bodies to match the shape of the melody.
Creative movement	"A la Rueda de San Miguel"
	CSP: C
	• **T** and **Ss** sing and play the game.
	• **Ss** perform the song with various beat motions.
	• **Ss** continue marching in a circle while singing the next song.
Review known songs and elements	"Rain, Rain"
	CSP: A
	• **Ss** sing the song and keep the beat.
	• **T**: "Let's sing 'Rain, Rain' and make the shape of the melody with our bodies."
	• **Ss** sing the song and identify the high and low sounds.
	• **Ss** sing the first phrase with "high" and "low."
	• **T** places multiple icons on the board and asks one **S** to make the icons into the melodic contour of the song.
	• **Ss** sing phrase 1 using the words *high* and *low* while pointing and sing phrase 2 with text and beat motions.
	• Repeat process but with each **S** having a set of icons to build the phrases.
	• Repeat with the first phrase of "Doggie, Doggie" and "Apple Tree."
SUMMARY ACTIVITIES	
Review lesson outcomes	"We Are Dancing in the Forest"
	CSP: A
Review the new song	

Grade 1, Unit 1, Kindergarten Review, Lesson 3

Outcome	Review kinesthetic and aural awareness of rhythm
	Review improvisation of high and low melody
INTRODUCTORY ACTIVITIES	
Warm-up	• Body warm-up
	• Beat activity
	"Fossils," from *Carnival of the Animals*, by Camille Saint-Saëns (1835–1921)
	• Breathing: **Ss** practice blowing up a balloon and watch how air is released when deflating the balloon.
	• Resonance: explore a cow sound using low and high voices. Make sure **Ss** are inhaling and exhaling correctly with the support muscles.
	• Posture: remind **Ss** of the correct posture for singing.

Sing known songs	"Bobby Shafto" CSP: A • **T** and **Ss** sing the song. • **Ss** sing and pat the beat. o **Ss** continue the beat while **T** sings the next song.
Develop tuneful singing Tone production Diction Expression	"Doggie, Doggie" CSP: A • **Ss** sing the song while performing the beat. • **Ss** perform the song singing on "koo" focusing on breath support and vowel sound. • **Ss** sing the song with a simple ostinato: $\frac{2}{4}$ ♩ ♩ | ♩ ♩ :| pat pat clap clap • **Ss** continue the ostinato into the next song.
Review known songs and elements	"Snail, Snail" CSP: A • **T** and **Ss** sing the song. • **T** places the contour of the song on the board with intentional mistakes. • **Ss** identify and correct the mistakes. • **T** points to the contour on the board and sings "Doggie, Doggie." • **Ss** identify and make the necessary corrections to the song.
CORE ACTIVITIES	
Teach a new song	"Queen, Queen Caroline" • **T** performs the rhyme with motions to represent each phrase. • **T**: "What was the queen's name?" (Caroline) • **Ss** perform phrases 1 and 4; **T** performs phrases 2 and 3. • **T**: "What did she wash her hair in?" (turpentine) • **Ss** perform phrases 1, 2, and 4; **T** performs phrase 3. • **T**: "Turpentine to make it _____?" (shine) • **Ss** perform all four phrases of the rhyme with the appropriate motions.
Review known songs and elements	"Rain, Rain" CSP: A • **Ss** sing the song and keep the beat; **T** sings and claps the rhythm. • **Ss** sing and "clap the way the words go." • **T** sings and pats the beat. • **T** presents a heart icon representing the beat. • If **T** points at the heart, **Ss** perform the beat. If **T** points at the clapping hands, **Ss** perform the rhythm. • **T** sings the song and keeps the beat or taps the words. **Ss** must identify if **T** has kept the beat or performed the rhythm. ("the words")
Creative movement	"Bow Wow Wow" CSP: D • **Ss** sing the song; **T** briefly reviews the rules of the game. • **Ss** sing and practice the motions. • **Ss** sing and play the game.

Review known songs and elements	"Snail, Snail" CSP: A • **Ss** sing "Snail, Snail" and keep the beat. • **Ss** sing phrase 1 using the words *high* and *low* and sing phrase 2 using the text while keeping the beat. • **T** improvises a new insect or animal for first phrase and **Ss** sing second phrase while keeping the beat (ex.: bear, bear, bear, bear, go around and round and round, etc.). • **Ss** improvise names of other animals and create high and low motions for their animals. Depending on the skills of the **Ss**, this improvisation activity may also be used: • **Ss** read the first phrase of "Snail, Snail" from icons on the board with "high" and "low." • **T**: "Let's pretend we're having a musical conversation. You ask me a question by singing the first phrase of 'Snail, Snail' with high and low, and then I'll answer you by singing something back with high and low." • **Ss** sing the first phrase of "Snail, Snail"; **T** replies with the first phrase of "Doggie, Doggie." • **T** shows an iconic representation of the first phrase of "Snail, Snail" with the first phrase of "Doggie, Doggie" on the board. • Switch. **T** sings the "question," and **Ss** sing the "answer." • Continue same type of activity using songs with similar patterns.
SUMMARY ACTIVITIES	
Review lesson outcomes Review the new song	"Queen, Queen Caroline"

Grade 1, Unit 1, Kindergarten Review, Lesson 4

Outcome	Review visual awareness and aural presentation of rhythm
INTRODUCTORY ACTIVITIES	
Warm-up	• Body warm-up • Beat activity "Fossils," from *Carnival of the Animals*, by Camille Saint-Saëns (1835–1921) • Breathing: **Ss** practice blowing up a balloon and watch how air is released when deflating the balloon. • Resonance: explore a cow sound using low and high voices. Make sure **Ss** are inhaling and exhaling correctly with the support muscles. • Posture: remind **Ss** of the correct posture for singing.

Sing known songs	"Down Came a Lady" CSP: F • **Ss** sing the song and play the game. • **Ss** continue marching the beat while **T** sings the next song.
Develop tuneful singing Tone production Diction Expression	"Lucy Locket" CSP: A • **Ss** sing the song while performing the beat. • **Ss** sing the song with dynamics, loud or soft (**T** may also review how to spell these words). • **Ss** may briefly play the game. • **Ss** continue the beat into the next song.
Review known songs and elements	"Snail, Snail CSP: A • **Ss** sing the song. • **T** directs **Ss** to sing and "clap the way the words go."
CORE ACTIVITIES	
Teach a new song	"Closet Key" CSP: F • **T** sings the song and shows the phrases with his or her body. **Ss** copy. • **Ss** identify the number of phrases in the song. (four) • **T** sings and draws the phrases on the board. • **T** sings and two or three **Ss** trace the phrases on the board. • **T** sings the first two phrases on a neutral syllable. • **T**: "Do the first phrase and the second phrase sound the same or different?" (different) • **T** places an apple icon by the first phrase (A) and a banana icon by the second phrase (B). (**T** may choose to use letters.) • **T** sings the third phrase on a neutral syllable; then the fourth. • **Ss** identify the form of the song. **T**: "What's the pattern of this song?" • **T** sings the A phrase and **Ss** sing the B phrase. Switch. • **Ss** sing the song and keep the beat. • **Ss** continue the beat into the next song.
Review known songs and elements	"Rain, Rain" CSP: A • **Ss** sing and pat the beat and then sing and clap the rhythm.. • Review kinesthetic and aural awareness activities. • **T** gives **Ss** long and short strips of paper or Unifix cubes. • **T**: "Show me what that phrase looks like with your Unifix cubes." • **T** selects one **S** to put the correct picture on the board, and **Ss** sing and point to the phrase. • **Ss** sing the song and clap the words. • **Ss** sing the song and **T** plays in canon on an Orff instrument. • **T** plays the next song on an Orff instrument and **Ss** identify the melody.

Creative movement	"We Are Dancing in the Forest" CSP: A • T and Ss sing the song. • T selects two or three Ss to play the beat on a hand drum, and two or three Ss to play the rhythm on claves. • T briefly explains the rules of the game. • T and Ss sing and play the game. • Ss continue the beat on the hand drum while T sings the next song.

Review known songs and elements	"Bounce High, Bounce Low"
	 CSP: A
	 • Ss sing and keep the beat.
	 • Review kinesthetic, aural, and visual awareness activities.
	 • T: "When we have long sounds and short sounds that make a pattern in music, we call it the rhythm."
	 • Ss sing the song and clap the rhythm while T plays the rhythm on an instrument.
	 • Ss sing the song and clap the rhythm of the song, and T chooses one S to play the rhythm on an instrument.
	 • Ss connect "rhythm" to related phrases in known song material:
	   o "Doggie, Doggie"
	   o "Snail, Snail"
	   o "We Are Dancing in the Forest"
	   o "Lucy Locket"
	   o "Bobby Shafto"

SUMMARY ACTIVITIES	
Review lesson outcomes Review the new song	"Closet Key" CSP: D

Grade 1, Unit 1, Kindergarten Review, Lesson 5

Outcome	Review aural presentation and notation of rhythm
INTRODUCTORY ACTIVITIES	
Warm-up	• Body warm-up • Beat activity "Fossils," from *Carnival of the Animals*, by Camille Saint-Saëns (1835–1921) • Breathing: Ss practice blowing up a balloon and watch how air is released when deflating the balloon. • Resonance: explore a cow sound using low and high voices. Make sure Ss are inhaling and exhaling correctly with the support muscles. • Posture: remind Ss of the correct posture for singing.

Sing known songs	"Lucy Locket" CSP: A • **Ss** sing song and keep the beat. • **Ss** sing song and play the game.
Develop tuneful singing Tone production Diction Expression	"Queen, Queen Caroline" • **T** and **Ss** perform the rhyme with the motions. • **Ss** choose which phrases will be performed loud, and which will be performed soft. • **Ss** choose which phrases they will inner-hear while clapping. • **Ss** tap the rhythm of rhyme on instruments while **T** hums "Bobby Shafto"; **Ss** identify it.
Review known songs and elements	"Bobby Shafto" CSP: A • **Ss** sing the song and keep the beat. • **T** directs **Ss** to sing each phrase and "clap the rhythm." • **T** directs **Ss** to sing and form a circle.
CORE ACTIVITIES	
Teach a new song	"On a Mountain" CSP: A • **T** sings the song and **Ss** keep the beat standing in a circle. • **T** sings the song and points to several **Ss** to jump into and out of the circle.

Review known songs and elements	"Rain, Rain"
	CSP: A
	• **Ss** sing and keep the beat.
	• Review kinesthetic, aural, and visual awareness activities.
	• **T**: "When we have long sounds and short sounds that make a pattern in music, we call it the rhythm."
	• **Ss** sing the song tap the beat.
	• **T** sings phrase 1 on "loo" and asks:
	  o "Andy, how many beats did we tap?" (four)
	  o Andy, which beat had two sounds?" (beat 3)
	  o "Let's sing our phrase like this: 'long, long, short, short, long.'"
	• **Ss** play the rhythm on an instrument.
	• **Ss** connect the learning to related song material:
	  o "Doggie, Doggie"
	  o "Snail, Snail"
	  o "We Are Dancing in the Forest"
	  o "Lucy Locket"
	  o "Bobby Shafto"

Creative movement	"Bee, Bee, Bumble Bee"
	  o **T** chants the rhyme and shows the motions for each phrase. **Ss** copy.
	  o **T**: "Where was the man stung?" (on his knee)
	  o **T** chants the rhyme and shows the motions for each phrase. **Ss** copy.

	o **T**: "Where was the pig stung?" (on his snout) o **Ss** perform the first phrase of the rhyme; **T** performs the remaining. o **Ss** and **T** switch performing phrases of the rhyme.
Review known songs and elements	"Bounce High, Bounce Low" CSP: A • **Ss** sing and pat the beat. • **Ss** identify the number of phrases. (two) • **Ss** sing and draw the phrases on the board. • **Ss** sing phrase 1 and keep the beat. • **Ss** identify the number of beats in the phrase. (four) • **Ss** sing and draw the beats in the phrase. • **Ss** sing on a neutral syllable and point to the beats. • **T** hums phrase 2. **T**: "Which beat has one sound? Which beat has more than one sound?" • **T**: "Let's sing the song with the words *long* and *short*." • **Ss** sing on a neutral syllable and point to a representation of the rhythm written on the board.
SUMMARY ACTIVITIES	
Review lesson outcomes Review the new song	"On a Mountain"

Unit 2: Teaching Quarter and Eighth Notes

Lessons for Teaching One and Two Sounds on a Beat

Sections 1 and 2, Unit 2, *ta tadi* table (revised)
Prepare: ♩ ♫
Focus song: "Rain, Rain"
Practice: high and low

SONG REPERTOIRE							
	Known Songs	Songs for Tuneful Singing	Songs to Review Known Rhythmic Elements	Songs to Prepare Next Concepts: *so-mi*	Songs to Prepare Concept: ♩ ♫	Creative Movement	Songs to Practice Known Elements: "High and Low"
Lesson 1	"Seesaw"	"Snail, Snail"	"Bee, Bee, Bumble Bee," "Engine, Engine, Number Nine"	"Ducks and Geese"	"Rain, Rain"	"Doggie, Doggie"	"Cobbler, Cobbler," "Seesaw," "Doggie, Doggie"

KODÁLY IN THE FIRST GRADE CLASSROOM

Lesson 2	"Bounce High, Bounce Low"	"Snail, Snail"	"Queen, Queen Caroline," "Cobbler, Cobbler"	"Ducks and Geese"	"Rain, Rain"	"Doggie, Doggie"	"Cobbler, Cobbler," "Snail, Snail," "Seesaw"
Lesson 3	"Tortillitas," "Ducks and Geese"	"Good Night, Sleep Tight"	"Bee, Bee, Bumble Bee," "Lucy Locket," "Cobbler, Cobbler"	"Lemonade"	"Rain, Rain"	"We Are Dancing in the Forest"	"Snail, Snail"
	Known Songs	**Songs for Tuneful Singing**	**Songs to Review Known Elements:** High and Low	**Songs to Prepare Next Concepts:** *so-mi*	**Songs to Present Concept:** ♩ ♫	**Creative Movement**	**Songs to Present Concept:** ♩ ♫
Lesson 4	"Queen, Queen Caroline," "Lemonade"	"Good Night, Sleep Tight"	"Seesaw"; "Cobbler, Cobbler"	"Lemonade"	"Rain, Rain"	"Lucy Locket"	"Bee, Bee, Bumble Bee," "Queen, Queen Caroline," "Cobbler, Cobbler," "Engine, Engine, Number Nine"
Lesson 5	"Doggie, Doggie"	"Snail, Snail"	"Engine, Engine, Number Nine"	"Witch, Witch"	"Rain, Rain"	"Lemonade"	"Bee, Bee, Bumble Bee," "Seesaw," "Doggie, Doggie," "Engine, Engine, Number Nine," "Snail, Snail"

Here is a chart of the primary musical skills that are developed in the five lessons associated with teaching the concept of *one and two sounds on a beat*. Remember, in the first three lessons, students *practice* the previous musical element, which in this case is the *melodic contour*, learned in kindergarten.

	Lesson 1	**Lesson 2**	**Lesson 3**	**Lesson 4**	**Lesson 5**
Reading	Ss read the melodic contour of "Snail, Snail" and "Bounce High, Bounce Low" and additional songs using icons on the board.				Ss read the rhythm of "Rain, Rain" from traditional rhythm notation.
Writing		Ss write the melodic contour of "Snail, Snail" and "Bounce High, Bounce Low" and additional songs using icons on the board.			Ss write the rhythm of "Rain, Rain" using traditional rhythm notation.
Improvisation			T sings a question phrase written on the board, with "high" and "low." Ss sing a response either from the board or improvising, using the words *high* and *low*.		
Movement	"Doggie, Doggie"		"We Are Dancing in the Forest"	"Lucy Locket"	"Lemonade"
Listening					

Grade 1, Unit 2, Quarter and Eighth Notes, Lesson 1

Outcome	Preparation: internalizing one and two sounds on a beat through kinesthetic activities Practice: reading melodic contour
INTRODUCTORY ACTIVITIES	
Warm-up	• Body warm-up • Beat activity "Dance of the Sugar Plum Fairies," from *Nutcracker Suite*, by Peter Ilyich Tchaikovsky (1840–1893) • Breathing: **Ss** practice blowing up a balloon and watch how air is released when deflating the balloon. • Resonance: explore a cow sound using low and high voices. Make sure **Ss** are inhaling and exhaling correctly with the support muscles. • Posture: remind **Ss** of the correct posture for singing.
Sing known songs	"Seesaw" CSP: A • **Ss** sing the song. • **Ss** sing and pat the beat. • **Ss** create other beat motions to perform while singing the song. • **Ss** continue the beat while **T** sings the next song.
Develop tuneful singing Tone production Diction Expression	"Snail, Snail" CSP: A • **Ss** sing "Snail, Snail" while performing the beat. • **Ss** sing song and change the vowels (ex.: "sneel, snile, snool, snawl") • **Ss** buzz like a bee to explore head voice. • **Ss** sing "Snail, Snail" on a [z] ("sing like a bee").
Review known songs and rhythmic elements	"Bee, Bee, Bumble Bee"; "Engine, Engine, Number Nine" • **Ss** chant the rhyme. • **T** chants one phrase at a time and **Ss** echo with text while clapping the rhythm; perform this echo game for each phrase of the rhymes. • **T** selects one **S** to play the beat on a hand drum. • **S** steps the beat and claps the rhythm of "Engine, Engine, Number Nine." • **S** continues the beat while **T** sings the next song.
CORE ACTIVITIES	
Teach a new song	"Ducks and Geese" CSP: A • **T** sings song with finger puppets to show call-and-response roles. • **T** sings calls and **Ss** chime in on the responses. • **T** and **Ss** may sing and play the game.

Develop knowledge of music concepts Internalize music through kinesthetic activities	"Rain, Rain" CSP: A • Ss sing "Rain, Rain" and pat the beat. • Ss sing "Rain, Rain" and clap the rhythm. • Ss sing and point to a representation of phrase 1 on the board: ♦ ♦ ♦♦ ♦ • Ss sing "Rain, Rain" while one S taps the representation. Line up several Ss and have them sing and tap the phrase. • Divide class in half; have one group walk the beat while the other claps the rhythm. Switch roles. • Choose individual Ss to walk the beat and clap the rhythm. • Ss inner-hear the song while performing beat against rhythm.
Creative movement	"Doggie, Doggie" CSP: A • Ss identify the song. • Ss sing and play the game. • After playing the game, Ss perform the song with various beat and rhythm motions. • Ss continue the beat while T claps the rhythm of another "mystery song."
Practice and performance of music skills Reading	"Cobbler, Cobbler"; "Doggie, Doggie" CSP: A • Ss identify the song. • Ss sing. • T writes a representation of the melodic contour for phrase 1 of the song on the board. • Ss sing and point to representation using "high" and "low." • T transforms the pattern into "Seesaw." • Ss read the new pattern and identify the song. • T transforms the pattern into phrase 1 of "Doggie, Doggie." • Ss read the new pattern and identify the song. • T transforms the pattern into other known songs as time permits.
SUMMARY ACTIVITIES	
Review lesson outcomes Review the new song	"Ducks and Geese" CSP: A

Grade 1, Unit 2, Quarter and Eighth Notes, Lesson 2

Outcome	Preparation: analyzing repertoire that contains one and two sounds on a beat Practice: writing high and low melodic contour

INTRODUCTORY ACTIVITIES	
Warm-up	• Body warm-up • Beat activity "Dance of the Sugar Plum Fairies," from *Nutcracker Suite*, by Peter Ilyich Tchaikovsky (1840–1893) • Breathing: **Ss** practice blowing up a balloon and watch how air is released when deflating the balloon. • Resonance: explore a cow sound using low and high voices. Make sure **Ss** are inhaling and exhaling correctly with the support muscles. • Posture: remind **Ss** of the correct posture for singing.
Sing known songs	"Bounce High, Bounce Low" CSP: A • **Ss** sing the song. • Add four-beat ostinato: pat, clap, pat, clap.
Develop tuneful singing Tone production Diction Expression	"Snail, Snail" CSP: A • **Ss** sing the song. • **Ss** sing song on "noo." • **Ss** sing song on "noo" staccato or legato. • **Ss** "sing" "Snail, Snail" on a hiss, articulating all the rhythms. • **Ss** "sing" "Doggie, Doggie" on a hiss, articulating all the rhythms.
Review known songs and rhythmic elements	"Queen, Queen Caroline"; "Cobbler, Cobbler" CSP: A • **Ss** chant "Queen, Queen Caroline." • **T** chants one phrase at a time and **Ss** echo with text while clapping the rhythm. • Repeat with "Cobbler, Cobbler." • **T** sings the first phrase of "Ducks and Geese"; **Ss** echo and clap the rhythm. • Repeat this activity with any four-beat pattern from the **Ss**' known repertoire.
CORE ACTIVITIES	
Teach a new song	"Ducks and Geese" CSP: A • **T** sings song with finger puppets to demonstrate call-and-response roles. • **T** sings calls and **Ss** join on responses. • **T** and **Ss** play the game. **Ss** sing all responses in order to continue playing. • **Ss** sing and pat the beat and continue the beat into the next song.

Develop knowledge of music literacy concepts Describe what you hear	"Rain, Rain" CSP: A • **Ss** sing "Rain, Rain." • Review kinesthetic awareness activities. • **Ss** and **T** sing the first phrase of "Rain, Rain" on "loo" and tap the beat before asking each question: • **T**: "Andy, how many beats did we tap?" (four) • **T**: "Andy, which beat had the most sounds?" (beat 3) • **T**: "Andy, how many sounds did we sing on beat 3?" (two) • **T**: "If we sang two sounds on beat 3, how many sounds did we sing on each of the other beats?" (one) • **Ss** sing "Rain, Rain" with text and inner-hear the beat with two sounds. • **Ss** sing "Rain, Rain" while **T** softly sings "Doggie, Doggie" as a partner song. Switch.
Creative movement	"Doggie, Doggie" CSP: A • **T** and **Ss** sing and play the circle game. • **Ss** may create accompaniment with a simple ostinato played on pitched or unpitched instruments (𝄞 ♩ ♩ | ♩ 𝄾 :|). • **T** continues ostinato into the next song. (It might be easier to establish the ostinato before moving to the game; allow those who are able to perform ostinato the opportunity to play it on an instrument.)
Practice and performance of music skills Writing	"Snail, Snail"; "Seesaw"; "Cobbler, Cobbler" CSP: A • **T** and **Ss** sing "Snail, Snail." • **Ss** sing the song with "high" and "low." • **T** distributes materials and **Ss** complete the writing worksheet on high and low. • **Ss** either draw or use manipulatives to show the high and low sounds of the song. • Repeat the process with "Seesaw" and "Cobbler, Cobbler."
SUMMARY ACTIVITIES	
Review lesson outcomes Review the new song	"Ducks and Geese" CSP: A

Grade 1, Unit 2, Quarter and Eighth Notes, Lesson 3

Outcome	Preparation: creating a visual representation of one and two sounds on a beat Practice: improvise high and low melodic contour

	INTRODUCTORY ACTIVITIES
Warm-up	• Body warm-up • Beat activity "Dance of the Sugar Plum Fairies," from *Nutcracker Suite*, by Peter Ilyich Tchaikovsky (1840–1893) • Breathing: **Ss** practice blowing up a balloon and watch how air is released when deflating the balloon. • Resonance: explore a cow sound using low and high voices. Make sure **Ss** are inhaling and exhaling correctly with the support muscles. • Posture: remind **Ss** of the correct posture for singing.
Sing known songs	"Ducks and Geese" CSP: A • **T** sings the calls and **Ss** sing the responses while patting the beat. "Tortillitas" CSP: A • **T** sings song alone while **Ss** pat the beat. • **Ss** will suggest ingredients with which to make tortillas. If they decide the ingredient is good, then finish the song with "para mama que esta contenta." If **Ss** decide the ingredient is bad, then finish the song with "para papa que esta nojado." • **T** and **Ss** will sing with **Ss**' suggestions. • **Ss** continue the beat while **T** sings the next song.
Develop tuneful singing Tone production Diction Expression	"Good Night, Sleep Tight" or " Star Light, Star Bright" CSP: A • **Ss** sing the song while keeping the beat. • **Ss** sing first phrase but only the vowel sounds (ex.: "ooo, ah, eee, ah").
Review known songs and rhythmic elements	"Lucy Locket"; "Cobbler, Cobbler"; "Bee, Bee, Bumble Bee" CSP: A • **Ss** chant song/rhyme. • **T** chants one phrase at a time and **Ss** echo with text while clapping the rhythm. Repeat this activity with any four-beat phrase from **Ss**' known repertoire.
	CORE ACTIVITIES
Teach a new song	"Lemonade" CSP: A • **T** sings song with puppets to show call-and-response roles. • **T** will sing the calls and **Ss** will sing the responses. • **T** and **Ss** sing and play the game. • **Ss** sing the song all together. • **T** sings the last phrase on a neutral syllable. This "reminds" **T** of part of another song. • **T** sings "Rain, Rain" on a neutral syllable and **Ss** must identify it.

Develop knowledge of music literacy concepts Create a visual representation of what you hear	"Rain, Rain" CSP: A • **Ss** sing "Rain, Rain." • Review and assess kinesthetic and aural awareness activities; ask the same questions from the previous lesson. • **T** sings the first phrase of "Rain, Rain" while **Ss** create a visual representation with Unifix cubes, demonstrating the number of sounds on a beat. • **Ss** share representations with each other and discuss similarities and differences. • One **S** shares a representation on the board. If necessary, corrections to the representation can be made by reviewing the aural awareness questions. • **Ss** sing the first phrase of "Rain, Rain" on "loo" and point to the representation.
Creative movement	"We Are Dancing in the Forest" CSP: A • **Ss** sing and play the game (either version of the game). • **T** selects **S** to play the beat on a hand drum or tambourine. • **T** selects another **S** to play the rhythm with the rhythm sticks. • **T** sings "Snail, Snail" as a partner song. Switch.
Practice and performance of music skills Improvisation	"Snail, Snail" CSP: A • **Ss** sing the song. • **Ss** read a representation of the melodic contour from the board with high and low. • One by one **T** presents, and **Ss** read, three additional representations of high and low melodic contour. • **Ss** sing the first example as a "question" phrase with the words *high* and *low*. • **T** "answers" with one of the three representations. Repeat several times. • **T** sings the "question" phrase and calls on individual **Ss** to respond with one of the three melodic contours, singing with words *high* and *low* or creating their own improvisation.
SUMMARY ACTIVITIES	
Review lesson outcomes Review the new song	"Lemonade" CSP: A

Grade 1, Unit 2, Quarter and Eighth Notes, Lesson 4

Outcome	Presentation: labeling one and two sounds on a beat with rhythm syllables

	INTRODUCTORY ACTIVITIES
Warm-up	• Body warm-up • Beat activity "Dance of the Sugar Plum Fairies," from *Nutcracker Suite*, by Peter Ilyich Tchaikovsky (1840–1893) • Breathing: **Ss** practice blowing up a balloon and watch how air is released when deflating the balloon. • Resonance: explore a cow sound using low and high voices. Make sure **Ss** are inhaling and exhaling correctly with the support muscles. • Posture: remind **Ss** of the correct posture for singing.
Sing known songs	"Queen, Queen Caroline"; "Lemonade" • **Ss** perform chant with steady beat motions. • **Ss** perform the chant with a four-beat ostinato: pat, clap, pat, clap.
Develop tuneful singing Tone production Diction Expression	"Good Night, Sleep Tight" CSP: A • **Ss** sing the song and continue the ostinato. • **Ss** sing the song with loud and soft singing voices. • **Ss** lightly hum the song (**T** monitors for proper vocal resonance). • **Ss** sing the song on a [z] (**T**: "Wow! You sound like a bunch of bees!") • **Ss** follow a bee with their voices, moving through head voice and chest voice.
Review known songs and rhythmic elements	"Seesaw"; "Cobbler, Cobbler" CSP: A • Sing song. • **T** sings one phrase at a time and **Ss** echo with text while clapping the rhythm. • Repeat this activity with any four-beat phrase from **Ss**' known repertoire.
	CORE ACTIVITIES
Teach a new song	"Lemonade" CSP: A • **T** sings song with puppets to show call-and-response roles. • **Ss** join on response singing. • **Ss** sing back and forth to one another in two groups. • **Ss** sing and play the game. • **T** sings "Rain, Rain" on a neutral syllable and **Ss** must identify it.
Develop knowledge of music literacy concepts Describe what you hear with rhythm syllables	"Rain, Rain" CSP: A • Sing first phrase of "Rain, Rain" and review and assess kinesthetic, aural, and visual awareness activities and questions. • **T**: "When we hear one sound on a beat we call it 'ta', and when we hear two sounds on a beat we can call it 'tadi.'" • **T** writes the words *ta* and *tadi* on the board (*not* the notation).

	• **T** sings first phrase of "Rain, Rain" with rhythm syllables and **Ss** echo-sing, "ta ta ta di ta," clapping the rhythm. • **T** sings first phrase of "Rain, Rain" with rhythm syllables and **Ss** echo-sing, "ta ta ta di ta," clapping the beat. • **T** performs the echo activity as a class and with individual **Ss**.
Creative movement	"Lucy Locket" CSP: A • **Ss** identify the song. • **Ss** sing and play the game for several rounds. • **T** chooses **Ss** to play the beat on a drum or tambourine and rhythm on rhythm sticks.
Presentation Describe what you hear with rhythm syllables	"Bee, Bee, Bumble Bee" • **Ss** chant the rhyme. • **T** continues the review aural presentation (**T**: "When we hear one sound on a beat we call it 'ta', and when we hear two sounds on a beat we can call it 'tadi'."). • **T** sings four-beat patterns from related songs with text and **Ss** echo with rhythm syllables: 　o "Seesaw" (phrase 1) 　o "Queen, Queen Caroline" (entire chant) 　o "Engine, Engine, Number Nine" (entire chant) 　o "Cobbler, Cobbler" (phrase 1) • **Ss** echo as a class and individually.
SUMMARY ACTIVITIES	
Review lesson outcomes Review the new song	"Lemonade" CSP: A

Grade 1, Unit 2, Quarter and Eighth Notes, Lesson 5

Outcome	Presentation: notation of one and two sounds on a beat
INTRODUCTORY ACTIVITIES	
Warm-up	• Body warm-up • Beat activity "Dance of the Sugar Plum Fairies," from *Nutcracker Suite*, by Peter Ilyich Tchaikovsky (1840–1893) • Breathing: **Ss** practice blowing up a balloon and watch how air is released when deflating the balloon. • Resonance: explore a cow sound using low and high voices. Make sure **Ss** are inhaling and exhaling correctly with the support muscles. • Posture: remind **Ss** of the correct posture for singing.

Sing known songs	"Doggie, Doggie" CSP: A • **T** and **Ss** sing the song while keeping a steady beat on the body. • **T** adds a four-beat ostinato: pat, rest, pat, rest.
Developing tuneful singing Tone production Diction Expression	"Snail, Snail" CSP: A • **T** and **Ss** sing the song while continuing the ostinato. • Sing the first four pitches and change the vowels (i.e., "sneel," "snole," "snool," "snawl"). • **T** draws a "snail trail" on the board and **Ss** follow it with finger and vocal inflection (high at the top of the trail and low at the bottom).
Review known songs and rhythmic elements	"Engine, Engine, Number Nine" • **Ss** chant the rhyme. • **T** chants one phrase at a time and **Ss** echo with rhythm syllables. • Repeat this activity with any four-phrase from the **Ss**' known repertoire.
CORE ACTIVITIES	
Teaching a new song	"Witch, Witch" CSP: A • **T** sings the song alone and acts out the call and response of the B section with a hand puppet. • **T** sings again, but **Ss** sing the responses of the B section. Switch. • **T** will be the "witch" for the first two to three rounds and then will allow **Ss** to take over the game.
Develop knowledge of music concepts Notate what you hear	"Rain, Rain" CSP: A • **Ss** sing "Rain, Rain" with rhythm syllables and keep the beat. • **T**: "We can represent one and two sounds on a beat using traditional notation. We can use a quarter note to represent one sound on a beat. A quarter note has a note head and a stem." Show on the board. • **T**: "We can use two eighth notes to represent two sounds on a beat. Two eighth notes have two note heads, two stems, and a beam." Show on the board. • **T**: "Our first phrase of "Rain, Rain" looks like this:" ♩ ♩ ♫ ♩ • **T**: "We can read this rhythm pattern using rhythm syllables." **T** sings rhythm syllables while pointing to heartbeats and **Ss** echo-sing and point. • **T**: "Stick notation is an easy way to write rhythmic notation. Stick notation is traditional notation without the note heads for quarter and eighth notes." ♩ ♩ ♫ ♩ • Sing "Rain, Rain" with rhythm syllables while pointing to the phrase written on the board. Individual **Ss** sing and point while class sings song with rhythm syllables. • **T** switches the pattern to represent phrase 1 of "Lemonade." • **Ss** read and identify the song.

Creative movement	"Lemonade" CSP: A • **T** and **Ss** sing the song. • **Ss** sing and play the game. • **Ss** sing the song with rhythm syllables.

Presentation of music skills
 	
Notate what you hear
	"Bee, Bee, Bumble Bee"
	• **Ss** chant the rhyme.
	• **Ss** chant with rhythm syllables and pat the beat.
	• **Ss** chant while pointing to standard rhythm notation.
	• **T** changes the rhythm into some of these songs (with **Ss** singing the rhythm syllables while pointing to the standard notation of each):
	  o "Rain, Rain"
	  o "Doggie, Doggie" (entire song)
	  o "Engine, Engine, Number Nine" (entire chant)
	  o "Queen, Queen Caroline"
	• Several **Ss** go up to the board and write the rhythm notation for a four-beat phrase from any of the previous songs/chants.
	• Review answers and call on more **Ss** until each has had a turn.

SUMMARY ACTIVITIES	
Review lesson outcomes Review the new song	"Witch, Witch"

Unit 3: Teaching a Two-Note Child's Chant *so-mi*

Lessons for Teaching *so-mi*

Sections 1 and 2, Unit 3, *so-mi* (revised)
Prepare: *so-mi*
Focus song: "Snail, Snail"
Practice: ♩ ♫

Song Repertoire:							
	Known Songs	Songs for Tuneful Singing	Songs to Review Known Melodic Elements	Songs to Prepare Next Concepts: Q	Songs to Prepare Concept: *so-mi*	Creative movement	Songs to Practice Known Elements ♩ ♫
Lesson 1	"Doggie, Doggie," "Witch, Witch"	"Good Night, Sleep Tight"	"Seesaw," "Cobbler, Cobbler"	"Bow Wow Wow"	"Snail, Snail"	"Witch, Witch"	"Rain, Rain," "Queen, Queen Caroline"
Lesson 2	"Bobby Shafto," "Bow Wow Wow"	"Witch, Witch"	"Cobbler, Cobbler"	"Hot Cross Buns"	"Snail, Snail"	"Ducks and Geese"	"Rain, Rain," "Doggie, Doggie"

KODÁLY IN THE FIRST GRADE CLASSROOM

Lesson 3:	"Seesaw," "Hot Cross Buns"	"Cobbler, Cobbler"	"Lemonade"	"All Around the Buttercup"	"Snail, Snail"	"Bow Wow Wow"	"Rain, Rain"
	Known Songs	Songs for Tuneful Singing	Songs to Review Known Elements: ♩ ♫	Songs to Prepare Next Concepts: Q	Songs to Present Concept: *so-mi*	Creative Movement	Songs to Present Concept: *so-mi*
Lesson 4	"Seesaw," "All Around the Buttercup"	"Good Night, Sleep Tight"	"Doggie, Doggie"	"Down Came a Lady"	"Snail, Snail"	"Witch, Witch"	"Rain, Rain," "Cobbler, Cobbler," "Seesaw"
Lesson 5	"Bobby Shafto," "Down Came a Lady"	"Tortillitas"	"Doggie, Doggie," "Rain, Rain," "Good Night, Sleep Tight," "Seesaw," "Doggie, Doggie"	"Pease Porridge Hot"	"Snail, Snail"	"All Around the Buttercup"	"Rain, Rain," "Tortillitas," "Doggie, Doggie," "Cobbler, Cobbler"

Here is a chart of the primary musical skills that are developed in the five lessons associated with teaching the concept of *so-mi*. Remember, in the first three lessons, students *practice* the previous musical element, in this case *one and two sounds on a beat*.

	Lesson 1	Lesson 2	Lesson 3	Lesson 4	Lesson 5
Reading	Ss read "Rain, Rain," "Bounce High, Bounce Low," and other duple meter songs from traditional rhythm notation.				Ss read "Snail, Snail" with hand signs from steps, traditional notation with solfège, and then staff notation.
Writing		Ss write "Rain, Rain," "Bounce High, Bounce Low," and other duple meter songs.			Ss write phrase 1 of "Snail, Snail" in rhythmic notation with solfège syllables and staff notation.

Improvisation			T sings a question phrase written on the board; Ss choose an answer phrase to sing from selections written on the board using rhythm syllables.		
Movement	"Witch, Witch"	"Ducks and Geese"	"Bow Wow Wow"	"Witch, Witch"	"All Around the Buttercup"
Listening	"Andante," from Symphony No. 94, *Surprise*, by Joseph Haydn (1732–1809)				

Grade 1, Unit 3, *so-mi*, Lesson 1

Outcome	Preparation: internalizing *so-mi* through kinesthetic activities Practice: reading quarter and eighth note patterns in known songs
INTRODUCTORY ACTIVITIES	
Warm-up	• Body warm-up • Beat activity "Stars and Stripes Forever," by John Philip Sousa (1854–1937) • Breathing: **Ss** practice blowing up a balloon and watch how air is released when deflating the balloon. • Resonance: explore a cow sound using low and high voices. Make sure **Ss** are inhaling and exhaling correctly with the support muscles. • Posture: remind **Ss** of the correct posture for singing.
Sing known songs	"Doggie, Doggie" CSP: A • **Ss** sing "Doggie, Doggie." • **Ss** sing with a simple ostinato (pat, clap, pat, clap).

Develop tuneful singing Tone production Diction Expression	"Good Night, Sleep Tight" CSP: A • **Ss** sing "Good Night, Sleep Tight" with words. • **T** may choose **Ss** to sing alone or in small groups. • Sing "Good Night, Sleep Tight" on "loo," "boo," "zoo."

Review known songs and melodic elements	"Seesaw"
	CSP: A
	• Sing "Seesaw"
	• **T** sings phrase by phrase, and **Ss** echo-sing using high and low.
	"Cobbler, Cobbler"
	CSP: A
	• Sing "Cobbler, Cobbler."
	• **T** sings phrases 1 and 2; **Ss** echo-sing using high and low while showing the melodic contour.
	• Repeat this activity with any of these songs:
	  o "Rain, Rain" (phrase 1)
	  o "Ducks and Geese" (phrase 1)
	  o "Snail, Snail" (phrase 1)
	  o "Doggie, Doggie" (phrase 1)
	  o "Good Night, Sleep Tight" (phrase 1)

CORE ACTIVITIES	
Teach a new song	"Bow Wow Wow" CSP: D • **T** sings "Bow Wow Wow" while **Ss** step the beat. • **T** sings "Bow Wow Wow" while **Ss** show the phrases in the air. • **Ss** identify the number of phrases. • **T** sings phrase by phrase demonstrating game motions. **Ss** echo. • **Ss** sing the song with a simple ostinato (pat, pat, clap, clap). • **Ss** continue the ostinato while T sings the next song.
Develop knowledge of musical concepts Internalize music through kinesthetic activities	"Snail, Snail" CSP: A • **Ss** sing "Snail, Snail." • **Ss** sing "Snail, Snail" and keep the beat. • **Ss** sing "Snail, Snail" and point to a representation of focus phrase. ○ ○ ○ ○ • **Ss** sing "Snail, Snail" and clap the melodic contour. • **Ss** sing "Snail, Snail" with rhythm syllables while showing contour. • **Ss** sing and pat the beat. • **Ss** continue the beat into the next song.

Creative movement	"Witch, Witch" CSP: A • **Ss** sing and play the game. • **Ss** sing and step the beat. • **Ss** continue the beat as **T** sings the next song on "loo."
Practice and performance of music skills Reading	"Rain, Rain" CSP: A • **Ss** sing the song. • **T** sings phrase 1 of "Rain, Rain" on "loo" and **Ss** identify the song. • **Ss** read the rhythm of "Rain, Rain" from the board and keep the beat. • **T** gradually adds additional phrases, turning "Rain, Rain" into "Queen, Queen Caroline." • **T** changes the rhythm into the main theme from "Allegretto," from Symphony No. 94, *Surprise*, by Joseph Haydn (1732–1809) ♫ ♫ | ♫ ♩ ♫ ♫ | ♫ ♩ ♫ ♫ | ♫ ♩ ♫ ♫ | ♩ ♩ • **Ss** listen to a recording while quietly tapping the rhythm.
SUMMARY ACTIVITIES	
Review lesson outcomes Review the new song	"Bow Wow Wow" CSP: D

Grade 1, Unit 3, *so-mi*, Lesson 2

Outcome	Preparation: analyzing repertoire that contains *so-mi* Practice: writing musical patterns that contain quarter and eighth notes
INTRODUCTORY ACTIVITIES	
Warm-up	• Body warm-up • Beat activity "Stars and Stripes Forever," by John Philip Sousa (1854–1937) • Breathing: **Ss** practice blowing up a balloon and watch how air is released when deflating the balloon. • Resonance: explore a cow sound using low and high voices. Make sure **Ss** are inhaling and exhaling correctly with the support muscles. • Posture: remind **Ss** of the correct posture for singing.

Sing known songs	"Bobby Shafto" CSP: A • Sing "Bobby Shafto" and pat the beat. • **T** adds a simple ostinato (2/4 ♩ ♩ | ♫ ♩ :|). **T** may allow a few **Ss** to play the ostinato on a percussion instrument. "Bow Wow Wow" CSP: D • **Ss** sing the song and keep the beat.
Develop tuneful singing Tone production Diction Expression	"Witch, Witch" CSP: A • **Ss** sing the song. • **Ss** sing "Witch, Witch" using a number of consonants as vocalizers ("yow," "cow," "dow," "pow," etc.). Switch.

Review known songs and melodic elements	"Cobbler, Cobbler"
	CSP: A
	• Sing "Cobbler, Cobbler."
	• **T** sings "Cobbler, Cobbler" phrase by phrase; **Ss** echo with rhythm syllables and clap the contour for phrases 1 and 2.
	• Repeat this activity with any of these songs:
	  o "Rain, Rain" (phrase 1)
	  o "Ducks and Geese" (phrase 1)
	  o "Snail, Snail" (phrase 1)
	  o "Doggie, Doggie" (phrase 1)
	  o "Good Night, Sleep Tight" (phrase 1)

CORE ACTIVITIES	
Teach a new song	"Hot Cross Buns" CSP: A • **T** sings "Hot Cross Buns." • **T** sings the song and **Ss** keep the beat on lap. • **T** sings the song and **Ss** show phrases. • **Ss** identify which phrases are the same. (1, 2, and 4) • **Ss** identify phrase 3 as B. • **Ss** sing only the A phrases; **T** sings B. • **Ss** continue their beat motions while **T** sings the next song.
Develop knowledge of music concepts Describe what you hear	"Snail, Snail" CSP: A • Review and assess kinesthetic awareness activities. • Sing first phrase of "Snail, Snail" on "loo" and keep the beat before asking each question: • **T**: "Andy, how many beats did we tap?" (four)

	- Sing first two beats only. **T**: "Andy, how many different pitches did we sing?" (two)
- **T**: "Andy, what words can we use to describe these two different pitches?" (the first is high and the second is low)
- **T**: "I'll sing the words and you sing [**T** sings] high and low."
- **T** sings phrase 1 with text; one **S** echo-sings with high and low.
- Repeat with large and small groups, and then with individual **Ss**.
Creative movement	"Ducks and Geese" CSP: A - **T** and **Ss** sing and play the game. - **T** selects one **S** to lead the singing. - **T** "realizes" he or she can sing this song with rhythm syllables.
Practice and performance of music skills Writing	"Rain, Rain" CSP: A - Sing "Rain, Rain" with words. - Sing "Rain, Rain" with rhythm syllables and keep the beat; one **S** draws eight-beat bars on the board. - Determine the number of sounds on each beat for phrase 1. - Ask **Ss** how we notate these sounds. - One **S** writes it on the board above the beat bars. - **Ss** sing phrase 1 with rhythm syllables while clapping the rhythm. - Repeat for phrase 2. - **Ss** sing "Rain, Rain" with rhythm syllables while clapping the rhythm. "Doggie, Doggie" CSP: A - Repeat the process with the first two phrases of "Doggie, Doggie." - Each **S** completes a writing activity.
	SUMMARY ACTIVITIES
Review lesson outcomes Review the new song	"Hot Cross Buns" CSP: A

Grade 1, Unit 3, *so-mi*, Lesson 3

Outcome	Preparation: creating a visual representation of *so-mi* Practice: improvise a rhythm pattern of quarter and eighth notes
INTRODUCTORY ACTIVITIES	
Warm-up	• Body warm-up • Beat activity "Stars and Stripes Forever," by John Philip Sousa (1854–1937) • Breathing: **Ss** practice blowing up a balloon and watch how air is released when deflating the balloon. • Resonance: explore a cow sound using low and high voices. Make sure **Ss** are inhaling and exhaling correctly with the support muscles. • Posture: remind **Ss** of the correct posture for singing.
Sing known songs	"Seesaw" CSP: A • **Ss** sing the song in unison. • **Ss** sing the song with an ostinato. "Hot Cross Buns" CSP: F-sharp • **Ss** sing the song.
Develop tuneful singing Tone production Diction Expression	"Cobbler, Cobbler" CSP: A • **Ss** sing the song in unison. • **Ss** sing using vowel sounds (ex.: "ooo, ah, eee, ah").

Review known songs and melodic elements	"Lemonade"
	 CSP: A
	 • **Ss** sing "Lemonade" with text and keep the beat.
	 • **Ss** sing "Lemonade" with text, then high and low.
	 • **T** hums *so-mi* motives from known songs and **Ss** echo-sing with high and low.
	 • Repeat this activity with any of these songs:
	   • "Rain, Rain" (phrase 1)
	   • "Ducks and Geese" (phrase 1)
	   • "Snail, Snail" (phrase 1)
	   • "Doggie, Doggie" (phrase 1)
	   • "Good Night, Sleep Tight" (phrase 1)

CORE ACTIVITIES	
Teach a new song	"All Around the Buttercup" CSP: F-sharp • **T** sings "All Around the Buttercup" while **Ss** pat the beat. • **T** sings the song while **Ss** march in a circle. • **T** sings the song while demonstrating the game. • **T** and **Ss** sing and play the game. • **Ss** continue marching to the beat while singing the next song.

Develop knowledge of music concepts Create a visual representation of what you hear	"Snail, Snail" CSP: A • **Ss** sing "Snail, Snail" while stepping the beat. • Review kinesthetic and aural awareness activities. • **T** hums or sings the first phrase of "Snail, Snail" on a neutral syllable. • **T**: "Using the Unifix cubes, pick up what you need in order to draw a picture of these pitches." • **Ss** share their examples with each other. • **T** asks one **S** to share an example with the class; corrections can be made by reviewing aural awareness questions. • **Ss** sing the first phrase of "Snail, Snail" with "high" and "low" while pointing to the representation. • **Ss** sing with rhythm syllables and pat the beat.
Creative movement	"Bow Wow Wow" CSP: D • **Ss** sing and play the game. • **Ss** create accompaniment with known rhythmic elements. • **Ss** continue their accompaniment into the next song.

Practice and performance of music skills
 	
Improvisation
	"Rain, Rain"
	CSP: A
	• **T** has the first phrase of "Rain, Rain" and four rhythm patterns of quarter notes and eighth notes prepared on board in standard notation.
	• **Ss** sing "Rain, Rain" with words.
	• **Ss** sing "Rain, Rain" with rhythm syllables.
	• **Ss** clap the first phrase of "Rain, Rain" as a "question."
	• Revealing only one at a time, **T** chooses one of four quarter or eighth note rhythms as an "answer."
	• Perform several times with each response.
	• **T** claps the first phrase of "Rain, Rain" and chooses one **S** to perform an answer or create his or her own.
	
	    <u>Teacher</u> <u>Student</u>
	    ♩ ♩ ♫ ♩ ♫ ♫ ♫ ♩
	                   ♫ ♫ ♩ ♩
	                   ♩ ♫ ♩ ♫
	                   ♩ ♫ ♫ ♩

SUMMARY ACTIVITIES	
Review lesson outcomes Review the new song	"All Around the Buttercup"

Grade 1, Unit 3, *so-mi*, Lesson 4

Outcome	Presentation: labeling the two pitches with solfège syllables *so-mi*
INTRODUCTORY ACTIVITIES	
Warm-up	• Body warm-up • Beat activity "Stars and Stripes Forever," by John Philip Sousa (1854–1937) • Breathing: **Ss** practice blowing up a balloon and watch how air is released when deflating the balloon. • Resonance: explore a cow sound using low and high voices. Make sure **Ss** are inhaling and exhaling correctly with the support muscles. • Posture: remind **Ss** of the correct posture for singing.
Sing known songs	"Seesaw" CSP: A • **Ss** sing the song and keep the beat. "All Around the Buttercup" CSP: F-sharp • **Ss** sing the song and keep the beat.
Develop tuneful singing Tone production Diction Expression	"Good Night, Sleep Tight" CSP: A • **Ss** sing the song while continuing the beat. • **T** models on a staccato "doo"; **Ss** copy. • **T** models on a legato "loo"; **Ss** copy.

Review known songs and melodic elements	"Doggie, Doggie"
	CSP: A
	• **Ss** sing song and keep beat.
	• **T** sing phrases 1 and 2, and **Ss** echo-sing each phrase with high and low.
	• Repeat this activity with any of these songs:
	  o "Rain, Rain" (phrase 1)
	  o "Ducks and Geese" (phrase 1)
	  o "Snail, Snail" (phrase 1)
	  o "Good Night, Sleep Tight" (phrase 1)

CORE ACTIVITIES	
Teach a new song	"Down Came a Lady" CSP: F • **Ss** continue the beat while **T** sings "Down Came a Lady." • **T** sings and demonstrates how to play the game. • **Ss** join in the singing after several rounds.

Presentation of music literacy concepts Describe what you hear with rhythm or solfège syllables	"Snail, Snail" CSP: A • Review kinesthetic, aural, and visual awareness activities with phrase 1 of "Snail, Snail." • **T**: "We can label the high and low pitches with solfège syllables. We call the high pitch *so* and the low pitch *mi*." Show hand signs spatially, using the whole arm. • **T** sings the first phrase of "Snail, Snail" with solfège syllables and hand signs. **Ss** echo. 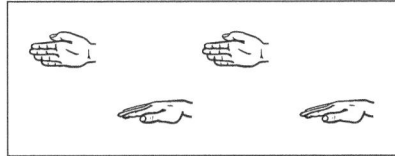 • **T** sings the target phrase with solfège syllables and hand signs to individual **Ss** who echo the pattern. • **T** sings "Snail, snail, snail, snail." **Ss** echo with "*so mi so mi*." • The pattern reminds **T** of another song.
Creative movement	"Witch, Witch" CSP: A • **Ss** sing and play the game.

Presentation of music literacy concepts
 	
Describe what you hear with rhythm or solfège syllables
	"Rain, Rain"
	CSP: A
	• **T** and **Ss** sing "Rain, Rain."
	• **Ss** sing the first phrase with solfège syllables and hand signs.
	• **T** labels *so* and *mi* in related songs.
	• **T** sings words and **Ss** echo with solfège and hands signs as a group and individually:
	  o "Snail, Snail" (first four beats)
	  o "Doggie, Doggie" (first four beats)
	  o "Cobbler, Cobbler" (first eight beats)
	  o "Seesaw" (whole song)
	  o "Lemonade" (first twelve beats)
	  o "Good Night, Sleep Tight" (first four beats)
	  o "Ducks and Geese" (first four beats; entire song except for the last four beats)

SUMMARY ACTIVITIES	
Review lesson outcomes Review the new song	"Down Came a Lady" CSP: F

Grade 1, Unit 3, *so-mi*, Lesson 5

Outcome	Presentation: notate *so-mi*
INTRODUCTORY ACTIVITIES	
Warm-up	• Body warm-up • Beat activity "Stars and Stripes Forever," by John Philip Sousa (1854–1937) • Breathing: **Ss** practice blowing up a balloon and watch how air is released when deflating the balloon. • Resonance: explore a cow sound using low and high voices. Make sure **Ss** are inhaling and exhaling correctly with the support muscles. • Posture: remind **Ss** of the correct posture for singing.
Sing known songs	"Bobby Shafto" CSP: A • **Ss** sing the song with the beat in their feet and rhythm in their hands. "Down Came a Lady" (rest at the end of song) CSP: F • **Ss** sing the song with the beat in their feet and rhythm in their hands.
Develop tuneful singing Tone production Diction Expression	"Tortillitas" CSP: A • **Ss** sing "Tortillitas" and continue the ostinato. • **Ss** follow a "tortilla" (**T** may use a poly spot or something round and flat as a prop) up and down with their voices as **T** tosses it in the air.

Review known songs and melodic elements	"Doggie, Doggie"
	CSP: A
	• **Ss** sing song and keep the beat.
	• **T** sings the first phrase and **Ss** echo with *so* and *mi* and hand signs.
	• **T** sings the second phrase with text and **Ss** echo with *so* and *mi* and hand signs.
	• **T** and **Ss** sing these songs, and then **T** sings the first phrase and **Ss** echo with *so* and *mi* and hand signs:
	  o "Rain, Rain" (phrase 1)
	  o "Good Night, Sleep Tight" (phrase 1)
	  o "Seesaw" (phrase 1)
	  o "Doggie, Doggie" (phrase 1)

CORE ACTIVITIES	
Teach a new song	"Pease Porridge Hot" CSP: A • **T** sings the song while **Ss** pat the beat.

	• **T** sings the song while **Ss** show the phrases and identify the number of phrases. • **Ss** create steady beat motions to accompany each phrase of the song. • **Ss** continue their beat motions into the next song.

Presentation of music literacy concepts
 	
Notate what you hear
	"Snail, Snail"
	CSP: A
	• **Ss** sing the song.
	• **Ss** sing the first phrase with solfège syllables and hand signs..
	• Review aural presentation:
	  o **T**: "We can label pitches with solfège syllables. We call the high sound *so* and the low sound *mi*." Show hand signs spatially, using the whole arm.
	  o **T** sings the first phrase of "Snail, Snail" with solfège syllables and hand signs. **Ss** echo.
	• Introduce the "musical steps":
	  o **T**: "*So* and *mi* look like this on our musical steps. From *so* to *mi* is a skip." (Hum *so-fa-mi* to prove that there is something else in the middle.)
	  o **T**: "We can write our phrase in traditional notation and put our solfège syllables under the notation."
	    ♩ ♩ |♩ ♩
	    s m s m
	• Introduce music staff and hand staff:
	  o Five lines and four spaces; **Ss** count the lines and spaces from bottom to top.
	• Rule of placement:
	  o **T**: "Sometimes notes are on a line and sometimes notes are in the space." **T** shows a note on a line and a note in a space. (Note to **T**: we find it best to place only the note head on the staff.)
	  o **T** chants, "If *so* is in a line, then *mi* is in a line below!" **Ss** echo and **T** shows the placement on the staff.
	  o **T** chants, "If *so* is on a space, then *mi* is on a space below!" **Ss** echo and **T** shows the placement on the staff.
	• **Ss** read "Snail, Snail" from the staff with solfège syllables and hand signs.
	• Individual **Ss** may read the song with solfège syllables and hand signs.

Creative movement	"All Around the Buttercup" CSP: F-sharp • **Ss** sing and play the game. • **Ss** create an accompaniment with known rhythmic elements. • **Ss** continue their accompaniment into the next song.

Presentation of music literacy concepts
 	
Notate what you hear
	"Rain, Rain"
	CSP: A
	- **Ss** sing song and keep the beat.
	- **Ss** sing song with rhythm syllables and pat the beat.
	- **Ss** sing with solfège syllables and hand signs.
	- **T** reviews the rule of placement and **Ss** read "Rain, Rain" from the staff on a number of staff placements.
	- **T** transforms the melody into other related patterns. **Ss** read with solfège syllables and hand signs:
	  o "Tortillitas" (phrase 1)
	  o "Doggie, Doggie" (phrase 1)
	  o "Cobbler, Cobbler" (phrases 1 and 2)
	- **Ss** may create patterns from other known songs. For example, transform the rhythm of "Rain, Rain" into " Snail, Snail" and then into "Apple Tree."

SUMMARY ACTIVITIES	
Review lesson outcomes Review the new song	"Pease Porridge Hot"

Unit 4: Teaching Quarter Note Rest

Lessons for Teaching Quarter Note Rest

Sections 1 and 2, Unit 4, Quarter Rest (revised)
Prepare: quarter rest
Focus song: "Hot Cross Buns"
Practice: *so-mi*

SONG REPERTOIRE							
	Known Songs	Songs for Tuneful Singing	Songs to Review Known Rhythmic Elements	Songs to Prepare Next Concepts: *la*	Songs to Prepare Concept: ᙅ	Creative Movement	Songs to Practice Known Elements *so-mi*
Lesson 1	"Pease Porridge Hot"	"Bow Wow Wow"	"Doggie, Doggie," "Rain, Rain," "Cobbler, Cobbler," "Seesaw"	"Nanny Goat"	"Hot Cross Buns"	"Lucy Locket"	"Snail, Snail," "Doggie, Doggie," "Rain, Rain," "Seesaw," "Ducks and Geese"

	Known Songs	Songs for Tuneful Singing	Songs to Review Known Elements: so-mi	Song to Prepare Next Concepts: la	Songs to Present Concept: ?	Creative Movement	Songs to Present Concept: ?
Lesson 2	"Rain, Rain"; "Nanny Goat"	"All Around the Buttercup"	"Doggie, Doggie," "Snail, Snail"	"A Tisket, a Tasket"	"Hot Cross Buns"	"Cut the Cake" (Clap Your Hands Together)	"Snail, Snail"
Lesson 3	"Bounce High, Bounce Low," "A Tisket, a Tasket"	"Bow Wow Wow"	"Doggie, Doggie"	"Hush, Baby, Hush"	"Hot Cross Buns"	"Lucy Locket"	"Snail, Snail"
Lesson 4	"Rain, Rain," "We Are Dancing in the Forest"	"All Around the Buttercup"	"Snail, Snail"	"Fudge Fudge"	"Hot Cross Buns"	"Cut the Cake" (Clap Your Hands Together)	"Bow Wow Wow," "All Around the Buttercup," "Pease Porridge Hot," "Naughty Kitty Cat," "Down Came a Lady," "Cut the Cake"
Lesson 5	"We Are Dancing in the Forest"	"Tortillitas"	"Down Came a Lady"	"La Vieja Inez"	"Hot Cross Buns"	"Lucy Locket"	"Bow Wow Wow," "Hot Cross Buns," "Naughty Kitty Cat," "All Around the Buttercup"

Here is a chart of the primary musical skills that are developed in the five lessons associated with teaching the concept of *a beat with no sound*. Remember, in the first three lessons, students *practice* the previous musical element, in this case *so-mi*.

	Lesson 1	**Lesson 2**	**Lesson 3**	**Lesson 4**	**Lesson 5**
Reading	Ss read "Snail, Snail" and other duple meter songs, reading from traditional rhythm notation with solfège and then staff notation.				Ss read "Hot Cross Buns" from traditional rhythm notation.
Writing		Ss write "Snail, Snail" and other duple meter songs, writing in traditional rhythm notation with solfège and then staff notation and indicate duple meter.			Ss write "Hot Cross Buns" using traditional rhythm notation.
Improvisation			T sings a question phrase written on the board with solfège syllables and hand signs; Ss sing an answer phrase written on the board using hand signs and solfège syllables.		

Movement	"Lucy Locket"	"Cut the Cake" (Clap Your Hands Together)	"Lucy Locket"	"Cut the Cake" (Clap Your Hands Together)	"Lucy Locket"
Listening	"Allegro," from *Toy Symphony*, by Joseph Haydn (1732–1809)				

Grade 1, Unit 4, Quarter Note Rest, Lesson 1

Outcome	Prepare: internalize quarter rest through kinesthetic activities Practice: reading *so-mi*
INTRODUCTORY ACTIVITIES	
Warm-up	• Body warm-up • Beat activity "In the Hall of the Mountain King," from *Peer Gynt*, by Edvard Grieg (1843–1907) • Breathing: **Ss** practice blowing up a balloon and watch how air is released when deflating the balloon. • Resonance: explore a cow sound using low and high voices. Make sure **Ss** are inhaling and exhaling correctly with the support muscles. • Posture: remind **Ss** of the correct posture for singing.
Sing known songs	"Pease Porridge Hot" CSP: A • **T** and **Ss** sing the song. • **Ss** perform steady beat motions to reflect the form of the song. (AABC)
Develop tuneful singing Tone production Diction Expression	"Bow Wow Wow" CSP: D • **Ss** sing the song with motions from the previous song. • **Ss** hum the song or a selected phrase. • **Ss** sing the song or a selected phrase on [z].

Review known songs and rhythmic elements	"Doggie, Doggie"
	 CSP: A
	 • **Ss** sing and keep the beat.
	 • **Ss** sing the first and second phrases with rhythm syllables and tap the beat.
	 • **T** sings known songs and **Ss** echo with rhythm syllables and tapping the beat:
	   o "Rain, Rain"
	   o "Cobbler, Cobbler"
	   o "Seesaw"

CORE ACTIVITIES	
Teach a new song	"Nanny Goat" (or "Naughty Kitty Cat") CSP: A • **T** sings song on "loo" to relate it to the previous song. • **T** sings the song with text. • **T** sings the song while demonstrating the game. • **Ss** sing and play.

Develop knowledge of music concepts
 Internalize music through kinesthetic activities
	"Hot Cross Buns"
	 CSP: A
	 • **Ss** sing the song.
	 • **Ss** sing the song on "loo" and keep the beat.
	 • **T** demonstrates how to clap rhythm. ("Put the beat with no sound on your shoulders." (**Ss** copy **T**'s motions; **T** does not tell them about the rest at this time.)
	 • **Ss** sing the song and point to a representation of the rhythm.
	 • **T**: "For the heartbeats with no lines (or buns, circles, etc.), tap the beat on your shoulders."
	
	     ― ― ― ―
	     ♥ ♥ ♥ ♥
	     ― ― ―
	     ♥ ♥ ♥ ♥
	     ― ― ― ― ― ― ― ―
	     ♥ ♥ ♥ ♥
	     ― ― ―
	     ♥ ♥ ♥ ♥

Creative movement	"Lucy Locket" CSP: A • **Ss** sing the song and play the game. • **Ss** create a rhythmic accompaniment with known elements using unpitched percussion instruments.
Practice and performance of music skills Reading	"Snail, Snail" CSP: A • **Ss** sing the song. • **Ss** sing first phrase with solfège syllables and hand signs. • **Ss** read the target phrase from standard rhythmic notation and solfège with inner hearing. • **Ss** read the target phrase from standard rhythmic notation and solfège.

	- **T** reviews rule of placement on hand staff.
	- **T** places target phrase on hand staff.
	- **Ss** read the target phrase from staff notation.
	- **T** transforms the phrase into related song material:
	  ○ "Rain, Rain" and "Seesaw"
	  ○ "Doggie, Doggie" and "Cobbler, Cobbler" and "Ducks and Geese"

SUMMARY ACTIVITIES	
Review lesson outcomes Review the new song	"Nanny Goat"

Grade 1, Unit 4, Quarter Note Rest, Lesson 2

Outcome	Prepare: analyze repertoire that contains a beat with no sound Practice: writing music with *so-mi*
INTRODUCTORY ACTIVITIES	
Warm-up	- Body warm-up - Beat activity *William Tell Overture,* Gioachino Rossini (1792–1868) - Breathing: **Ss** practice blowing up a balloon and watch how air is released when deflating the balloon. - Resonance: explore a cow sound using low and high voices. Make sure **Ss** are inhaling and exhaling correctly with the support muscles. - Posture: remind **Ss** of the correct posture for singing.

Sing known songs	"Rain, Rain"
	CSP: A
	- **Ss** sing the song with an ostinato:
	  $\frac{2}{4}$ ♫ ♫ | ♩ ♩ :|
	"Nanny Goat"
	CSP: A
	- **Ss** sing the song.
	- Add an ostinato using either body percussion or instruments:
	  ($\frac{2}{4}$ ♩ ♩ | ♩ ♩ :|).

Develop tuneful singing Tone production Diction Expression	"All Around the Buttercup" CSP: F-sharp - **Ss** hum the song. - **Ss** "sing" the song on a hiss. - **Ss** sing the song on a unified pure vowel ("nee," "neh," "nah," "noh" or "noo").

Review known songs and rhythm elements	"Doggie, Doggie" and "Snail, Snail"
	CSP: A
	• **Ss** read from the board and identify each song.
	• **Ss** sing each song and pat the beat.
	• **Ss** sing with rhythm syllables and tap the beat.
	• **T** sings known songs and **Ss** echo with rhythm syllables and tapping the beat:
	  o "Rain, Rain"
	  o "Cobbler, Cobbler"
	  o "Seesaw"

CORE ACTIVITIES	
Teach a new song	"A Tisket, a Tasket" CSP: A • **T** sings the song. • **T** sings again and asks **Ss** to figure out how to play the game on the basis of the lyrics of the song. • **T** and **Ss** sing and play the game. • **T** may transfer the accompaniment to instruments. • **Ss** continue their accompaniment into the next song.
Develop knowledge of music concepts Describe what you hear	"Hot Cross Buns" CSP: A • **Ss** sing the song. • Review kinesthetic awareness activities. • **T** and **Ss** sing first phrase of song on "loo" while performing the beat before asking each question. • **T**: "Andy, how many beats did we tap?" (four) • **T**: "Andy, which beat has no sound?" (the last one, beat 4) • **T**: "Andy, if beat 4 has no sound, how many sounds are on each of the other beats?" (one) • **Ss** sing the song and put the rest on their shoulders.
Creative Movement	"Cut the Cake" CSP: A • Note: this will be a new song. • **T** sings while demonstrating the game. • After two or three cycles, **Ss** join the singing and **T** drops out.
Practice and performance of music skills Writing	"Snail, Snail" CSP: A • **Ss** sing the song and pat the beat. • **Ss** sing with rhythm syllables and pat the beat. • **Ss** sing first phrase with solfège syllables and hand signs. • One **S** writes solfège syllables under the rhythmic notation on the board. • **T** reviews rules of placement. • **Ss** fill in the blanks on the staff for "Snail, Snail" on their worksheets. • **T** explains rules for adding stems to note heads.

SUMMARY ACTIVITIES	
Review the new song Review lesson outcomes	"A Tisket, a Tasket" CSP: A

Grade 1, Unit 4, Quarter Note Rest, Lesson 3

Outcome	Prepare: create a visual representation of a quarter rest Practice: improvise a melody using *so* and *mi*
INTRODUCTORY ACTIVITIES	
Warm-up	• Body warm-up • Beat activity "In the Hall of the Mountain King," from *Peer Gynt*, by Edvard Grieg (1843–1907). • Breathing: **Ss** practice blowing up a balloon and watch how air is released when deflating the balloon. • Resonance: explore a cow sound using low and high voices. Make sure **Ss** are inhaling and exhaling correctly with the support muscles. • Posture: remind **Ss** of the correct posture for singing.
Sing known songs	"Bounce High, Bounce Low" CSP: A • **Ss** sing the song with an ostinato: $\frac{2}{4}$ ♫ ♩ | ♫ ♩ :| "A Tisket, a Tasket" CSP: A • **Ss** sing the song. • Add a simple ostinato: ($\frac{2}{4}$ ♫ ♩ | ♫ ♩ :|)
Develop tuneful singing Tone production Diction Expression	"Bow Wow Wow" CSP: D • **Ss** sing the song. • **T** directs **Ss** to sing the song with various musical elements (staccato or legato, crescendo or decrescendo, etc.).
Review Known Songs and Rhythm Elements	"Doggie, Doggie" CSP: A • **Ss** sing song and pat the beat. • **Ss** sing the song with rhythm syllables and pat the bat. • **T** sings phrases from "Doggie, Doggie" and **Ss** echo-sing with rhythm syllables while patting the beat. • **T** sings known songs and **Ss** echo with rhythm syllables and tapping the beat: o "Rain, Rain" o "Cobbler, Cobbler" o "Seesaw" o "We Are Dancing in the Forest"

\	CORE ACTIVITIES
Teach a new song	"Hush, Baby, Hush" CSP: A • **T** sings the song on "loo" while **Ss** pat the beat. • **T** sings again while **Ss** show the phrases and identify the song. • **Ss** identify the number of phrases. (four) • **Ss** sing the whole song with **T**.
| **Develop knowledge of music concepts**<br>Create a visual representation of what you hear | "Hot Cross Buns"<br>CSP: A<br>• Review kinesthetic and aural awareness activities.<br>• **T** hums first phrase of "Hot Cross Buns."<br>• **Ss** create a visual representation for the rhythm of phrase 1 of "Hot Cross Buns" on top of the heart beats on their worksheet. ("Draw the number of sounds you hear on each heart beat.")<br>Example:<br><br>```
___  ___  ___  ___
 ♥    ♥    ♥    ♥
___  ___  ___  ___
 ♥    ♥    ♥    ♥
___  ___  ___  ___
 ♥    ♥    ♥    ♥
___  ___  ___  ___
 ♥    ♥    ♥    ♥
```<br><br>• Have **Ss** share their visuals with their neighbor. Invite one **S** to share their visual with the class.<br>• **Ss** sing "Hot Cross Buns" on "loo" and point to the representation. |
| **Creative movement** | "Lucy Locket"
CSP: A
• **Ss** sing and play the game.
• **T** selects one **S** to play the beat on a hand drum or tambourine and another to play the rhythm on rhythm sticks. |
| **Practice and performance of music skills**
Improvisation | "Snail, Snail"
CSP: A
• **Ss** sing song with words.
• **Ss** sing with solfège syllables and hand signs.
• **Ss** read phrase 1 of "Snail, Snail" from staff notation.
• **T** changes the fourth pitch to make the phrase end on *so*.
• **T**: "That sounds a lot like a musical question. You ask me the musical question, and I'll tell you a musical answer. . . ."
• **Ss** sing the question phrase; **T** responds with a *so-mi* motive from known song material. **T** reveals the answer on the board written in staff notation with stems.
• **T** and **Ss** switch.
• **T** repeats the process with two additional "answers."
• **T** sings the question phrase and chooses one **S** to respond with an answer phrase. |
```

SUMMARY ACTIVITIES	
Review lesson outcomes	"We Are Dancing in the Forest"
Review the new song	CSP: A

Grade 1, Unit 4, Quarter Note Rest, Lesson 4

Outcome	Present: label the quarter rest
INTRODUCTORY ACTIVITIES	
Warm-up	• Body warm-up • Beat activity *William Tell Overture,* Gioachino Rossini (1792–1868) • **Breathing: Ss** practice blowing up a balloon and watch how air is released when deflating the balloon. • **Resonance:** explore a cow sound using low and high voices. Make sure **Ss** are inhaling and exhaling correctly with the support muscles. • **Posture:** remind **Ss** of the correct posture for singing.
Sing known songs	"Rain, Rain" CSP: A • **Ss** sing the song with a simple ostinato: $\frac{2}{4}$ ♫ ♫ | ♩ ♩ :| "We Are Dancing in the Forest" or "Hush, Baby, Hush." CSP: A • **Ss** sing song and pat the beat. • **Ss** sing song in canon with **T**.
Develop tuneful singing Tone production Diction Expression	"All Around the Buttercup" CSP: F-sharp • **Ss** sing song and pat the beat. • **Ss** sing the song on a staccato "doo." • **Ss** sing the song on a legato "loo." • Practice crescendo and/or diminuendo.

Review known songs and rhythm elements	"Snail, Snail"
	CSP: A
	• **Ss** sing song and pat the beat.
	• **Ss** sing each phrase with rhythm syllables and pat the beat.
	• **T** sings known songs and **Ss** echo with rhythm syllables and tapping the beat:
	  o "Rain, Rain"
	  o "Cobbler, Cobbler"
	  o "Seesaw"
	  o "We Are Dancing in the Forest"

CORE ACTIVITIES	
Teach a new song	"Fudge Fudge" CSP: A • **T** sings the song while **Ss** pat the beat. • **Ss** practice singing and jumping to the beat. • **Ss** sing and play the game.
Presentation of music concepts Describe what you hear with rhythm syllables	"Hot Cross Buns" CSP: A • **Ss** sing and walk the beat. • Review kinesthetic, aural, and visual awareness activities. • **T**: "When we have a beat with no sound on it, we call it a *rest*." • **T** immediately sings the song with rhythm syllables, touching finger to lips every time there is a rest in the music. **Ss** copy.
Creative movement	"Clap Your Hands Together" CSP: A • **Ss** sing the song. • Play and sing the circle game. • **Ss** create a rhythmic accompaniment with known elements.

Presentation of music skills
 	
 Describe what you hear with rhythm syllables
	"Bow Wow Wow"
	 CSP: A
	 • **Ss** sing the song and show the rests by putting fingers to lips.
	 • **T**: "Can someone remind me what we call it when we have a beat with no sound?"
	 • **T** taps the rhythm of "Bow Wow Wow," and **Ss** identify the song and where the rests are placed.
	 • **Ss** sing the song with rhythm syllables and show the rests by touching fingers to lips.
	 • **Ss** identify and sing other known songs containing rests:
	   o "All Around the Buttercup"
	   o "Pease Porridge Hot"
	   o "Naughty Kitty Cat"
	   o "Down Came a Lady"
	   o "Cut the Cake"

SUMMARY ACTIVITIES	
Review lesson outcomes Review the new song	"Fudge Fudge" CSP: A

Grade 1, Unit 4, Quarter Note Rest, Lesson 5

Outcome	Present: notate the quarter rest
INTRODUCTORY ACTIVITIES	
Warm-up	• Body warm-up • Beat activity

	"In the Hall of the Mountain King," from *Peer Gynt*, by Edvard Grieg (1843–1907).
	• Breathing: **Ss** practice blowing up a balloon and watch how air is released when deflating the balloon.
	• Resonance: explore a cow sound using low and high voices. Make sure **Ss** are inhaling and exhaling correctly with the support muscles.
	• Posture: remind **Ss** of the correct posture for singing.
Sing known songs	"We Are Dancing in the Forest"
	CSP: A
	• **Ss** sing the song and briefly play the game.
	"Fudge Fudge"
	CSP: A
	• **Ss** sing song with motions.
Develop tuneful singing Tone production Diction Expression	"Tortillitas"
	CSP: A
	• **Ss** sing the song.
	• **Ss** sing song on "loo."
	• **Ss** sing the song and keep the beat.
Review known songs and rhythm elements	"Down Came a Lady"
	CSP: A
	• **Ss** sing "Down Came a Lady" and pat the beat.
	• **Ss** sing with rhythm syllables and pat the beat.
	• **T** sings individual phrases of the song and **Ss** echo-sing with rhythm syllables while keeping the beat.
CORE ACTIVITIES	
Teach a new song	"La Vieja Inez"
	CSP: B
	• **T** sings the song and **Ss** identify three rests in the song.
	• **T** writes names of colors in English and Spanish on board.
	• **T** sings song while acting out the call and response between La Vieja Inez and **Ss**.
	• **T** introduces the color guessing game.
	• **T** and **Ss** sing the song and play the game.
	• **S** play the game, singing the responses.
Presentation of music concepts Notate what you hear	"Hot Cross Buns"
	CSP: A
	• Review awareness activities and aural presentation.
	• **T**: "Our first phrase of 'Hot Cross Buns' looks like this." **T** shows the traditional rhythmic notation for quarter notes and quarter rests.
	• Point to notation and sing first phrase of "Hot Cross Buns."
	• **T**: "We represent a *rest* on a beat with traditional notation. Point to the *rest*. This is what it looks like when we read *rest*."
	• **T**: "We represent a *rest* in stick notation with a z when we are writing."
	• "Let's sing 'Hot Cross Buns' with rhythm syllables and pat the beat."

Creative movement	"Lucy Locket" CSP: A • **Ss** sing the song. • Play and sing the circle game. • **Ss** create a rhythmic accompaniment with known elements.

Presentation of music concepts
Notate what you hear
	"Bow Wow Wow"
	CSP: D
	• **Ss** sings the song and pat the beat.
	• **Ss** sing with rhythm syllables and pat the beat.
	• **T** writes the rhythm on the board; **Ss** clap the rhythm, sing the song with rhythm syllables, and pat the beat.
	• **T** transforms the rhythm into other related song material:
	  o "Pease Porridge Hot"
	  o "Naughty Kitty Cat"
	  o "All Around the Buttercup"
	  o "Cut the Cake"

SUMMARY ACTIVITIES	
Review lesson outcomes Review the new song	"La Vieja Inez" CSP: B

Unit 5: Teaching a Three-Note Child's Chant *la*

Lessons for Teaching *la*

Sections 1 and 2, Unit 5, *la*
Prepare: *la*
Practice: quarter rest
Focus song: "Bounce High, Bounce Low"

Song Repertoire							
	Known Songs	Songs for Tuneful Singing	Songs to Review Known Melodic Elements	Songs to Prepare Next Concept: 2/4 Meter	Songs to Prepare Concept: *la*	Creative Movement	Songs to Practice Known Concepts: ♩
Lesson 1	"Tortillitas," "La Vieja Inez"	"Lucy Locket"	"Rain, Rain"	"Apple Tree"	"Bounce High, Bounce Low"	"We Are Dancing in the Forest"	"Hot Cross Buns"
Lesson 2	"Witch, Witch," "Apple Tree"	"Bobby Shafto"	"Snail, Snail"	"El Perrito Goloso"	"Bounce High, Bounce Low"	"Cut the Cake" (Clap Your Hands Together)	"Hot Cross Buns"

Unit Plans and Lesson Plans

Lesson 3	"Cobbler, Cobbler," "El Perrito Goloso"	"Doggie, Doggie"	"Snail, Snail"	"Naughty Kitty Cat"	"Bounce High, Bounce Low"	"No Robbers Out Today"	"Hot Cross Buns," "Naughty Kitty Cat," "Pease Porridge Hot"
	Known Songs	Songs for Tuneful Singing	Songs to Review Known Elements: ⸰	Songs to Prepare Next Concept: 2/4 Meter	Songs to Present Concept: *la*	Creative Movement	Songs to Present Concept: *la*
Lesson 4	"Snail, Snail," "Naughty Kitty Cat"	"Bobby Shafto"	"Seesaw"	"Just from the Kitchen"	"Bounce High, Bounce Low"	"We Are Dancing in the Forest"	"Lucy Locket," "Snail Snail," "We Are Dancing in the Forest"
Lesson 5	"Doggie, Doggie," "Just from the Kitchen"	"Snail, Snail"	"Seesaw"	"A la Ronda, Ronda"	"Bounce High, Bounce Low"	"Lucy Locket"	"Bobby Shafto," "Lucy Locket," "Snail Snail," "We Are Dancing in the Forest"

Here is a chart of the primary musical skills that are developed in the five lessons associated with teaching the concept of *la*. Remember, in the first three lessons students *practice* the previous musical element, in this case *a beat with no sound*.

	Lesson 1	Lesson 2	Lesson 3	Lesson 4	Lesson 5
Reading	**Ss** read "Hot Cross Buns" and other duple meter songs with rests, reading from traditional rhythm notation.				**Ss** read "Bounce High, Bounce Low" with hand signs from steps, traditional notation with solfège, and then staff notation.

Writing		Ss write "Hot Cross Buns" and other duple meter songs with rests using traditional rhythm notation.			Ss write "Bounce High, Bounce Low" in rhythmic notation with solfège syllables and staff notation.
Improvisation			T sings a question phrase written on the board; one S sings an answer phrase written on the board using rhythm syllables.		
Movement	"We Are Dancing in the Forest"	"Cut the Cake" (Clap Your Hands Together)	"No Robbers Out Today"	"We Are Dancing in the Forest"	"Lucy Locket"
Listening	"In the Hall of the Mountain King," from *Peer Gynt*, by Edvard Grieg (1843–1907)				

Grade 1, Unit 5, *la*, Lesson 1

Outcome	Preparation: internalizing a pitch a step higher than *so* through kinesthetic activities
	Practice: reading rhythmic patterns that contain rests
INTRODUCTORY ACTIVITIES	
Warm-up	• Body warm-up • Beat activity

	"Fossils," from *Carnival of the Animals*, by Camille Saint-Saëns (1835–1921)
	• Breathing: **Ss** practice blowing up a balloon and watch how air is released when deflating the balloon.
	• Resonance: explore a cow sound using low and high voices. Make sure **Ss** are inhaling and exhaling correctly with the support muscles.
	• Posture: remind **Ss** of the correct posture for singing.
Sing known songs	"Tortillitas" CSP: A • **Ss** sing the song and keep the beat by pretending to make tortillas. "La Vieja Inez" CSP: B • **Ss** sing the song. • **T** adds a simple ostinato in the B section ("rojo, negro, verde, azul...") of the song: $\frac{2}{4}$ ♫ ♩ | ♫ ♩ :|
Develop tuneful singing Tone production Diction Expression	"Lucy Locket" CSP: A • **Ss** sing song with text. • **Ss** sing song with "koo" sound for each syllable. • **Ss** sing and inner-hear beat 4 of each phrase. • **Ss** sing and inner-hear beats 3 and 4 of each phrase. • **Ss** sing with text and show the phrase.

Review known songs and melodic elements	"Rain, Rain"
	 CSP: A
	 • **Ss** sing song.
	 • **Ss** sing the first phrase of "Rain, Rain" with solfège syllables and hand signs.
	 • **T** sings the first phrase of "Rain, Rain" on "loo"; **Ss** echo the phrase singing with solfège syllables and hand signs.
	 • **T** sings phrases of these songs, and **Ss** echo with solfège syllables and hand signs:
	  o "Doggie, Doggie" (phrase 1)
	  o "Snail, Snail" (phrase 1)
	  o "Seesaw" (phrase 1)
	  o "Ducks and Geese" (phrase 1)
	  o "Tortillitas" (phrase 1)

CORE ACTIVITIES	
Teach a new song	"Apple Tree" CSP: A • **Ss** move into a circle while **T** sings the song. • **Ss** pat the beat while listening. • **Ss** show the phrases while listening, and identify the number of phrases.

	• **Ss** create new beat motions for each repetition of the song. • **Ss** sing and play the game. • **Ss** sing "Apple Tree" while **T** sings "Bounce High, Bounce Low" as a partner song.
Develop knowledge of music concepts Internalize music through kinesthetic activities	"Bounce High, Bounce Low" CSP: A • **Ss** sing the song. • **Ss** sing the song on "loo" while **T** points to a representation of the melodic contour on the board. [melodic contour dot diagram] • **Ss** point to the representation from their seat while singing. • One **S** comes to the board to tap the representation; **S** points to the representation while singing with rhythm syllables. • **Ss** clap the contour of the song, mirroring **T**. • **Ss** clap the contour of the song, mirroring with a partner. • **Ss** clap the contour of the song with their eyes closed. • **Ss** clap the last four beats of the song as a rhythmic ostinato into the next song.
Creative movement	"We Are Dancing in the Forest" CSP: A • **Ss** use rhythmic or melodic elements to create an accompaniment.
Practice and performance of music skills Reading	"Hot Cross Buns" CSP: F-sharp • **Ss** sing song and pat the beat. • **Ss** sing song with rhythm syllables and pat the beat. • **Ss** read the rhythm of "Hot Cross Buns" from the board with rhythm syllables using inner hearing. • **Ss** read the rhythm of "Hot Cross Buns" from the board with rhythm syllables. • **T** gradually changes the rhythm of phrases 2 and 3; **Ss** identify and make the necessary changes to turn "Hot Cross Buns" into "Bow Wow Wow." • **T** uses same process; **Ss** identify and make the necessary changes to turn "Bow Wow Wow" into "All Around the Buttercup." • **T** changes the rhythm of "All Around the Buttercup" into the rhythm of "In the Hall of the Mountain King," movement 4 from *Peer Gynt Suite* No. 1, Op. 46, by Edvard Grieg: ♫♫ | ♫ ♩ ♫ ♩ | ♫ ♩ ♫♫ | ♫♫ ♫♫ | ♩ 𝄽 • **Ss** identify the rhythm on the board while listening to the musical example.

SUMMARY ACTIVITIES	
Review lesson objectives	"Apple Tree"
	CSP: A
Review new song	

Grade 1, Unit 5, *la*, Lesson 2

Outcome	Preparation: analyzing repertoire that contains a pitch a step higher than *so*
	Practice: writing musical patterns that contain a rest
INTRODUCTORY ACTIVITIES	
Warm-up	• Body warm-up
	• Beat activity
	"Fossils," from *Carnival of the Animals,* by Camille Saint-Saëns (1835–1921)
	• Breathing: **Ss** practice blowing up a balloon and watch how air is released when deflating the balloon.
	• Resonance: explore a cow sound using low and high voices. Make sure **Ss** are inhaling and exhaling correctly with the support muscles.
	• Posture: remind **Ss** of the correct posture for singing.
Sing known songs	"Witch, Witch"
	CSP: A
	• **Ss** sing the song and may briefly play the game.
	"Apple Tree"
	CSP: A
	• **Ss** sing the song.
	• **Ss** add a simple ostinato:
	2/4 ♫ ♫ | ♩ ♩ :‖
Develop tuneful singing	"Bobby Shafto"
	CSP: A
Tone production	• **Ss** sing the song.
Diction	• **T** tosses a ball from one **S** to another, and **Ss** have to follow the movement of the ball with their voices, using different vowel sounds.
Expression	• **Ss** sing the song and show phrase.
	• **Ss** sing the song and inner-hear beat 2 while showing phrase.
	• **Ss** sing beats 1 and 3; **T** sings 2 and 4. (Show phrase.) Switch.
Review known songs and melodic elements	"Snail, Snail"
	CSP: A
	• **Ss** sing the song and pat the beat.
	• **Ss** sing phrase 1 with solfège syllables and hand signs.
	• **T** sings phrases of these songs, as **Ss** echo with solfège syllables and hand signs:
	o "Doggie, Doggie" (phrase 1)
	o "Rain, Rain" (phrase 1)
	o "Seesaw" (phrase 1)
	o "Ducks and Geese" (phrase 1)
	o "Tortillitas" (phrase 1)

CORE ACTIVITIES	
Teach a new song	"El Perrito Goloso" CSP: A • **T** speaks the dialogue and translates. • **T** sings the response, and **Ss** echo. • **T** speaks the dialogue, and **Ss** sing the response. • **Ss** continue the response while moving into a line. • **T** briefly explains the rules of the game. • **T** and **Ss** sing and play. • **Ss** sing the response while **T** sings the next song.
Develop knowledge of music concepts Describe what you hear	"Bounce High, Bounce Low" CSP: A • Review kinesthetic awareness activities. • **T** and **Ss** sing the first phrase of "Bounce High, Bounce Low" on "loo" and tap the beat. • **T**: "Andy, how many beats did we tap?" (four) • **T**: "Andy, what solfège syllables do we use for beats 3 and 4?" (*so-mi*) • **T**: "Andy, which beat had the highest pitch?" (beat 2) • **T**: "Andy, which hand sign do our songs begin with?" (*so*) • **T**: "Let's sing the first phrase of 'Bounce High, Bounce Low' using our hand signs and solfège syllables and say 'high' for beat 2." (*so high so mi*) • **T** sings the words; **Ss** echo with solfège syllables singing "high" for beat 2. (**T** "Bounce High, Bounce Low"; **S** "*so high so mi*") • **T** sings words while six to eight **Ss** echo individually using hand signs.
Creative movement	"Clap Your Hands Together" CSP: A • **T** and **Ss** sing and play the game. • **Ss** sing with rhythm syllables and play the game. • **Ss** create an accompaniment by choosing a phrase from the song to play on rhythm instruments or a xylophone. • **Ss** continue their accompaniment into the next song.
Practice and performance of music skills Writing	"Hot Cross Buns" CSP: F-sharp • **Ss** sing and pat the beat. • **Ss** sing "Hot Cross Buns" with rhythm syllables. • **Ss** read the song from the board: ♩ ♩ | ♩ 𝄽 ♩ ♩ | ♩ 𝄽 ♫ ♫ | ♫ ♫ ♩ ♩ | ♩ 𝄽 • **T** erases the second measure of each phrase: ♩ ♩ | | ♩ ♩ | | ♫ ♫ | | ♩ ♩ | | • **Ss** fill in the blank beats on their worksheets.

	SUMMARY ACTIVITIES
Review the new song Review lesson outcomes	"El Perrito Goloso" CSP: A

Grade 1, Unit 5, *la*, Lesson 3

Outcome	Preparation: creating a visual representation of a pitch a step above *so* Practice: improvise a four-beat rhythm including quarter notes, eighth notes, and quarter rests
	INTRODUCTORY ACTIVITIES
Warm-up	• Body warm-up • Beat activity "Fossils," from *Carnival of the Animals*, by Camille Saint-Saëns (1835–1921) • Breathing: **Ss** practice blowing up a balloon and watch how air is released when deflating the balloon. • Resonance: explore a cow sound using low and high voices. Make sure **Ss** are inhaling and exhaling correctly with the support muscles. • Posture: remind **Ss** of the correct posture for singing.
Sing known songs	"Cobbler, Cobbler" CSP: A • **Ss** sing the song and step the beat. "El Perrito Goloso" CSP: A • **Ss** sing the song while keeping the beat.
Develop tuneful singing Tone production Diction Expression	"Doggie, Doggie" CSP: A • **Ss** sing the song and clap the rhythm. • **Ss** sing and explore the upper and lower ranges of the voice by singing like dogs of various types (large and small). • **Ss** may "bark" the melody of the song.

Review known songs and melodic elements	"Snail, Snail"
	 CSP: A
	 • **Ss** sing song and pat the beat.
	 • **Ss** sing song with solfège syllables and hand signs.
	 • **T** sings phrases of these songs, and **Ss** echo with solfège syllables and hand signs:
	   o "Doggie, Doggie" (phrase 1)
	   o "Rain, Rain" (phrase 1)
	   o "Seesaw" (phrase 1)
	   o "Ducks and Geese" (phrase 1)
	   o "Tortillitas" (phrase 1)
	   o "Cobbler, Cobbler" (phrases 1 and 2)

CORE ACTIVITIES	
Teach a new song	"Naughty Kitty Cat" (this is a known song, but singing it here gives the **T** an opportunity to work on **Ss**' intonation) CSP: A • **T** sings the song while **Ss** continue the ostinato. • **Ss** listen and show the phrases of the song in the air. • **Ss** sing the first two phrases. • **T** and **Ss** sing and play the game.
Develop knowledge of music concepts Create a visual representation of what you hear	"Bounce High, Bounce Low" CSP: A • **Ss** sing the song. • Review kinesthetic and aural activities. • **T** sings the target phrase on "loo" and asks the class to create a visual representation of the target phrase. **Ss** may use manipulatives. • **T**: "Pick up Unifix cubes and recreate what you heard." **Ss** share their representations with each other. • **T** invites one **S** to the board to share a representation with the class. If necessary, corrections to the representation can be made by reviewing the aural awareness questions. • **Ss** sing the first phrase of "Bounce High, Bounce Low" on "loo" and point to the representation. • **Ss** sing with rhythm syllables and pat the beat.
Creative movement	"No Robbers Out Today" CSP: A • *Note: this will be a new song.* • **T** sings the song and demonstrates the game. • **Ss** play the game while **T** sings. • After two or three cycles, **Ss** sing and play game. • **Ss** sing and march the beat.
Practice and performance of music skills Improvisation	"Hot Cross Buns" CSP: F-sharp • **Ss** sing the song and pat the beat. • **Ss** read the target phrase from the board: ♩ ♩ |♩ ≹ • **T** labels this as a "question" phrase. • **Ss** clap the question phrase and **T** claps a four-beat response. Perform several times. • **T** presents the "answer" phrase on the board: ♫ ♫ |♩ ≹ ("Naughty Kitty Cat," phrase 1) • **T** asks the question; **Ss** perform the answer. • Repeat with a second option. ♩ ♫ |♩ ≹ ("Pease Porridge Hot," phrase 2) • **T** reveals more answer choices. • Perform a call-and-response game with **T** performing questions and individual **Ss** choosing an answer.

SUMMARY ACTIVITIES	
Review lesson outcomes Review the new song	"No Robbers Out Today" CSP: A

Grade 1, Unit 5, *la*, Lesson 4

Outcome	Presentation: label the sound of a pitch a step above *so* as *la*
INTRODUCTORY ACTIVITIES	
Warm-up	• Body warm-up • Beat activity "Fossils," from *Carnival of the Animals*, by Camille Saint-Saëns (1835–1921) • Breathing: **Ss** practice blowing up a balloon and watch how air is released when deflating the balloon. • Resonance: explore a cow sound using low and high voices. Make sure **Ss** are inhaling and exhaling correctly with the support muscles. • Posture: remind **Ss** of the correct posture for singing.
Sing known songs	"Snail, Snail" CSP: A • **Ss** sing the song with an ostinato. "Naughty Kitty Cat" CSP: A • **Ss** sing the song. • **T** adds a simple rhythmic ostinato and **Ss** sing the song.
Developing tuneful singing Tone production Diction Expression	"Bobby Shafto" CSP: A • **Ss** sing song and keep the beat. • **Ss** sing text, then the song using the syllable "koo," and then "no" and other vowel sounds.

Review known songs and melodic elements	"Seesaw"
	CSP: A
	• **Ss** sing song.
	• **Ss** sing phrase 1 with solfège syllables and hand signs.
	• **T** sings phrases of these songs, as **Ss** echo with solfège syllables and hand signs:
	  o "Doggie, Doggie" (phrase 1)
	  o "Snail, Snail" (phrases 1 and 2)
	  o "Rain, Rain" (phrase 1)
	  o "Tortillitas" (phrase 1)

CORE ACTIVITIES	
Teaching a new song	"Just from the Kitchen" CSP: E • **T** sings the song while **Ss** continue the ostinato. • On the second listening, **Ss** sing the responses ("shoo-li-loo"). • **T** and **Ss** sing and play the game, clapping on beats 2 and 4.
Presentation of music concepts Describe what you hear with solfège syllables	"Bounce High, Bounce Low" CSP: A • **Ss** sing the song. • Review kinesthetic, aural, and visual awareness activities. • **T**: "When we have a sound that is a step higher than *so*, we call it *la*." • **T** shows the hand sign. • **T** sings "*so la so mi*" (phrase 1 of "Bounce High, Bounce Low") to individual **Ss** who echo with solfège and hand signs. • **T** sings phrase 1 of the song with text, and **Ss** echo using solfège syllables and hand signs. • Repeat with at least six to eight **Ss**.
Creative movement	"We Are Dancing in the Forest" CSP: A • **Ss** create accompaniment with rhythmic or melodic elements. • **Ss** sing and play the game.

Presentation of music concepts
 	
Describe what you hear with rhythm or solfège syllables
	"Lucy Locket"
	CSP: A
	• **Ss** sing the song.
	• **T**: "When we have a sound that is a step higher than *so*, we call it *la*."
	• **Ss** sing the song with solfège syllables and hand signs.
	• **T** labels the sound *la* in related patterns:
	  o "Snail, Snail" (entire song)
	  o "Cobbler, Cobbler" (phrases 1 and 2)
	  o "We Are Dancing in the Forest" (entire song)

SUMMARY ACTIVITIES	
Review the new song Review lesson outcomes	"Just from the Kitchen" CSP: E

Grade 1, Unit 5, *la*, Lesson 5

Outcome	Presentation: notation techniques for *la*, a pitch higher than *so*
INTRODUCTORY ACTIVITIES	
Warm-up	• Body warm-up • Beat activity "The Aquarium," from *Carnival of the Animals*, by Camille Saint-Saëns (1835–1921) • Breathing: **Ss** practice blowing up a balloon and watch how air is released when deflating the balloon. • Resonance: explore a cow sound using low and high voices. Make sure **Ss** are inhaling and exhaling correctly with the support muscles. • Posture: remind **Ss** of the correct posture for singing.
Sing known songs	"Doggie, Doggie" CSP: A • **Ss** sing the song and step the beat. "Just from the Kitchen" CSP: D • **Ss** sing and play the game.
Develop tuneful singing Tone production Diction Expression	"Snail, Snail" CSP: A • **Ss** sing the song. • **Ss** read each phrase from **T's** hand signs. • Individual **Ss** sing the song with solfège syllables and hand signs. • **Ss** sing song on "loo."

Review known songs and melodic elements	"Seesaw"
	CSP: A
	• **Ss** sing the song.
	• **T** sings phrases of these songs, and **Ss** echo with solfège syllables and hand signs:
	  o "Doggie, Doggie" (phrase 1)
	  o "Snail, Snail" (phrases 1 and 2)
	  o "Rain, Rain" (phrases 1 and 2)
	  o "Tortillitas" (phrase 1)
	  o "Bounce High, Bounce Low" (whole song, phrase by phrase)
	  o "Lucy Locket" (whole song, phrase by phrase)
	  o "Bobby Shafto" (whole song, phrase by phrase)

CORE ACTIVITIES	
Teach a new song	"A la Ronda, Ronda" CSP: A • **T** sings and demonstrates the game. **T**: "It's a bit like 'Ring Around the Rosie.'"

| **Presentation of music concepts**<br><br>Notate what you hear | "Bounce High, Bounce Low"<br>CSP: A<br><br>• Review aural presentation.<br>• Present the position of *la* on the tone ladder.<br><br>```
 l
  s
      m
```<br><br>• **T** sings the quality of each interval and **Ss** echo (sung: "*la* and *so* are a step apart... *so* and *mi* are a skip apart...")<br>• Present standard rhythmic notation with solfège syllables. **T**: "We can write our phrase using rhythm notation and put our solfège syllables under it."<br><br>♩ ♩ \| ♩ ♩ \|<br>s  l    s  m<br><br>♫ ♫ \| ♩ ♩<br>ss ll   s  m<br><br>• Explain the rule of placement. **T**: "If *so* is in a space, then *la* is on the line above. If *so* is in a space, then *mi* is in the space below."<br>• Present the position of *la* on the staff and apply the rule of placement. Relate the position to the finger staff. |
Creative movement	"Lucy Locket" CSP: A • **Ss** sing and play the game.

Presentation of music skills
 	
Notate what you hear
	"Bobby Shafto"
	CSP: A
	• **Ss** sing song
	• **Ss** read the song from staff notation:
	  • **Ss** clap and say the rhythm syllables and keep the beat.
	  • **Ss** identify the *la-so-mi*. They sing with solfège syllables and hand signs.
	• **T** alters the rhythm of the phrases until the song becomes "Bounce High, Bounce Low."
	• **Ss** read "Bounce High, Bounce Low" from the staff with solfège syllables and hand signs.

SUMMARY ACTIVITIES	
Review lesson outcomes Review the new song	"A la Ronda, Ronda" CSP: A

Unit 6: Teaching Duple Meter

Sections 1 and 2, Unit 6, duple meter (revised)
```

Prepare: duple meter
Focus song: "Bobby Shafto"
Practice: *la*

Song Repertoire							
	Known Songs	Songs for Tuneful Singing	Songs to Review Known Rhythmic Elements	Songs to Prepare Next New Concepts: *do*	Songs to Prepare Concept: $\frac{2}{4}$ Meter	Creative Movement	Songs to Practice Known Elements *la*
Lesson 1	"A la Ronda, Ronda"	"Star Light, Star Bright"	"Bow Wow Wow"	"Closet Key"	"Bobby Shafto"	"No Robbers Out Today"	"Bounce High, Bounce Low"
Lesson 2	"Down Came a Lady," "Closet Key"	"Cobbler, Cobbler"	"Pease Porridge Hot"	"Plainsies, Clapsies"	"Bobby Shafto"	"Cut the Cake" (Clap Your Hands Together)	"Bounce High, Bounce Low"
Lesson 3	"Naughty Kitty Cat," "Plainsies Clapsies"	"Lucy Locket"	"Hot Cross Buns"	"Thread Follows the Needle"	"Bobby Shafto"	"No Robbers Out Today"	"Bounce High, Bounce Low,"
	Known Songs	Songs for Tuneful Singing	Songs to Review Known Elements	Songs to Prepare Next New Concepts: *do*	Songs to Present Concept: $\frac{2}{4}$ Meter	Creative Movement	Songs to Present Concept: $\frac{2}{4}$ Meter
Lesson 4	"Thread Follows the Needle"	"Cobbler, Cobbler"	"Hot Cross Buns"	"¡Que Llueva!"	"Bobby Shafto"	"Lemonade"	"Doggie, Doggie," "Bobby Shafto," "Bounce High, Bounce Low," "Cut the Cake," "Fudge Fudge," "Good Night, Sleep Tight," "Lucy Locket," "Nanny Goat," "Naughty Kitty Cat," "Rain, Rain," "Snail, Snail," "We Are Dancing in the Forest"

| Lesson 5 | "Pease Porridge Hot," "¡Que Llueva!" | "Lucy Locket" | "Naughty Kitty Cat" | "Rocky Mountain" | "Bobby Shafto" | "¡Que Llueva!" | "Doggie, Doggie," "Bobby Shafto," "Bounce High, Bounce Low," "Cut the Cake," "Fudge Fudge," "Good Night, Sleep Tight," "Lucy Locket," "Nanny Goat," "Naughty Kitty Cat," "Rain, Rain," "Snail, Snail," "We Are Dancing in the Forest" |

Here is a chart of the primary musical skills that are developed in the five lessons associated with teaching the concept of *duple meter*. Remember, in the first three lessons, students *practice* the previous musical element, in this case *la*.

	Lesson 1	Lesson 2	Lesson 3	Lesson 4	Lesson 5
Reading	Ss read "Bounce High, Bounce Low" and other duple meter songs, reading from traditional rhythm notation with solfège, and then staff notation.				Ss read "Bounce High, Bounce Low" written in traditional rhythm notation, and staff notation with a time signature and bar lines.

Writing		Ss write "Bounce High, Bounce Low" and other duple meter songs in traditional rhythm notation with solfège, and then staff notation.			Ss write "Bounce High, Bounce Low" in traditional rhythm notation, and staff notation with a time signature and bar lines.
Improvisation			T sings a question phrase written on the board; Ss sing an answer phrase written on the board using hand signs and solfège syllables.		
Movement	"No Robbers Out Today"	"Cut the Cake" (Clap Your Hands Together)	"No Robbers Out Today"	"Lemonade"	"¡Que Llueva!"
Listening	"Rain, Rain, Go Away," recorded by Ella Jenkins (1924–)				

Grade 1, Unit 6, Duple Meter, Lesson 1

Outcome	Preparation: internalizing duple meter through kinesthetic activities Practice: read melodies that include *la*
INTRODUCTORY ACTIVITIES	
Warm-up	• Body warm-up • Beat activity Concerto for Four Harpsichords, BWV 1065, by J. S. Bach (1685–1750) • Breathing: **Ss** practice blowing up a balloon and watch how air is released when deflating the balloon. • Resonance: explore a cow sound using low and high voices. Make sure **Ss** are inhaling and exhaling correctly with the support muscles. • Posture: remind **Ss** of the correct posture for singing.
Sing known songs	"A la Ronda, Ronda" CSP: A • **Ss** sing song. • **Ss** sing and briefly play the game. • **T** adds a simple ostinato: $\frac{2}{4}$ ♩ 𝄽 ｜ ♫ ♩ ⫶｜ • **Ss** continue the ostinato into the next song.
Develop tuneful singing Tone production Diction Expression	"Star Light, Star Bright" CSP: A • **Ss** sing the song. • **Ss** sing song on a unison neutral vowel ("nee," "neh," "nah," "noh," or "noo").
Review known songs and rhythmic elements	"Bow Wow Wow" CSP: D • **Ss** sing song and pat the beat. • **Ss** sing with rhythm syllables and tap the beat. • **T** sings phrases from this and other known songs, and **Ss** echo-sing using rhythm syllables.
CORE ACTIVITIES	
Teach a new song	"Closet Key" CSP: D • **T** sings the song while **Ss** listen and tap the beat. • **T** sings and **Ss** listen and show the phrases with arm motions. • **Ss** identify the number of phrases. (four) • **T** sings while **Ss** show the phrases. • **T**: "Which phrases were the same?" (1 and 3) • **T** isolates the difference between phrases 2 and 4. • **T** and **Ss** sing and play the game.

Develop knowledge of music concepts Internalize music through kinesthetic activities	"Bobby Shafto" CSP: A - T: "Let's sing 'Bobby Shafto' and pretend to row a boat." (use a strong and weak motion) - Ss sing and perform the motions. - T and Ss sing the song and pat their knees on the strong beats and touch their shoulders on the weak. - Ss point to a representation of strong and weak beats (not rhythm) on the board. (T can keep the beats the same size or make the strongs beats larger.) ◆ · ◆ · ◆ · ◆ · - Ss sing the song with rhythm syllables and step the strong beats and snap the weak.
Creative movement	"No Robbers Out Today" CSP: A - T selects Ss to play the beat on unpitched percussion instruments. - T selects additional Ss to "play the words" on rhythm sticks. - Ss sing and play the game.
Practice and performance of music skills Reading	"Bounce High, Bounce Low" CSP: A - Ss sing the song and pat the beat. - Ss first read the song from the board in standard rhythmic notation with solfège syllables and hand signs using inner hearing. - Ss then read the song from the board in standard rhythmic notation with solfège syllables and hand signs. - T doubles the song. Ss read the changes: ♩ ♩ | ♩ ♩ s l s m ♫ ♫ | ♩ ♩ ss ll s m ♩ ♩ | ♩ ♩ s l s m ♫ ♫ | ♩ ♩ ss ll s m - T modifies the rhythm and solfège until the song becomes "Plainsies, Clapsies." (If this song has not been taught yet, T can still do the activity, or use known songs such as "We Are Dancing in the Forest.")

SUMMARY ACTIVITIES	
Review lesson outcomes Review the new song	"Closet Key" CSP: D

Grade 1, Unit 6, Duple Meter, Lesson 2

Outcome	Preparation: analyzing repertoire written in duple meter Practice: writing melodies that include the solfège syllable *la*
INTRODUCTORY ACTIVITIES	
Warm-up	• Body warm-up • Beat activity Concerto for Four Harpsichords, BWV 1065, by J. S. Bach (1685–1750) • Breathing: **Ss** practice blowing up a balloon and watch how air is released when deflating the balloon. • Resonance: explore a cow sound using low and high voices. Make sure **Ss** are inhaling and exhaling correctly with the support muscles. • Posture: remind **Ss** of the correct posture for singing.
Sing known songs	"Down Came a Lady" CSP: D • **Ss** sing the song. "Closet Key" CSP: D • **Ss** sing the song. • **T** adds an ostinato: $\frac{2}{4}$ ♩ 𝄽 | ♫ ♩ :|| • **Ss** sing the song with the ostinato.
Develop tuneful singing Tone production Diction Expression	"Cobbler, Cobbler" CSP: A • **Ss** pretend they're falling off a cliff and say "aaaahhhhhhhhhh!" • **T** uses a ball. Toss a ball from one S to another; **Ss** have to follow the movement of the ball with their voices. • **Ss** sing "Cobbler, Cobbler" on "loo" and draw the phrases in the air.
Review known songs and rhythmic elements	"Pease Porridge Hot" CSP: A • **Ss** sing and keep the beat. • **Ss** sing with rhythm syllables and tap the beat. • **T** sings phrases from this song and other known songs; **Ss** echo-sing with rhythm syllables.

	CORE ACTIVITIES
Teach a new song	"Plainsies, Clapsies" CSP: A • **T** sings while **Ss** continue the rhythm of the previous song. • **T** sings the song and demonstrates the motions with a scarf or ball. • **T** may select **Ss** to practice the motions while **T** sings. • **Ss** join in the song. • **T** sings the last phrase and "realizes" it sounds like another song. (**Ss** guess: "Bobby Shafto")
Develop knowledge of music concepts Describe what you hear	"Bobby Shafto" CSP: A • **Ss** sing song and keep the beat. • Review kinesthetic activities. • **T** and **Ss** sing phrase 1 of the song on "loo" while keeping the beat by patting on beats 1 and 3, snapping or clapping on beats 2 and 4. Or the teacher my accompany song with a beat, emphasizing beats 1 and 3. • **T**: "Andy, how many beats did we tap?" (four) • **T**: "Andy, which beats are stronger?" (1 and 3) • **T**: "Andy, if beats 1 and 3 are strong, beats 2 and 4 are _____?" (weak) • **T**: and **Ss** sing and show the strong and weak beats. • **Ss** sing and inner-hear the weak beats.
Creative movement	"Cut the Cake" CSP: A • **Ss** sing the song. • **T** adds a simple ostinato. • **Ss** sing and play the game with the ostinato.
Practice and performance of music skills Writing	"Bounce High, Bounce Low" CSP: A • **Ss** sing the song and keep the beat. • **Ss** sing the song with solfège syllables and hand signs. • **Ss** fill in the solfège syllables beneath the standard rhythmic notation prepared on the board: ♩ ♩ | ♩ ♩ s l s m ♫ ♫ | ♩ ♩ ss ll s m • **T** erases the solfège on the board, and **Ss** complete the *la* writing worksheet. • **Ss** fill in the solfège syllables beneath the staff notation prepared on the board.

SUMMARY ACTIVITIES	
Review lesson outcomes	"Plainsies, Clapsies"
	CSP: A
Review the new song	

Grade 1, Unit 6, Duple Meter, Lesson 3

Outcome	Preparation: creating a visual representation of strong and weak beats
	Practice: improvising melodies that include *la*
INTRODUCTORY ACTIVITIES	
Warm-up	• Body warm-up
	• Beat activity
	Concerto for Four Harpsichords, BWV 1065, by J. S. Bach (1685–1750)
	• Breathing: **Ss** practice blowing up a balloon and watch how air is released when deflating the balloon.
	• Resonance: explore a cow sound using low and high voices. Make sure **Ss** are inhaling and exhaling correctly with the support muscles.
	• Posture: remind **Ss** of the correct posture for singing.
Sing known songs	"Naughty Kitty Cat"
	CSP: A
	• **Ss** sing the song and keep the beat continuing into the next song.
	"Plainsies, Clapsies"
	CSP: A
	• **Ss** sing the song.
	• **Ss** sing and briefly play the game.
Develop tuneful singing	"Lucy Locket"
Tone production	CSP: A
Diction	• As **T** moves a flashlight beam projected onto the board, **Ss** are asked to follow the contour of the moving beam of light on an "oh" sound. Transition into "Lucy Locket."
Expression	• **Ss** sing song with text and keep the beat.
Review known songs and rhythmic elements	"Hot Cross Buns"
	CSP: D
	• **T** sings song on "loo." **Ss** recognize and sing the song with text.
	• **Ss** sing with rhythm syllables and keep the beat.
	• **T** sings phrases from this song and other known songs; **Ss** echo-sing the phrase with rhythm syllables and keep the beat.
CORE ACTIVITIES	
Teach a new song	"Thread Follows the Needle"
	CSP: A
	• **T** sings song and demonstrates movements for the game.
	• **T** sings while **Ss** play the game.

Develop knowledge of music concepts Create a visual representation of what you hear	"Bobby Shafto" CSP: A • **Ss** sing the song. • Review kinesthetic and aural awareness activities. • **T** sings the target phrase and asks **Ss** to create a visual representation of the beat. (**Ss** may use manipulatives.) • **T**: "Pick up what you need to create a representation of the strong and weak beats you heard" or "Draw what you heard." • **Ss** share their representations with each other. (Some teachers like to use paper and crayons for this activity.) • **T** invites one **S** to the board to share a representation with the class. If necessary, corrections to the representation can be made by viewing the aural awareness questions. • **Ss** sing the first phrase of "Bobby Shafto" while pointing to the representation of strong and weak beats. **Ss** can perform this activity with other known repertoire. • **Ss** sing with solfège syllables and hand signs.
Creative movement	"No Robbers Out Today" CSP: A • **Ss** read the song from **T**'s hand signs; **Ss** sing and play the game.
Practice and performance of music skills Improvisation	"Bounce High, Bounce Low" CSP: A • **Ss** sing the song and keep the beat. • **Ss** sing the song with solfège syllables and hand signs. • **Ss** read the song from standard rhythmic notation with solfège syllables and hand signs and/or from staff notation. • **T** adds additional phrases, one at a time, to the song. **Ss** read from rhythmic notation with solfège and/or from staff notation: ♩ ♩ | ♩ ♩ s l s m ♫ ♫ | ♩ ♩ ss ll s m ♫ ♫ | ♫ ♩ ss ll ss m ♩ ♫ | ♩ ♩ s ml s m • **T** labels phrase 1 above as the question and the others as answer 1, answer 2, and answer 3. • **T** sings the question phrase and directs **Ss** as to which phrase they should use to answer. • **Ss** may also create their own four-beat answer to include *la*.

SUMMARY ACTIVITIES

Review lesson outcomes Review the new song	"Thread Follows the Needle" CSP: A

Grade 1, Unit 6, $\frac{2}{4}$ Meter, Lesson 4

Outcome	Presentation: label the metric pattern of one strong beat followed by one weak beat as duple meter
INTRODUCTORY ACTIVITIES	
Warm-up	• Body warm-up • Beat activity Concerto for Four Harpsichords, BWV 1065, by J. S. Bach (1685–1750) • Breathing: **Ss** practice blowing up a balloon and watch how air is released when deflating the balloon. • Resonance: explore a cow sound using low and high voices. Make sure **Ss** are inhaling and exhaling correctly with the support muscles. • Posture: remind **Ss** of the correct posture for singing.
Sing known songs	"All Around the Buttercup" CSP: F-sharp • **Ss** sing the song and march in a circle to the beat. • **Ss** continue marching to the beat while singing the next song. "Thread Follows the Needle" CSP: A • **Ss** sing the song. • **Ss** perform the song with a simple ostinato.
Develop tuneful singing Tone production Diction Expression	"Cobbler, Cobbler" CSP: A • **Ss** sing the song. • **Ss** sing phrases of songs on "noh"; **T** makes sure that the tone is very light and relaxed. • Explore the upper and lower ranges of the voice by using a Slinky toy.
Review known songs and rhythmic elements	"Bounce High, Bounce Low" CSP: A • **Ss** sing song and pat the beat. • **Ss** sing song with rhythm syllables and pat the beat. • **T** sings phrases from "Pease Porridge Hot" and other known songs; **Ss** echo-sing with rhythm syllables and pat the beat.
CORE ACTIVITIES	
Teach a new song	"¡Que Llueva!" CSP: A • **T** sings the song while **Ss** listen. • **T** sings the song and **Ss** perform the chant. • **T** sings the song and demonstrates the game. • **T** and **Ss** sing and play.

Presentation of music concepts Describe what you hear with rhythm or solfège syllables	"Bobby Shafto" CSP: A • **Ss** sing the song and show the strong and weak beats. • **Ss** inner-hear the weak beats. • Review kinesthetic, aural, and visual awareness activities. • **T**: "When we have beats in a strong-weak pattern, we say that this piece of music is written in duple meter. We can show strong and weak beats by conducting." • **T** demonstrates duple meter conducting, and **Ss** copy. • **Ss** sing the song and conduct a two-beat pattern. • **Ss** continue conducting while **T** sings the next song.
Creative movement	"Lemonade" CSP: A • **Ss** sing the song and conduct. • **Ss** sing and play the game.

Presentation of music concepts
 	
Describe what you hear with rhythm or solfège syllables
	"Doggie, Doggie"
	CSP: A
	• **Ss** sing the song and keep the beat.
	• **T** reviews aural presentation.
	• **Ss** identify other known songs that may be in duple meter.
	• **Ss** sing these songs and conduct (select individual **Ss** to lead the class in conducting):
	  o "Bounce High, Bounce Low"
	  o "Cut the Cake"
	  o "Fudge, Fudge"
	  o "Good Night, Sleep Tight"
	  o "Lucy Locket"
	  o "Nanny Goat"
	  o "Naughty Kitty Cat"
	  o "Rain, Rain"
	  o "Snail, Snail"
	  o "We Are Dancing in the Forest"

SUMMARY ACTIVITIES	
Review lesson outcomes Review the new song	"¡Que Llueva!" CSP: A

Grade 1, Unit 6, 2/4 Meter, Lesson 5

Outcome	Presentation: notation of duple meter
INTRODUCTORY ACTIVITIES	
Warm-up	- Body warm-up - Beat activity Concerto for Four Harpsichords, BWV 1065, by J. S. Bach (1685–1750) - Breathing: **Ss** practice blowing up a balloon and watch how air is released when deflating the balloon. - Resonance: explore a cow sound using low and high voices. Make sure **Ss** are inhaling and exhaling correctly with the support muscles. - Posture: remind **Ss** of the correct posture for singing.
Sing known songs	"Pease Porridge Hot" CSP: A - **Ss** sing the song and conduct. "¡Que Llueva!" CSP: A - **T** sings the song and **Ss** perform the chant ("¡Que sí, que no, que llueva chaparron!"). - **Ss** perform the song with an ostinato.
Develop tuneful singing Tone production Diction Expression	"Lucy Locket" CSP: A - **Ss** sing song with the ostinato. - **Ss** sing the song on "loo" and show the strong and weak beats. - **T** directs **Ss** to sing on "loo" and conduct. - **Ss** sing and conduct a two-beat pattern. - **Ss** continue conducting into the next song.
Review known songs and rhythmic elements	"Naughty Kitty Cat" CSP: A - **Ss** sing and conduct without assistance. - **T** selects several **Ss** to "be the teacher" and conduct the class. - **Ss** sing with rhythm syllables and conduct. - **T** sings songs in duple meter; **Ss** echo-sing with rhythm syllables and conduct.
CORE ACTIVITIES	
Teach a new song	"Rocky Mountain" CSP: D - **T** sings and **Ss** move into a circle for the game. - **T** sings and **Ss** show the phrases. - Continue singing and playing the game until **Ss** can sing all four phrases. - **Ss** sing the last four beats as a melodic ostinato into the next song.

Presentation of music concepts Notate what you hear	"Bobby Shafto" CSP: A - Ss sing the song. - Review awareness activities and aural presentation. - Ss sing and conduct the song. - T reveals the rhythm of the song, without bar lines or time signature. - T: "We can show strong beats by writing bar lines." - T: "We are going to draw a bar line after every weak beat. This tells us that the next beat will be strong." - Ss fill in bar lines for the remaining phrases. - T: "When we get to the end of a song, we draw a double bar to show that the song is finished." - Ss identify the number of beats per measure. (two) - T: "Musicians call the space between bar lines a 'measure.'" - T: "Musicians show the number of beats in each measure by writing a time signature. When there are two beats in a measure and each beat is a quarter note, the time signature is $\frac{2}{4}$." - T draws $\frac{2}{4}$ time signature at the beginning of the song. - Ss sing the song and show $\frac{2}{4}$ by conducting: $\frac{2}{4}$ ♫ ♫ | ♫ ♩ | ♫ ♫ | ♫ ♩ | ♫ ♫ | ♫ ♩ | ♫ ♫ | ♩ ♩ ‖
Creative movement	"¡Que Llueva!" CSP: A - Ss sing and play the game and create a simple ostinato.

Presentation of music concepts
 	
Notate what you hear
	"Doggie, Doggie"
	CSP: A
	- Ss sing the song and keep the beat.
	- Ss sing song with rhythm syllables and keep the beat.
	- T presents the rhythmic notation of "Doggie, Doggie" without bar lines or time signature.
	- Ss fill in the bar lines and time signature.
	- Ss sing the song with solfège and hand signs.
	- Ss write the solfège underneath the notes.
	- T presents the notation for the song on the staff in different positions.
	- T connects learning to other related song material:
	  o "Bobby Shafto"
	  o "Bounce High, Bounce Low"
	  o "Cut the Cake"
	  o "Lucy Locket"
	  o "Naughty Kitty Cat"
	  o "We Are Dancing in the Forest"

SUMMARY ACTIVITIES	
Review lesson outcomes Review the new song	"Rocky Mountain" CSP: D

Chapter 6

Assessment and Evaluation

The purpose of assessment in the classroom is to evaluate the work of both students and teachers. This chapter contains examples of assessments for evaluating each musical concept and element taught in first grade. By assessing a student's skill development and the teacher's classroom teaching, we can develop strategies to improve music learning and music teaching. Effective assessments lead to development of a more effective music program.

There are five steps to developing assessment rubrics in the first grade classroom:

1. Decide on the areas of assessment.
2. Determine the activities you will use to assess these areas.
3. Create assessment rubrics for each area.
4. Create a class profile that summarizes the children's scores.
5. Have the teacher review the results of assessments and decide how to modify the teaching to help students develop their knowledge of music.

For a more comprehensive view of assessment, consult *Kodály Today*.

We have included assessment rubric samples for units two through six for grade one. The assessments for each unit cover singing, reading, writing, and improvisation. The teacher can select some or all of the assessment activities for the unit being taught.

Grade 1 Assessments

Melodic Contour Assessments

Melodic contour singing assessment is for a student's singing of "Snail, Snail" (see Table 6.1).

Table 6.1 Melodic Contour Singing Assessment

Student Name:	Date:	Class:
Criteria	Levels	Comments
Student sings the text of "Snail, Snail" with accurate intonation, pure vowel sounds, clear pronunciation, and tall, balanced posture, giving a musically sensitive performance that shows evidence of excellent vocal technique.	**Advanced** 4	
Student sings the text of "Snail, Snail" with mostly accurate intonation, primarily pure vowel sounds, some use of clear pronunciation, and tall, balanced posture, giving an overall musical performance.	**Proficient** 3	
Student sings the text of "Snail, Snail" with some accurate intonation, few pure vowel sounds, unclear pronunciation, and generally poor posture, giving a performance that lacks musicality.	**Basic** 2	
Student sings the text of "Snail, Snail" without accurate intonation, pure vowel sounds, clear pronunciation, or tall posture, giving a performance that lacks musicality and shows evidence of poor vocal technique.	**Emerging** 1	

Melodic contour reading assessment is for a student's reading of a four-beat melodic motive that includes icons showing high and low (Table 6.2).

Table 6.2

Student Name:	Date:	Class:
Criteria	Levels	Comments
Student reads the first phrase of "Snail, Snail" while showing the melodic contour and reading icons for high low high low, making no errors.	**Advanced** 4	
Student reads the first phrase of "Snail, Snail" while showing the melodic contour and reading icons for high low high low, making some errors that do not detract from the overall performance.	**Proficient** 3	

(Continued)

Table 6.2 (continued)

Student reads the first phrase of "Snail, Snail" while showing the melodic contour and reading icons for high low high low, making errors that detract from the overall performance.	Basic 2	
Student does not read the first phrase of "Snail, Snail" while showing the melodic contour and reading from icons for high low high low.	Emerging 1	

Melodic contour writing assessment is for a student's writing of a four-beat melodic motive that includes icons showing high and low (Table 6.3).

Table 6.3

Student Name: _____	Date: _____	Class: _____
Criteria	Levels	Comments
Student writes the first phrase of "Snail, Snail" showing the melodic contour using icons for high low and high low making no errors.	Advanced 4	
Student writes the first phrase of "Snail, Snail" while showing the melodic contour using icons for high low high low, making some errors that do not detract from the overall performance.	Proficient 3	
Student writes the first phrase of "Snail, Snail" while showing the melodic contour using icons for high low high low, making errors that detract from the overall performance.	Basic 2	
Student does not write the first phrase of "Snail, Snail" while showing the melodic contour using icons for high low high low.	Emerging 1	

Melodic contour improvisation assessment is for a student's improvising of a four-beat melodic motive that includes icons showing high and low (Table 6.4).

Table 6.4

Student Name:	Date:	Class:
Criteria	Levels	Comments
Student improvises a four-beat melodic motive that includes icons showing high and low, making no errors.	Advanced 4	
Student improvises a four-beat melodic motif that includes icons showing high and low, making a few errors that do not detract from the overall performance.	Proficient 3	
Student improvises a four-beat melodic motive that includes icons showing high and low, making errors that detract from the overall performance.	Basic 2	
Student does not improvise a four-beat melodic motive that includes icons showing high and low.	Emerging 1	

Quarter and Eighth Note Assessments

In the *singing assessment*, a student sings "Rain, Rain," using a quarter note and two eighth notes (Table 6.5).

Table 6.5

Student Name:	Date:	Class:
Criteria	Levels	Comments
Student sings the text of "Rain, Rain" with accurate intonation, pure vowel sounds, clear pronunciation, and tall, balanced posture, giving a musically sensitive performance that shows evidence of excellent vocal technique.	Advanced 4	
Student sings the text of "Rain, Rain" with mostly accurate intonation, primarily pure vowel sounds, some use of clear pronunciation, and tall, balanced posture, giving an overall musical performance.	Proficient 3	
Student sings the text of "Rain, Rain" with some accurate intonation, few pure vowel sounds, unclear pronunciation, and generally poor posture, giving a performance that lacks musicality.	Basic 2	

(Continued)

Table 6.5 (continued)

Student sings the text of "Rain, Rain" without accurate intonation, pure vowel sounds, clear pronunciation, or tall posture, giving a performance that lacks musicality and shows evidence of poor vocal technique.	Emerging 1	

In *reading assessment*, a student reads a four-beat rhythm pattern that includes a quarter note and two eighth notes (Table 6.6).

Table 6.6

Student Name:	Date:	Class:
Criteria	**Levels**	**Comments**
Student reads the first phrase of "Rain, Rain" from traditional notation, speaking and clapping rhythm syllables and making no errors.	Advanced 4	
Student reads the first phrase of "Rain, Rain" from traditional notation, speaking and clapping rhythm syllables and making only a few errors that do not detract from the performance.	Proficient 3	
Student reads the first phrase of "Rain, Rain" from traditional notation, speaking and clapping rhythm syllables and making errors that detract from the performance.	Basic 2	
Student does not read and clap the rhythm of the first phrase of "Rain, Rain."	Emerging 1	

In the *writing assessment*, a student writes a four-beat rhythm pattern that includes a quarter note and two eighth notes (Table 6.7).

Table 6.7

Student Name:	Date:	Class:
Criteria	**Levels**	**Comments**
Student writes a four-beat rhythmic pattern with rhythmic notation of the first phrase of "Rain, Rain," making no errors.	Advanced 4	

(Continued)

Table 6.7 (continued)

Criteria	Levels	
Student writes a four-beat rhythmic pattern with rhythmic notation of the first phrase of "Rain, Rain," making only a few errors that do not detract from the writing activity.	**Proficient** 3	
Student writes a four-beat rhythmic pattern with rhythmic notation of the first phrase of "Rain, Rain," making errors that detract from the writing activity.	**Basic** 2	
Student does not write a four-beat rhythmic pattern with rhythmic notation of the first phrase of "Rain, Rain."	**Emerging** 1	

In the *improvisation assessment*, a student improvises a four-beat rhythm pattern that includes a quarter note and two eighth notes (Table 6.8).

Table 6.8

Student Name: _____	Date: _____	Class: _____
Criteria	**Levels**	**Comments**
Student improvises a four-beat rhythm pattern that includes a quarter note and two eighth notes on rhythm syllables, making no errors.	**Advanced** 4	
Student improvises a four-beat rhythm pattern that includes a quarter note and two eighth notes on rhythm syllables, making a few errors that do not detract from the performance.	**Proficient** 3	
Student improvises a four-beat rhythm pattern that includes a quarter note and two eighth notes on rhythm syllables, making errors that detract from the performance.	**Basic** 2	
Student does not improvise a four-beat rhythm pattern that includes a quarter note and two eighth notes.	**Emerging** 1	

so-mi Assessments

In *so-mi* singing assessment, a student sings "Snail, Snail" (Table 6.9).

Table 6.9

Student Name:	Date:	Class:
Criteria	**Levels**	**Comments**
Student sings the text of "Snail, Snail" with accurate intonation, pure vowel sounds, clear pronunciation, and tall, balanced posture, giving a musically sensitive performance that shows evidence of excellent vocal technique.	**Advanced** 4	
Student sings the text of "Snail, Snail" with mostly accurate intonation, primarily pure vowel sounds, some use of clear pronunciation, and tall, balanced posture, giving an overall musical performance.	**Proficient** 3	
Student sings the text of "Snail, Snail" with some accurate intonation, few pure vowel sounds, unclear pronunciation, and generally poor posture, giving a performance that lacks musicality.	**Basic** 2	
Student sings the text of "Snail, Snail" without accurate intonation, pure vowel sounds, clear pronunciation, or tall posture, giving a performance that lacks musicality and shows evidence of poor vocal technique.	**Emerging** 1	

In *so-mi reading assessment*, a student reads a four-beat melodic motif that includes *so-mi* (Table 6.10).

Table 6.10

Student Name:	Date:	Class:
Criteria	**Levels**	**Comments**
Student sings the first phrase of "Snail, Snail" with solfège syllables and hand signs from the staff or traditional notation, making no errors.	**Advanced** 4	

(Continued)

Table 6.10 (continued)

Criteria	Levels	Comments
Student sings the first phrase of "Snail, Snail" with solfège syllables and hand signs from the staff or traditional notation, making only a few errors that do not detract from the performance.	Proficient 3	
Student sings the first phrase of "Snail, Snail" with solfège syllables and hand signs from the staff or traditional notation, making errors that detract from the performance.	Basic 2	
Student does not sing the first phrase of "Snail, Snail" with solfège syllables and hand signs from the staff or traditional notation.	Emerging 1	

In *so-mi writing assessment*, a student writes a four-beat melodic motive that includes *so-mi* (Table 6.11).

Table 6.11

Student Name:	Date:	Class:
Criteria	**Levels**	**Comments**
Student writes a four-beat melodic motive with solfège syllables underneath the traditional notation of the first phrase of "Snail, Snail," making no errors.	Advanced 4	
Student writes a four-beat melodic motive with solfège syllables underneath the traditional notation of the first phrase of "Snail, Snail," making only a few errors that do not detract from the writing activity.	Proficient 3	
Student writes a four-beat melodic motive with solfège syllables underneath the traditional notation of the first phrase "Snail, Snail," making errors that detract from the writing activity.	Basic 2	
Student does not write a four-beat melodic motive with solfège syllables underneath the traditional notation of the first phrase of "Snail, Snail."	Emerging 1	

In *so-mi improvisation assessment*, a student improvises a four-beat melodic motive that includes *so-mi* (Table 6.12).

Table 6.12

Student Name:	Date:	Class:
Criteria	Levels	Comments
Student improvises a four-beat melodic motive that includes *so-mi* on solfège, making no errors.	Advanced 4	
Student improvises a four-beat melodic motive that includes *so-mi* on solfège, making a few errors that do not detract from the performance.	Proficient 3	
Student improvises a four-beat melodic motive that includes *so-mi* on solfège, making errors that detract from the performance.	Basic 2	
Student does not improvise a four-beat melodic motif that includes *so-mi*.	Emerging 1	

Rest Assessments

In *quarter rest tuneful singing assessment*, a student sings "Hot Cross Buns" (Table 6.13).

Table 6.13

Student Name:	Date:	Class:
Criteria	Levels	Comments
Student sings the text of "Hot Cross Buns" with accurate intonation, pure vowel sounds, and tall, balanced posture, giving a musically sensitive performance that shows evidence of excellent vocal technique.	Advanced 4	
Student sings the text of "Hot Cross Buns" with mostly accurate intonation, primarily pure vowel sounds, and balanced posture, giving an overall musical performance.	Proficient 3	

(*Continued*)

Table 6.13 (continued)

Student sings the text of "Hot Cross Buns" with some accurate intonation, few pure vowel sounds, and generally poor posture, giving a performance that lacks musicality.	**Basic** 2	
Student sings the text of "Hot Cross Buns" without accurate intonation, pure vowel sounds, or tall posture, giving a performance that lacks musicality and shows evidence of poor vocal technique.	**Emerging** 1	

In *quarter rest reading assessment*, a student reads a four-beat rhythm pattern that includes a quarter rest (Table 6.14).

Table 6.14

Student Name: _____	Date: _____	Class: _____
Criteria	**Levels**	**Comments**
Student reads the first phrase of "Hot Cross Buns" from traditional notation, speaking and clapping rhythm syllables, making no errors.	**Advanced** 4	
Student reads the first phrase of "Hot Cross Buns" from traditional notation, speaking and clapping rhythm syllables, making only a few errors that do not detract from the performance.	**Proficient** 3	
Student reads the first phrase of "Hot Cross Buns" from traditional notation, speaking and clapping rhythm syllables, making errors that detract from the performance.	**Basic** 2	
Student does not read and clap the rhythm of the first phrase of "Hot Cross Buns."	**Emerging** 1	

In *quarter rest writing assessment*, a student writes a four-beat rhythm pattern that includes a quarter rest (Table 6.15).

Table 6.15

Student Name:	Date:	Class:
Criteria	**Levels**	**Comments**
Student writes a four-beat rhythm pattern with rhythmic notation of the first phrase of "Hot Cross Buns," making no errors.	**Advanced** 4	
Student writes a four-beat rhythm pattern with rhythmic notation of the first phrase of "Hot Cross Buns," making only a few errors that do not detract from the writing activity.	**Proficient** 3	
Student writes a four-beat rhythm pattern with traditional notation of the first phrase of "Hot Cross Buns," making errors that detract from the writing activity.	**Basic** 2	
Student does not write a four-beat rhythm pattern with traditional notation of the first phrase of "Hot Cross Buns."	**Emerging** 1	

In *quarter rest improvisation assessment*, a student improvises a four-beat rhythm pattern that includes a quarter rest (Table 6.16).

Table 6.16

Student Name:	Date:	Class:
Criteria	**Levels**	**Comments**
Student improvises a four-beat rhythm pattern that includes a quarter rest on rhythm syllables, making no errors.	**Advanced** 4	
Student improvises a four-beat rhythm pattern that includes a quarter rest on rhythm syllables, making a few errors that do not detract from the performance.	**Proficient** 3	
Student improvises a four-beat rhythm pattern that includes a quarter note on rhythm syllables, making errors that detract from the performance.	**Basic** 2	
Student does not improvise a four-beat rhythm pattern that includes a quarter rest.	**Emerging** 1	

la Assessments

In *la singing assessment,* a student sings "Bounce High, Bounce Low" (Table 6.17).

Table 6.17

Student Name:	Date:	Class:
Criteria	**Levels**	**Comments**
Student sings the text of "Bounce High, Bounce Low" with accurate intonation, pure vowel sounds, clear pronunciation, and tall, balanced posture, giving a musically sensitive performance that shows evidence of excellent vocal technique.	**Advanced** 4	
Student sings the text of "Bounce High, Bounce Low" with mostly accurate intonation, primarily pure vowel sounds, some use of clear pronunciation, and balanced posture, giving an overall musical performance.	**Proficient** 3	
Student sings the text of "Bounce High, Bounce Low" with some accurate intonation, few pure vowel sounds, unclear pronunciation, and generally poor posture, giving a performance that lacks musicality.	**Basic** 2	
Student sings the text of "Bounce High, Bounce Low" without accurate intonation, pure vowel sounds, clear pronunciation, or tall posture, giving a performance that lacks musicality and shows evidence of poor vocal technique.	**Emerging** 1	

In *la reading assessment,* a student reads a melodic motive that includes "la" (Table 6.18).

Table 6.18

Student Name:	Date:	Class:
Criteria	Levels	Comments
Student sings the first phrase of "Bounce High, Bounce Low" with solfège syllables and hand signs reading from the staff or traditional notation, making no errors.	Advanced 4	
Student sings the first phrase of "Bounce High, Bounce Low" with solfège syllables and hand signs reading from the staff or traditional notation, making only a few errors that do not detract from the performance.	Proficient 3	
Student sings the first phrase of "Bounce High, Bounce Low" with solfège syllables and hand signs reading from the staff or traditional notation, making errors that detract from the performance.	Basic 2	
Student does not sing the first phrase of "Bounce High, Bounce Low" with solfège syllables and hand signs reading from the staff or traditional notation.	Emerging 1	

In *la writing assessment*, a student writes a melodic motive that includes *la* (Table 6.19).

Table 6.19

Student Name:	Date:	Class:
Criteria	Levels	Comments
Student writes a four-beat melodic motive with solfège syllables underneath the traditional notation of the first phrase of "Bounce High, Bounce Low," making no errors.	Advanced 4	
Student writes a four-beat melodic motive with solfège syllables underneath the traditional notation of the first phrase of "Bounce High, Bounce Low," making only a few errors that do not detract from the writing activity.	Proficient 3	

(*Continued*)

Table 6.19   (continued)

Student writes a four-beat melodic motive with solfège syllables underneath the traditional notation of the first phrase of "Bounce High, Bounce Low," making errors that detract from the writing activity.	Basic 2	
Student does not write a four-beat melodic motive with solfège syllables underneath the traditional notation of the first phrase of "Bounce High, Bounce Low."	Emerging 1	

In *la improvisation assessment*, a student improvises a melodic motive that includes *la* (Table 6.20).

Table 6.20

Student Name: _____	Date: _____	Class: _____
Criteria	**Levels**	**Comments**
Student improvises a four-beat melodic motive with solfège syllables that includes *la*, making no errors.	Advanced 4	
Student improvises a four-beat melodic motive with solfège syllables that includes *la*, making few errors do not detract from the performance.	Proficient 3	
Student improvises a four-beat melodic motive with solfège syllables that includes *la*, making errors that detract from the performance.	Basic 2	
Student does not improvise a four-beat melodic motive with solfège syllables that includes *la*.	Emerging 1	

Duple Meter Assessments

In *duple meter tuneful singing assessment*, a student sings "Bounce High, Bounce Low" (Table 6.21).

Table 6.21

Student Name:	Date:	Class:
Criteria	Levels	Comments
Student sings the text of "Bounce High, Bounce Low" using accurate intonation, pure vowel sounds, clear pronunciation, and tall, balanced posture, giving a musically sensitive performance that shows evidence of excellent vocal technique.	Advanced 4	
Student sings the text of "Bounce High, Bounce Low" using mostly accurate intonation, primarily pure vowel sounds, some use of clear pronunciation, and balanced posture, giving an overall musical performance.	Proficient 3	
Student sings the text of "Bounce High, Bounce Low" using some accurate intonation, few pure vowel sounds, unclear pronunciation, and generally poor posture, giving a performance that lacks musicality.	Basic 2	
Student sings the text of "Bounce High, Bounce Low" but without accurate intonation, pure vowel sounds, clear pronunciation, or tall posture, giving a performance that lacks musicality and shows evidence of poor vocal technique.	Emerging 1	

In *duple meter reading assessment*, a student reads an eight-beat rhythm pattern in duple meter while conducting (Table 6.22).

Table 6.22

Student Name:	Date:	Class:
Criteria	Levels	Comments
Student reads "Bounce High, Bounce Low" from traditional notation, singing rhythm syllables while conducting in $\frac{2}{4}$, making no errors.	Advanced 4	

(Continued)

Table 6.22 (continued)

Criteria	Levels	Comments
Student reads "Bounce High, Bounce Low" from traditional notation, singing rhythm syllables while conducting in 2/4, making only a few errors that do not detract from the performance.	Proficient 3	
Student reads "Bounce High, Bounce Low" from traditional notation, singing rhythm syllables while conducting in 2/4, making errors that detract from the performance.	Basic 2	
Student does not sing the rhythm syllables or conduct "Bounce High, Bounce Low" in 2/4.	Emerging 1	

In *duple meter writing assessment*, a student writes an eight-beat rhythm pattern with traditional notation in duple meter (Table 6.23).

Table 6.23

Student Name: _____	Date: _____	Class: _____
Criteria	**Levels**	**Comments**
Student writes an eight-beat rhythm pattern using a time signature and bar line for "Bounce High, Bounce Low," making no errors.	Advanced 4	
Student writes an eight-beat rhythm pattern using a time signature and bar line for "Bounce High, Bounce Low," making only a few errors that do not detract from the writing activity.	Proficient 3	
Student writes an eight-beat rhythm pattern using a time signature and bar line for "Bounce High, Bounce Low," making errors that detract from the writing activity.	Basic 2	
Student does not write an eight-beat rhythm pattern using a time signature and bar line for "Bounce High, Bounce Low."	Emerging 1	

In *duple meter improvisation assessment*, a student improvises a four-beat rhythm pattern in duple meter while conducting (Table 6.24).

Table 6.24

Student Name:	Date:	Class:
Criteria	**Levels**	**Comments**
Student improvises a four-beat rhythm pattern with rhythm syllables while conducting in duple meter, making no errors.	**Advanced** 4	
Student improvises a four-beat rhythm pattern with rhythm syllables while conducting in duple meter, making a few errors that do not detract from the performance.	**Proficient** 3	
Student improvises a four-beat rhythm pattern with rhythm syllables while conducting in duple meter, making errors that detract from the performance.	**Basic** 2	
Student does not improvise a four-beat rhythm pattern with rhythm syllables while conducting in duple meter.	**Emerging** 1	

Notes

Introduction

1. "Education for Life and Work Developing Transferable Knowledge and Skills in the 21st Century," July 12, 2012, National Research Council. http://www8.nationalacademies.org/onpinews/newsitem.aspx?RecordID=13398.

Chapter 1

1. Pink, *A Whole New Mind: Why Right Brainers Will Rule the Future.*
2. Trevarthen and Malloch, "Musicality and Musical Culture: Sharing Narratives of Sound from Early Childhood," *The Oxford Handbook of Music Education*, vol. 1, p. 254.

Chapter 2

1. Elliott, *Praxial Music Education: Reflections and Dialogues*, p. 258.
2. Barrett, "Commentary: Music Learning and Teaching in Infancy and Early Childhood," in *The Oxford Handbook of Music Education*, vol. 1, p. 228.
3. Chen-Hafteck and Mang, "Music and Language in Early Childhood Development and Learning," in *The Oxford Handbook of Music Education*, vol. 1, p. 274.
4. Jeanneret and Degraffenreid, "Music Education in the Generalist Classroom," in *The Oxford Handbook of Music Education*, vol. 1, p. 404.
5. Young and Ilari, "Musical Participation from Birth to Three: Toward a Global Perspective," in *The Oxford Handbook of Music Education*, vol. 1, p. 281.

Chapter 5

1. Kodály, "Children's Choirs," *Selected Writings*, pp. 121–122.

Index

"A la Ronda, Ronda"
    in duple meter unit plan, 201*t*, 204*t*
    in *la* unit plan, 189*t*, 199*t*, 200*t*
"A la Rueda de San Miguel"
    directions for playing, 23*t*
    in Kindergarten review lessons unit plan, 140*t*, 143*t*, 145*t*
"All Around the Buttercup"
    directions for playing, 24*t*
    in duple meter unit plan, 210*t*
    in *la* unit plan, 192*t*
    in preparation/practice lesson, 129*t*
    in presentation lesson plan, 52*t*, 132*t*
    in quarter note rest unit plan, 177*t*, 181*t*, 185*t*, 186*t*
    in *so-mi* unit plan, 164*t*, 165*t*, 170*t*, 171*t*, 172*t*, 175*t*
    in teaching rest, 71
"Allegretto," from Symphony No. 7 in A, Op. 92 (Beethoven), 72
"Allegretto," from Symphony No. 94, "Surprise" (Haydn), 95*t*, 138*t*, 167*t*
"Allegro," from "Toy Symphony" (Haydn), 68, 179*t*
"Allegro," from "Toy Symphony" (Mozart), 126
"Allegro assai," from *Brandenburg Concerto No. 2* (Bach), 81
alternate ending, and developing improvisation skills, 110, 111
"Andante, from Symphony No. 94, "Surprise" (Haydn), 63, 126, 165*t*
antiphonal singing, 116
"Apple, Peach, Pear, Plum," 24*t*
"Apple Tree"
    in Kindergarten review lessons unit plan, 143*t*, 145*t*
    in *la* unit plan, 188*t*, 191*t*, 192*t*, 193*t*
    in *so-mi* unit plan, 176*t*
"Aquarium, The," from *Carnival of the Animals* (Saint-Saëns), 199*t*
assessment and evaluation, 215
    for duple meter, 228–31
    for *la*, 226–28
    for melodic contour, 215–18
    for quarter and eighth notes, 218–20
    for rest, 223–25
    for *so-mi*, 221–23

assimilative phase of learning
    connecting lesson plans to, 82*t*
    description of, 81
    for teaching beat, 56–57
    for teaching duple meter, 80–81
    for teaching melodic contour, 59
    for teaching quarter and eighth notes, 62–64
    for teaching rest, 70–72
    for teaching three-note child's chant, 75–77
    for teaching two-note child's chant, 66–68
associative phase of learning
    connecting lesson plans to, 82*t*
    description of, 81
    for teaching beat, 56
    for teaching duple meter, 79
    for teaching melodic contour, 58–59
    for teaching quarter and eighth notes, 61–62
    for teaching rest, 69–70
    for teaching three-note child's chant, 74
    for teaching two-note child's chant, 65–66
    template for preparation/practice lesson plan framework for, 89–94*t*
aural practice
    in teaching beat, 56–57
    in teaching duple meter, 80
    in teaching melodic contour, 59
    in teaching quarter and eighth notes, 62
    in teaching rest, 70–71
    in teaching three-note child's chant, 75
    in teaching two-note child's chant, 66–67

Bach, Johann Sebastian
    "Allegro assai," from *Brandenburg Concerto No. 2*, 81
    Concerto for Four Harpsichords, 45*t*, 204*t*, 206*t*, 208*t*, 210*t*, 212*t*
beat
    and developing creative movement skills, 121
    in developing part-work skills, 115, 116
    lessons for teaching one and two sounds on, 84–94*t*, 151–63
    listening examples for one and two sounds on, 125–26
    reinforcing, using instruments, 119
    teaching strategies for, 54–57

Index

"Bee, Bee, Bumblebee"
  directions for playing, 24*t*
  in Kindergarten review lessons unit plan, 141*t*, 150*t*
  and labeling one and two sounds on beat, 91*t*
  and notation of one and two sounds on beat with quarter and eighth notes, 93*t*
  in quarter and eighth notes unit plan, 151*t*, 152*t*, 154*t*, 158*t*, 161*t*, 163*t*
  in teaching beat, 55
  in teaching quarter and eighth notes, 62
Beethoven, Ludwig van, "Allegretto," from Symphony No. 7 in A, Op. 92, 72
"Billy, Billy," 25*t*
"Bobby Shafto"
  directions for playing, 25*t*
  in duple meter unit plan, 201*t*, 202*t*, 205*t*, 207*t*, 209*t*, 211*t*, 213*t*
  in Kindergarten review lessons unit plan, 141*t*, 146*t*, 149*t*, 150*t*
  in *la* unit plan, 188*t*, 189*t*, 193*t*, 197*t*, 198*t*, 199*t*, 200*t*
  in preparation/practice lesson plan, 46*t*
  in presentation lesson plan, 48*t*, 49*t*, 51*t*
  in *so-mi* unit plan, 163*t*, 164*t*, 168*t*, 174*t*
body warm-up exercises, 100
"Bounce High, Bounce Low"
  directions for playing, 25–26*t*
  in duple meter assessments, 228–31
  in duple meter unit plan, 201*t*, 202*t*, 203*t*, 205*t*, 207*t*, 209*t*, 210*t*, 211*t*, 213*t*
  in Kindergarten review lessons unit plan, 141*t*, 149*t*, 151*t*
  in *la* singing assessments, 226–28
  in *la* unit plan, 188*t*, 189*t*, 190*t*, 192*t*, 194*t*, 196*t*, 198*t*, 199*t*, 200*t*
  in preparation/practice lesson plan, 46*t*
  in presentation lesson plan, 49*t*
  in quarter and eighth notes unit plan, 152*t*, 153*t*, 156*t*
  in quarter note rest unit plan, 177*t*, 183*t*
  in *so-mi* unit plan, 164*t*
  in teaching beat, 55*t*
  in teaching duple meter, 78
  in teaching melodic contour, 58
  in teaching three-note child's chant, 73, 74–76
"Bow Wow Wow"
  directions for playing, 26*t*
  in duple meter unit plan, 201*t*, 204*t*
  in Kindergarten review lessons unit plan, 140*t*, 141*t*, 142*t*, 146*t*
  in *la* unit plan, 192*t*
  and performing rhythm canons based on simple rhythms, 117
  in presentation lesson that includes music skills, 132*t*
  in quarter note rest unit plan, 176*t*, 177*t*, 179*t*, 183*t*, 186*t*, 188*t*
  in *so-mi* lesson plan, 136*t*, 137*t*, 138*t*
  in *so-mi* unit plan, 163*t*, 164*t*, 165*t*, 166*t*, 167*t*, 168*t*, 171*t*
  in teaching rest, 71
breathing, 100–101
"Bye, Bye, Baby," 26*t*

call-and-response singing, 116
canons, and developing instrumental performance skills, 119–20
"Charlie over the Ocean," 116
"Chicka-Ma, Chicka-Ma Craney Crow," 26–27*t*
child's chant
  teaching strategies for three-note, 72–77
  teaching strategies for two-note, 64–68
  unit plan for three-note *la*, 188–200
  unit plan for two-note *so-mi*, 163–76
"Circle 'Round the Zero," 27*t*
"Clap Your Hands Together"
  directions for playing, 27*t*
  in *la* unit plan, 194*t*
  in quarter note rest unit plan, 186*t*
"Closet Key, The"
  in duple meter unit plan, 201*t*, 204*t*, 206*t*
  in Kindergarten review lessons unit plan, 141*t*, 148*t*, 149*t*
  in preparation/practice lesson plan, 45*t*
  in teaching beat, 55*t*
"Cobbler, Cobbler"
  directions for playing, 27–28*t*
  in duple meter unit plan, 201*t*, 206*t*, 210*t*
  in *la* unit plan, 189*t*, 195*t*, 198*t*
  in preparation/practice lesson plan, 46*t*
  in presentation lesson plan, 49*t*, 52*t*
  in quarter and eighth notes unit plan, 151*t*, 152*t*, 155*t*, 156*t*, 157*t*, 158*t*, 160*t*
  in quarter note rest unit plan, 176*t*, 180*t*, 181*t*, 182*t*, 183*t*, 185*t*
  in *so-mi* lesson plan, 135*t*, 137*t*
  in *so-mi* unit plan, 163*t*, 164*t*, 166*t*, 168*t*, 170*t*, 173*t*, 176*t*
  in teaching beat, 55
  in teaching quarter and eighth notes, 62
cognitive phase of learning
  connecting lesson plans to, 82*t*
  description of, 81
  for teaching beat, 55–56
  for teaching duple meter, 78–79
  for teaching melodic contour, 58
  for teaching quarter and eighth notes, 60–61
  for teaching rest, 68–69
  for teaching three-note child's chant, 73–74
  for teaching two-note child's chant, 64–65

template for preparation/practice lesson plan framework for, 82–89t
composition
  in sample curriculum for grade one, 7–8
  in teaching melodic contour, 59
Concerto for Four Harpsichords (Bach), 45t, 204t, 206t, 208t, 210t, 212t
consonants, unvoiced, 102
creativity. See also movement
  improvisation and composition and, 7–8
  in Kodály method, 3
critical thinking
  in Kodály method, 3
  music literacy and, 6–7
cultural heritage, students as stewards of, 3, 4
curriculum
  prompt questions for constructing, 9–10
  sample, for grade one, 4–9
  student development and designing, 2
"Cut the Cake"
  in duple meter unit plan, 201t, 202t, 203t, 207t, 211t, 213t
  in *la* unit plan, 188t, 190t
  in preparation/practice lesson plan, 46t, 129t
  in quarter note rest unit plan, 177t, 179t, 182t, 186t
  in teaching rest, 71

"Dance of the Sugar Plum Fairies," from *Nutcracker Suite* (Tchaikovsky), 154t, 156t, 158t, 160t, 161t
"Deedle, Deedle Dumpling," 28t
diction, 102
"Do, Do, Pity My Case," 28t
"Doggie, Doggie"
  directions for playing, 28t
  in duple meter unit plan, 201t, 202t, 211t, 213t
  in Kindergarten review lessons unit plan, 140t, 141t, 142t, 143t, 145t, 146t, 147t, 149t, 150t
  in *la* unit plan, 189t, 191t, 193t, 195t, 197t, 199t
  in lesson framework for practicing writing quarter and two eighth note patterns, 96t
  in preparation/practice lesson, 129t
  in presentation lesson plan, 51t, 52t
  in quarter and eighth notes unit plan, 151t, 152t, 153t, 155t, 156t, 157t, 162t, 163t
  in quarter note rest unit plan, 176t, 177t, 180t, 181t, 182t, 183t
  in *so-mi* lesson plan, 135t, 137t
  in *so-mi* unit plan, 163t, 164t, 165t, 166t, 168t, 169t, 170t, 172t, 173t, 174t, 176t
  in teaching duple meter, 80
  in teaching quarter and eighth notes, 62
"Down Came a Lady"
  directions for playing, 28t
  in duple meter unit plan, 201t, 206t

  in Kindergarten review lessons unit plan, 141t, 148t
  in preparation/practice lesson plan, 45t
  in presentation lesson that includes music skills, 131t, 132t
  in quarter note rest unit plan, 177t, 186t, 187t
  in *so-mi* unit plan, 164t, 172t, 173t, 174t
drones, in developing part-work skills, 118
"Ducks and Geese"
  in *la* unit plan, 191t, 193t, 195t
  in quarter and eighth notes unit plan, 151t, 152t, 154t, 155t, 156t, 157t, 158t
  in quarter note rest unit plan, 176t, 181t
  in *so-mi* unit plan, 163t, 165t, 166t, 168t, 169t, 170t, 172t, 173t
duple meter
  assessment of, 228–31
  listening examples for, 127
  teaching strategies for, 77–81
  unit plan for, 200–214
dynamic markings, 102

ear, memorization by, 114
eighth notes
  assessment of, 218–20
  lesson for notation of one and two sounds on beat with, 92–98t
  preparation/practice lesson for practicing improvisation using, 97–98t
  teaching strategies for, 60–64
  unit plan for, 151–63
"El Perrito Goloso," 188t, 194t, 195t
"Engine, Engine, Number Nine"
  directions for playing, 29t
  in Kindergarten review lessons unit plan, 140t, 142t
  in quarter and eighth notes unit plan, 151t, 152t, 154t, 162t, 163t
  in teaching beat, 55
error identification, 104, 106

"Farmer in the Dell," 29t
fill in the blank, and developing writing skills, 108, 109
"Finale," from Symphony No. 4 (Tchaikovsky), 81
final note, singing, in developing part-work skills, 116
finger staff, reading from, 105
focus songs, 47
folk songs and music
  changing form of, 115
  identifying form of, 114
  in Kodály method, 1–2
  performing simple rhythm canons based on, 118
  in repertoire, 17

Index

form
- and developing creative movement skills, 121
- and developing improvisation skills, 111, 112
- in developing reading skills, 103, 105
- in sample curriculum for grade one, 7
- techniques for understanding, 114–15

"Fossils," from *Carnival of the Animals* (Saint-Saëns)
- in Kindergarten review lessons unit plan, 141*t*, 143*t*, 145*t*, 147*t*, 149*t*
- in *la* unit plan, 191*t*, 193*t*, 195*t*, 197*t*

"Four White Horses," 116

"Frog in the Meadow," 29*t*

"Fudge, Fudge"
- in duple meter unit plan, 201*t*, 202*t*, 211*t*
- in quarter note rest unit plan, 177*t*, 185*t*, 186*t*

games, list of, for grade one, 21–37

"Good Night, Sleep Tight"
- in duple meter unit plan, 201*t*, 202*t*, 211*t*
- in presentation lesson plan, 51*t*
- in quarter and eighth notes unit plan, 152*t*, 158*t*, 160*t*
- in *so-mi* lesson plan, 135*t*, 137*t*
- in *so-mi* unit plan, 163*t*, 164*t*, 166*t*, 168*t*, 170*t*, 172*t*, 173*t*, 174*t*
- in teaching beat, 55*t*

Grieg, Edvard, "In the Hall of the Mountain King," 64, 72, 131*t*, 179*t*, 183*t*, 186*t*, 190*t*, 192*t*

hand signs
- in developing inner hearing, 106–7
- and developing musical memory, 112–13
- in developing reading skills, 104
- in introducing songs, 42–43
- and labeling sounds, 65, 73
- reading from, 67, 71, 76
- writing melody from, and developing writing skills, 109–10

"Handy, Dandy," 29–30*t*

Haydn, Franz Joseph
- "Allegretto," from Symphony No. 94, "Surprise," 95*t*, 138*t*, 167*t*
- "Allegro," from "Toy Symphony," 68, 179*t*
- "Andante, from Symphony No. 94, "Surprise," 63, 126, 165*t*

"Here Comes a Bluebird," 30*t*

"Here We Go 'Round the Mulberry Bush," 30*t*

"Hey, Hey, Look at Me," 140*t*, 144*t*

"Hop, Old Squirrel," 30*t*

"Hot Cross Buns"
- in duple meter unit plan, 201*t*, 208*t*
- in *la* unit plan, 188*t*, 189*t*, 190*t*, 192*t*, 194*t*, 196*t*
- in preparation/practice lesson, 129*t*
- in presentation lesson, 132*t*
- in quarter note rest assessments, 223–25
- in quarter note rest unit plan, 176*t*, 177*t*, 178*t*, 180*t*, 182*t*, 184*t*, 186*t*, 187*t*
- in *so-mi* unit plan, 163*t*, 168*t*, 169*t*, 170*t*
- in teaching rest, 68–70, 71

humming, in teaching tone production, 101–2

"Hunt the Slipper," 55*t*

"Hush, Baby, Hush," 177*t*, 184*t*, 185*t*

improvisation
- duple meter assessment, 231
- in duple meter unit plan, 203*t*, 209*t*
- *la* assessment, 228
- in *la* unit plan, 190*t*, 196*t*
- lesson segment for practicing, 97–98*t*
- melodic contour assessment, 217–18
- quarter and eighth note assessment, 220
- in quarter and eighth notes unit plan, 153*t*, 159*t*
- quarter note rest assessment, 225
- in quarter note rest unit plan, 178*t*, 184*t*
- in sample curriculum for grade one, 7–8
- *so-mi* assessment, 222
- in *so-mi* unit plan, 165*t*, 171*t*
- in teaching beat, 57
- in teaching duple meter, 80, 81
- in teaching melodic contour, 59
- in teaching quarter and eighth notes, 62, 63
- in teaching rest, 71, 72
- in teaching three-note child's chant, 75, 77
- in teaching two-note child's chant, 66–67, 68
- techniques for developing, 110–12
- and understanding form, 114

inner hearing
- and developing musical memory, 113
- in developing reading skills, 103, 106
- in sample curriculum for grade one, 7
- in teaching beat, 57
- in teaching duple meter, 80
- in teaching melodic contour, 59
- in teaching quarter and eighth notes, 62
- in teaching rest, 70
- in teaching three-note child's chant, 75
- in teaching two-note child's chant, 66
- techniques for developing, 106–7

instruments
- appropriate, 119
- and developing creative movement skills, 121
- learning to play, 4–5
- in sample curriculum for grade one, 5
- teaching progression for, 119
- techniques for developing performance skills, 118–21

"In the Hall of the Mountain King" (Grieg)
- in assimilative phase, 64
- in *la* unit plan, 190*t*, 192*t*
- in presentation lesson that includes music skills, 131*t*
- in quarter note rest unit plan, 179*t*, 183*t*, 186*t*
- in teaching rest, 72

Jenkins, Ella, 127, 203*t*
"Johnny's It," 30*t*
"Johnny Works with One Hammer," 30*t*
"Just From the Kitchen"
    directions for playing, 30*t*
    in *la* unit plan, 189*t*, 198*t*, 199*t*
    in presentation lesson plan, 49*t*

Kindergarten review, 140–51
kinesthetic activities
    for teaching beat, 55
    for teaching duple meter, 78
    in teaching melodic contour, 58
    in teaching quarter and eighth notes, 60
    for teaching rest, 68–69
    for teaching three-note child's chant, 73
    for teaching two-note child's chant, 64
kinesthetic canon, performing, and developing part-work skills, 117
Kodály, Zoltán, on teaching technique, 133
Kodály method, 1–2

la
    assessment of, 226–28
    listening examples for, 126–27
    sample presentation plan for, 48–49*t*
    unit plan for, 188–200
"Lemonade"
    directions for playing, 31*t*
    in duple meter unit plan, 201*t*, 203*t*, 211*t*
    in quarter and eighth notes unit plan, 152*t*, 153*t*, 158*t*, 159*t*, 160*t*, 161*t*, 162*t*, 163*t*
    in *so-mi* unit plan, 164*t*, 170*t*, 173*t*
lesson plan(s). *See also* preparation/practice lessons; presentation lessons; unit plan(s)
    creating, 43–53
    developing, 10–11
    developing, based on teaching strategies, 81–98
    evaluating, 139–40
    general points for, 139
    key components of, 11–16
    transitions in, 134–38
listening
    and developing creative movement skills, 122–25
    and developing instrumental performance skills, 120
    in duple meter unit plan, 203*t*
    in Kodály method, 3
    in *la* unit plan, 190*t*
    in quarter note rest unit plan, 179*t*
    in sample curriculum for grade one, 8–9
    in *so-mi* unit plan, 165*t*
    in teaching beat, 57
    in teaching duple meter, 81
    in teaching quarter and eighth notes, 63–64
    in teaching rest, 72
    in teaching three-note child's chant, 77
    in teaching two-note child's chant, 68
literacy, in sample curriculum for grade one, 6–7
"Little Sally Water," 31–32*t*
"London Bridge"
    directions for playing, 32*t*
    in Kindergarten review lessons unit plan, 140*t*, 144*t*
"Looby Loo," 32*t*
"Lucy Locket"
    directions for playing, 32*t*
    in duple meter unit plan, 201*t*, 202*t*, 208*t*, 211*t*, 212*t*, 213*t*
    in Kindergarten review lessons unit plan, 140*t*, 141*t*, 144*t*, 148*t*, 149*t*, 150*t*
    in *la* unit plan, 188*t*, 189*t*, 190*t*, 191*t*, 198*t*, 199*t*, 200*t*
    in presentation lesson plan, 49*t*, 132*t*
    in quarter and eighth notes unit plan, 152*t*, 153*t*, 158*t*, 161*t*
    in quarter note rest unit plan, 176*t*, 177*t*, 179*t*, 180*t*, 184*t*, 187*t*
    in teaching three-note child's chant, 77

manipulatives, 108
matching, in developing reading skills, 104, 106
melodic activities, 107
melodic canons, 120
melodic contour
    assessment of, 215–18
    teaching strategies for, 57–59
melodic elements
    introducing songs using, 42–43
    lesson plan template for notating, 50*t*
    reading and writing, in sample curriculum for grade one, 7
    song list for grade one, 38–42*t*
melodic ostinato
    and developing improvisation skills, 111
    in developing part-work skills, 118
    reinforcing, using instruments, 119
melody
    and developing improvisation skills, 111–12
    and developing writing skills, 108–9
    reading activities, 104–6
memory. *See* musical memory
movement
    and developing improvisation skills, 112
    introducing songs using, 42
    in sample curriculum for grade one, 5
    techniques for developing, 121–25
Mozart, Leopold, "Allegro," from "Toy Symphony," 126
musical memory
    in sample curriculum for grade one, 7
    techniques for developing, 112–14
music literacy, 6–7. *See also* reading; writing

Index

"Nanny Goat"
   in duple meter unit plan, 201t, 202t, 211t
   in preparation/practice lesson, 128t
   in quarter note rest unit plan, 176t, 180t, 181t

"Naughty Kitty Cat"
   directions for playing, 32t
   in duple meter unit plan, 201t, 202t, 208t, 211t, 212t, 213t
   in *la* unit plan, 189t, 196t, 197t
   in presentation lesson plan, 48t
   in presentation lesson that includes music skills, 132t
   in quarter note rest unit plan, 177t, 180t, 186t

"No Robbers Out Today"
   directions for playing, 32–33t
   in duple meter unit plan, 201t, 203t, 205t, 209t
   in *la* unit plan, 189t, 190t, 196t, 197t

notation
   in developing inner hearing, 107
   and developing musical memory, 113
   in developing reading skills, 104
   and developing writing skills, 108–10
   in teaching beat, 56
   in teaching duple meter, 79
   in teaching melodic contour, 59
   in teaching quarter and eighth notes, 61–62
   in teaching rest, 70
   in teaching three-note child's chant, 74
   in teaching two-note child's chant, 65–66

"Oliver Twist," 33t
"On a Mountain," 33t, 141t, 150t, 151t
"One, Two, Buckle My Shoe," 33t
"One, Two, Three, Four, Five," 33–34t
ostinati. *See also* melodic ostinato; rhythmic ostinato
   defined, 116
   and developing creative movement skills, 122

"Paige's Train," 34t
part work
   in sample curriculum for grade one, 5
   in teaching beat, 56
   techniques for developing, 115–18

"Pease Porridge Hot"
   in duple meter unit plan, 201t, 202t, 206t, 210t, 212t
   in *la* unit plan, 189t, 196t
   in preparation/practice lesson plan, 46t
   in presentation lesson plan, 51t, 53t, 132t
   in quarter note rest unit plan, 176t, 177t, 179t, 186t
   in *so-mi* unit plan, 164t, 174–75t, 176t

performance
   in Kodály method, 3
   in preparation/practice lesson plan, 43, 44t
   in sample curriculum for grade one, 4–5

"Pizza, Pizza," 116

"Plainsies, Clapsies"
   directions for playing, 34–35t
   in duple meter unit plan, 201t, 205t, 207t, 208t
   in preparation/practice lesson plan, 46t, 47t

posture, 99–100
preparation/practice lessons, 11
   for cognitive phase, 82–89t
   components of basic, 12t
   creating plan for, 43–47
   designing, that includes music skills, 127–30
   explanation of basic, 12–13t
   for practicing improvisation using quarter and two eighth note patterns, 97–98t
   for practicing reading quarter and two eighth note patterns, 94–95t
   for practicing writing quarter and two eighth note patterns, 95–97t

presentation lessons, 11
   for associative phase, 89–94t
   components of basic, 14t, 15t
   creating plan for, 47–53
   designing, that includes music skills, 130–32
   explanation of basic, 14–15t, 16t

problem solving, 6–7
props, and developing creative movement skills, 122
"Pumpkin, Pumpkin," 35t

"Quaker, Quaker," 35t
quarter note rest
   assessment of, 223–25
   unit plan for, 176–88

quarter notes
   assessment of, 218–20
   lesson for notation of one and two sounds on beat with, 92–98t
   preparation/practice lesson for practicing improvisation using, 97–98t
   teaching strategies for, 60–64
   unit plan for, 151–63

"Queen, Queen Caroline"
   in Kindergarten review lessons unit plan, 141t, 146t, 147t, 150t
   in lesson framework for practicing reading quarter and two eighth note patterns, 95t
   in presentation lesson for notation of one and two sounds on beat with quarter and eighth notes, 94t
   in quarter and eighth notes unit plan, 152t, 156t, 160t, 163t
   in *so-mi* lesson plan, 138t
   in *so-mi* unit plan, 163t, 167t
   in teaching quarter and eighth notes, 62

"¡Que Llueva!"
   directions for playing, 35t
   in duple meter unit plan, 201t, 202t, 203t, 210t, 211t, 212t, 213t

Index

question and answer
    and developing improvisation skills, 111
    and understanding form, 114–15

"Rain, Rain"
    in duple meter unit plan, 201*t*, 202*t*, 203*t*, 211*t*
    in Kindergarten review lessons unit plan, 140*t*, 141*t*, 143*t*, 145*t*, 146*t*, 148*t*, 150*t*
    and labeling one and two sounds on beat, 91*t*
    in *la* unit plan, 188*t*, 191*t*, 193*t*, 195*t*, 197*t*, 199*t*
    as listening example for *la*, 127
    and notation of one and two sounds on beat with quarter and eighth notes, 93*t*
    and practicing improvisation using quarter and two eighth note patterns, 98*t*
    and practicing reading quarter and two eighth note patterns, 95*t*
    and practicing writing quarter and two eighth note patterns, 96*t*
    in preparation/practice lesson, 128*t*
    in presentation lesson plan, 51*t*, 52*t*
    in quarter and eighth note assessments, 218–20
    in quarter and eighth notes unit plan, 151*t*, 152*t*, 153*t*, 155*t*, 157*t*, 158*t*, 159*t*, 160–61*t*, 162*t*, 163*t*
    in quarter note rest unit plan, 176*t*, 177*t*, 180*t*, 181*t*, 182*t*, 183*t*, 185*t*
    in *so-mi* lesson plan, 136*t*, 137*t*, 138*t*
    in *so-mi* unit plan, 163*t*, 164*t*, 166*t*, 167*t*, 168*t*, 169*t*, 170*t*, 171*t*, 172*t*, 173*t*, 174*t*, 176*t*
    in teaching duple meter, 80
    in teaching melodic contour, 58
    and teaching one and two sounds on beat, 84*t*, 86*t*, 88*t*
    in teaching quarter and eighth notes, 60, 61–62, 93*t*
reading
    duple meter assessment, 229–30
    in duple meter unit plan, 202*t*, 205*t*
    in Kodály method, 2
    la assessment, 226–27
    in *la* unit plan, 189*t*, 192*t*
    lesson segment for practicing, 94–95*t*
    melodic contour assessment, 216–17
    quarter and eighth note assessment, 219
    in quarter and eighth notes unit plan, 153*t*, 155*t*
    quarter note rest assessment, 224
    in quarter note rest unit plan, 178*t*, 180*t*
    so-mi assessment, 221–22
    in *so-mi* lesson plan, 136*t*, 138*t*
    in *so-mi* unit plan, 164*t*, 167*t*
    in teaching beat, 57
    in teaching duple meter, 80
    in teaching melodic contour, 59
    in teaching quarter and eighth notes, 62–63
    in teaching rest, 71, 72
    in teaching three-note child's chant, 76
    in teaching two-note child's chant, 67, 68
    techniques for developing skills in, 102–6
repertoire
    and critical listening, 8–9
    and curriculum construction, 9–10
    in Kodály method, 1–2
    in preparation/practice lesson plan, 12–13*t*, 44*t*, 128*t*
    in presentation lesson plan, 47*t*, 130*t*
    selecting, 17–18
    singing games, for grade one, 21–37
    song list for grade one, 18–20
    and students as stewards of cultural heritage, 4
resonance, 101
rest
    assessment of, 223–25
    listening examples for, 126
    teaching strategies for, 68–72
    unit plan for quarter note, 176–88
retrograde, 104
rhythm
    activities for developing inner hearing, 107
    clapping, in developing part-work skills, 116
    and developing improvisation skills, 110–11
    and developing writing skills, 108
    reading activities, 102–4
    reinforcing, using instruments, 119
    transforming, in developing reading skills, 103
rhythm canons, 117–19
rhythmic concepts and elements
    and developing creative movement skills, 121–22
    introducing songs using, 42
    in lesson plan development, 11
    lesson plan template for notating, 50*t*
    listening examples for, 125–27
    in preparation/practice lesson plan, 44*t*
    in presentation lesson plan, 48*t*
    reading and writing, in sample curriculum for grade one, 6
    song list for grade one, 38–42*t*
rhythmic ostinato
    and developing improvisation skills, 110
    in developing part-work skills, 116–17
    reinforcing, using instruments, 119
rhythm syllables
    performing aural rhythm canon with, 118
    performing visual rhythm canon with, 117–18
"Ring Around the Rosie," 35*t*
"Rocky Mountain," 202*t*, 212*t*, 213*t*
Rossini, Gioachino, *William Tell Overture*, 128*t*, 181*t*, 185*t*

Saint-Saens, Camille
    "Aquarium, The," from *Carnival of the Animals*, 199*t*
    Carnival of the Animals, 48*t*
    "Fossils," from *Carnival of the Animals*, 141*t*, 143*t*, 145*t*, 147*t*, 149*t*, 191*t*, 193*t*, 195*t*, 197*t*

Index

"Sally Go 'Round the Sun," 36t
"Seesaw"
   directions for playing, 36t
   in *la* unit plan, 189t, 191t, 193t, 195t, 197t, 199t
   in presentation lesson plan, 49t, 51t
   in quarter and eighth notes unit plan, 151t, 152t, 154t, 157t, 160t
   in quarter note rest unit plan, 176t, 180t, 182t, 183t, 185t
   in *so-mi* lesson plan, 135t, 137t
   in *so-mi* unit plan, 163t, 164t, 166t, 170t, 172t, 173t, 174t
   in teaching quarter and eighth notes, 62
singing
   and developing creative movement skills, 122
   duple meter assessment, 228–29
   in Kodály method, 1
   la assessment, 226
   melodic contour assessment, 215–16
   in music education, 4
   quarter and eighth note assessment, 218–19
   quarter note rest assessment, 223–24
   so-mi assessment, 221
   in teaching beat, 57
   in teaching duple meter, 80
   in teaching melodic contour, 59
   in teaching rest, 70
   in teaching three-note child's chant, 75
   in teaching two-note child's chant, 66
singing games, list of, for grade one, 21–37
"Skin and Bones," 116
"Snail, Snail"
   directions for playing, 36t
   in duple meter unit plan, 201t, 202t, 211t
   in Kindergarten review lessons unit plan, 140t, 141t, 142t, 143t, 144t, 146t, 147t, 148t, 149t, 150t
   in *la* unit plan, 188t, 189t, 191t, 193t, 195t, 197t, 198t, 199t
   in melodic contour assessments, 215–18
   in preparation/practice lesson, 129t, 130t
   in presentation lesson plan, 48t, 49t, 51t, 52t
   in quarter and eighth notes unit plan, 151t, 152t, 153t, 154t, 156t, 157t, 159t, 162t
   in quarter note rest unit plan, 176t, 177t, 178t, 180t, 182t, 184t, 185t
   in *so mi* assessments, 221–23
   in *so-mi* lesson plan, 136t, 137t, 138t
   in *so-mi* unit plan, 163t, 164t, 166t, 168–69t, 170t, 171t, 172t, 173t, 175t, 176t
   in teaching beat, 55, 56
   in teaching melodic contour, 58–59
   in teaching quarter and eighth notes, 62
   in teaching two-note child's chant, 64, 65, 66, 67
solfège symbols
   and developing musical memory, 113
   in developing reading skills, 104
   rhythmic notation with, and developing writing skills, 108–9
so-mi
   assessment of, 221–23
   listening examples for, 126
   preparation lesson for, 97–98t
   presentation lesson for, 50–53t, 94–95t
   transitions in lesson plans for, 135–38t
   and tuneful singing, 102
   unit plan for, 163–76
songs
   focus, 47
   introducing, 42–43
   list of, for grade one, 18–20
   for teaching rhythmic and melodic concepts and elements, 38–42t
Sousa, John Philip, "Stars and Stripes Forever," 50t, 135t, 137t, 165t, 167t, 170t, 172t, 174t
staff notation
   and developing musical memory, 113
   in developing reading skills, 105
   and inner hearing skills, 107
   and writing melody, 109–10
"Star Light, Star Bright," 55t, 158t, 201t, 204t
"Stars and Stripes Forever" (Sousa)
   in presentation lesson plan, 50t
   in *so-mi* lesson plan, 135t, 137t
   in *so-mi* unit plan, 165t, 167t, 170t, 172t, 174t

Tchaikovsky, Peter Ilyich
   "Dance of the Sugar Plum Fairies," from *Nutcracker Suite*, 154t, 156t, 158t, 160t, 161t
   "Finale," from Symphony No. 4, 81
teaching strategies, 54
   for beat, 54–57
   developing lesson plan based on, 81–98
   for duple meter, 77–81
   for melodic contour, 57–59
   for quarter and eighth notes, 60–64
   for rest, 68–72
   for three-note child's chant, 72–77
   for two-note child's chant, 64–68
"Teddy Bear," 36t, 137t
"Thread Follows the Needle"
   directions for playing, 36t
   in duple meter unit plan, 201t, 208t, 209t, 210t
three-note child's chant
   teaching strategies for, 72–77
   unit plan for, 188–200
"Tisket, a Tasket, A"
   directions for playing, 37t
   in preparation/practice lesson, 129t, 130t
   in quarter note rest unit plan, 177t, 183t
tone ladder, 104, 107

tone production, 101–2
tone set, 108
tongue twisters, 102
"Tortillitas"
    directions for playing, 37*t*
    in *la* unit plan, 188*t*, 191*t*, 193*t*, 195*t*, 197*t*, 199*t*
    in presentation lesson plan, 51*t*, 52*t*, 131*t*
    in quarter and eighth notes unit plan, 152*t*, 158*t*
    in quarter note rest unit plan, 177*t*, 187*t*
    in *so-mi* lesson plan, 137*t*
    in *so-mi* unit plan, 164*t*, 174*t*, 176*t*
transitions
    and developing instrumental performance skills, 120
    in lesson plans, 134–38
tuneful singing
    in sample curriculum for grade one, 5
    techniques for developing, 99–102
2/4 meter. *See* duple meter
two-note child's chant
    teaching strategies for, 64–68
    unit plan for, 163–76

unit plan(s), 133–34. *See also* lesson plan(s)
    for duple meter, 200–214
    Kindergarten review, 140–51
    for quarter and eighth notes, 151–63
    for quarter note rest, 176–88
    for three-note child's chant *la*, 188–200
    for two-note child's chant *so-mi*, 163–76
unvoiced consonants, 102

"La Vieja Inez"
    directions for playing, 37*t*
    in *la* unit plan, 188*t*, 191*t*
    in presentation lesson, 131*t*, 132*t*
    in quarter note rest unit plan, 177*t*, 187*t*, 188*t*
visual practice
    in teaching beat, 57
    in teaching duple meter, 80–81
    in teaching melodic contour, 59
    in teaching quarter and eighth notes, 62–64
    in teaching rest, 71
    in teaching three-note child's chant, 75–77
    in teaching two-note child's chant, 67–68
visual representation
    in duple meter unit plan, 209*t*
    in *la* unit plan, 196*t*
    in quarter and eighth notes unit plan, 159*t*
    in quarter note rest unit plan, 184*t*
    in *so-mi* unit plan, 171*t*
    in teaching beat, 56
    in teaching melodic contour, 58
    in teaching quarter and eighth notes, 61
    in teaching rest, 69
    in teaching three-note child's chant, 73–74
    in teaching two-note child's chant, 65
visuals, introducing songs using, 42
vowel sounds, in teaching tone production, 102

warm-up exercises, 100
"We Are Dancing in the Forest"
    directions for playing, 37*t*
    in duple meter unit plan, 201*t*, 202*t*, 205*t*, 211*t*, 213*t*
    in Kindergarten review lessons unit plan, 140*t*, 141*t*, 144*t*, 145*t*, 149*t*, 150*t*
    in *la* unit plan, 188*t*, 189*t*, 190*t*, 192*t*, 198*t*
    in presentation lesson plan, 49*t*, 131*t*
    in quarter and eighth notes unit plan, 152*t*, 153*t*, 159*t*
    in quarter note rest unit plan, 177*t*, 183*t*, 184*t*, 185*t*, 187*t*
    in teaching three-note child's chant, 77
William Tell Overture (Rossini), 128*t*, 181*t*, 185*t*
"Witch, Witch"
    in *la* unit plan, 188*t*, 193*t*
    in quarter and eighth notes unit plan, 152*t*, 162*t*, 163*t*
    in *so-mi* lesson plan, 136*t*, 138*t*
    in *so-mi* unit plan, 163*t*, 164*t*, 165*t*, 167*t*, 168*t*, 173*t*
writing
    and developing instrumental performance skills, 121
    duple meter assessment, 230
    in duple meter unit plan, 203*t*, 207*t*
    in Kodály method, 2
    la assessment, 227–28
    in *la* unit plan, 190*t*, 194*t*
    lesson segment for practicing, 95–97*t*
    melodic contour assessment, 217
    in preparation/practice lesson plan, 46–47*t*, 129–30*t*
    quarter and eighth note assessment, 219–20
    in quarter and eighth notes unit plan, 153*t*, 157*t*
    quarter note rest assessment, 224–25
    in quarter note rest unit plan, 178*t*, 182*t*
    so-mi assessment, 222
    in *so-mi* unit plan, 164*t*, 169*t*
    in teaching beat, 57
    in teaching duple meter, 80–81
    in teaching melodic contour, 59
    in teaching quarter and eighth notes, 63
    in teaching rest, 71–72
    in teaching three-note child's chant, 77
    in teaching two-note child's chant, 67–68
    techniques for developing, 108–10

www.ingramcontent.com/pod-product-compliance
Lightning Source LLC
Chambersburg PA
CBHW052353290825
31867CB00029B/1329